NAVIGATING THE FUTURE TRENDS

Supply Chain 5.0

The Next Generation of Business Success Through Customer Centricity, Sustainability & Human Rights and Digitalization

NAVIGATING THE FUTURE TRENDS

Supply Chain 5.0

The Next Generation of Business Success Through Customer Centricity, Sustainability & Human Rights and Digitalization

Prateek Jain
EvolveWithUsNow, Singapore

Mabel C. Chou
National University of Singapore, Singapore

World Scientific

NEW JERSEY • LONDON • SINGAPORE • BEIJING • SHANGHAI • HONG KONG • TAIPEI • CHENNAI • TOKYO

Published by

World Scientific Publishing Co. Pte. Ltd.
5 Toh Tuck Link, Singapore 596224
USA office: 27 Warren Street, Suite 401-402, Hackensack, NJ 07601
UK office: 57 Shelton Street, Covent Garden, London WC2H 9HE

British Library Cataloguing-in-Publication Data
A catalogue record for this book is available from the British Library.

SUPPLY CHAIN 5.0
The Next Generation of Business Success Through Customer Centricity, Sustainability & Human Rights and Digitalization

ISBN 978-981-12-7865-5 (hardcover)
ISBN 978-981-12-7866-2 (ebook for institutions)
ISBN 978-981-12-7867-9 (ebook for individuals)

For any available supplementary material, please visit
https://www.worldscientific.com/worldscibooks/10.1142/13480#t=suppl

Desk Editor: Sandhya Venkatesh

Typeset by Stallion Press
Email: enquiries@stallionpress.com

ABOUT THE BOOK

"Supply Chain 5.0: The Next Generation of Business Success through Customer Centricity, Sustainability & Human Rights and Digitalization" unveils a transformative era in supply chain management, presenting a groundbreaking business model that integrates three pivotal elements: Customer Centricity, Sustainability & Human Rights, and the interplay of Advanced Digitalization. This insightful book guides businesses through the evolving landscape, showcasing how they can synchronize these elements to revolutionize their operations and unlock unparalleled value, ensuring future success. As consumer expectations shift and the world demands responsible practices, embracing the new generation of Supply Chain isn't just an option—it's the only way for organizations to thrive and shape a profitable and sustainable future.

PREFACE

Not long ago, the world witnessed the birth of organized supply chains. If we move back in time to the early 1900s, supply chains were much simpler and more straightforward. Goods were produced in one location and then transported to another for distribution within a few weeks. But as demand grew, supply chains became more complex, spanning multiple countries and continents. The evolution of supply chains was not a linear process, but rather a dramatic story with twists and turns.

In 1913, Henry Ford revolutionized the automotive industry, with the introduction of the assembly line. By standardizing parts and production processes, Ford was able to produce cars on a massive scale, but he also faced the challenge of getting his products to customers quickly and cost-effectively. To solve this, Ford built his own transportation system, including railroads and ships, to move raw materials and finished goods around the world.

However, as the demand for automobiles continued to grow, supply chains became more complex. In 1923, General Motors (GM) saw an opportunity to differentiate themselves from Ford by introducing new models and customizations, but this meant that they had to manage an increasingly complex supply chain. To solve this, GM developed a system called the "flying squad" that allowed them to quickly identify and resolve production issues at their suppliers.

In the 1950s, Toyota introduced the concept of Just-In-Time (JIT) manufacturing. JIT focused on producing only what was needed when it was needed, reducing waste and inventory costs. JIT also required a high level of coordination and communication between suppliers and manufacturers. Toyota's approach to supply chain management helped them become one of the most efficient and profitable car manufacturers globally.

As the years went by, supply chains continued to evolve and adapt to new challenges. In the 1980s, the rise of globalization led to the creation of even more complex and dispersed supply chains, with manufacturers and suppliers located around the world. This created new challenges in terms of managing logistics, communication, and quality control.

To meet these challenges, companies began to invest in new technologies and processes, such as Enterprise Resource Planning (ERP) systems, which allowed them to manage their supply chains more efficiently. They also started to work more closely with their suppliers, developing long-term partnerships and sharing information and best practices.

But the evolution of supply chains was not just about technology and processes. It was also about understanding the needs and preferences of customers. In the 1990s, companies began to focus more on customer-centric supply chains, which were designed to meet the specific needs of individual customers. This required a greater level of flexibility and agility, with companies able to quickly adjust their production and logistics to meet the changing demand.

In recent years, the concept of "Supply Chain 4.0," which focuses on the digitalization of supply chains, has emerged. This includes the use of advanced analytics, automation, and artificial intelligence to improve supply chain visibility and efficiency. By integrating data from multiple sources and using predictive analytics to anticipate demand, companies can optimize their production and logistics, reducing costs and improving customer service. Companies such as Amazon and Alibaba revolutionized the retail industry with their use of data analytics and automation, enabling them to offer fast and low-cost delivery to customers.

In addition to Amazon and Alibaba, there are many other examples of companies implementing Supply Chain 4.0 to improve their operations. For instance, Gebhardt Group, a provider of intralogistics solutions, launched the Galileo IoT platform, which provides real-time condition monitoring for its customers (Hero, 2021). Other companies, such as Maersk, a global logistics and transportation provider, have used blockchain technology to improve transparency and security in their supply chains (Ferrantino & Koten, 2019). ALBIS PLASTICS GmbH, a leading company in the distribution and compounding of technical thermoplastics and thermoplastic elastomers, can now identify quality risks before they arise and understand complex interdependencies in production by intelligently connecting and visualizing IoT data. These intelligent insights are also used for future product development (Hero, 2021).

The key elements of Supply Chain 4.0 include integrated planning and execution, logistics visibility, procurement 4.0, smart warehousing, efficient spare parts management, autonomous and B2C logistics, prescriptive supply chain analytics, and digital supply chain enablers (*Supply Chain 4.0: A Luxury or a Necessity,* 2023). Integrated planning and execution involve the integration of different data sources to provide real-time information on demand, inventory levels, and production capacity, enabling companies to make better decisions about production and logistics. Logistics visibility refers to the ability to track products in real-time throughout the supply chain, providing greater transparency and enabling a faster response to disruptions. Procurement 4.0 involves the use of data analytics and automation to optimize procurement processes, reduce costs, and improve supplier relationships. Smart warehousing refers to the use of automation and data analytics to optimize warehouse operations, reduce inventory costs, and improve order fulfillment. Efficient spare parts management involves the use of predictive analytics to anticipate demand for spare parts and reduce the risk of stockouts. Autonomous and B2C logistics refer to the use of autonomous vehicles and drones to enable faster and more efficient delivery to customers. Prescriptive supply chain analytics involves the use of artificial intelligence to analyze data and provide recommendations for improving supply chain performance. Finally, digital supply chain enablers refer to the use of technologies such as blockchain, cloud computing, and the Internet of Things (IoT) to support the other key elements of Supply Chain 4.0 (*Supply Chain 4.0: A Luxury or a Necessity,* 2023).

As the pace of technological advancement continues, Supply Chain 4.0 is expected to progress even further, with more companies adopting digital technologies to improve their supply chain operations. For instance, the COVID-19 pandemic has highlighted the importance of supply chain resilience, leading many companies to invest in new technologies and processes to better manage risk and disruptions (*How the COVID-19 Pandemic Has Changed Supply Chain Practices*, 2022). Undoubtedly, Supply Chain 4.0 has the potential to revolutionize supply chain management, enabling companies to improve their efficiency, reduce costs, and provide better service to their customers.

The supply chain has been reorganized in the era of Industry 4.0, with new technologies that are changing traditional ways of working (*Supply Chain 4.0 — The Next-Generation Digital Supply Chain*, 2020).

Although the focus on digitalization yielded numerous advantages, it overlooked some essential factors such as

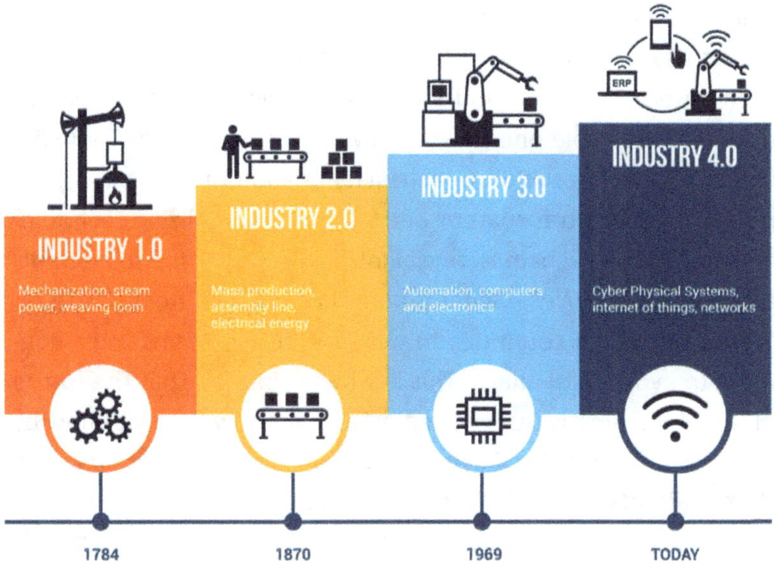

Figure 1.

Source: https://www.treatstock.fr/blog/business-with-treatstock

customer-centricity, sustainability and human rights. As companies begin to incorporate digitalization into their supply chains, the first step can appear overwhelming. However, recent supply chain shocks such as the pandemic, climate issues, and shipping port backups have been a wake-up call for companies and supply chain leaders to rethink their operations (Hadavi, 2021).

Supply Chain 4.0 focused on the reorganization of supply chains using Industry 4.0 technologies, such as smart manufacturing, smart production systems, smart warehouse management systems, smart logistics, and dynamic routing (Alicke *et al.*, 2019). However, most of the previous research studies ignored the social aspects of supply chain sustainability (*Industry 4.0 and Supply Chain Sustainability: Framework and Future Research Directions*, 2018).

The missing elements of sustainability, human rights, and customer-centricity in Supply Chain 4.0 will become integral components of Supply Chain 5.0. In this new era, digitalization will still play a major role but will be paired with a stronger emphasis on sustainability. Companies will be required to lessen their carbon footprint and embrace greener practices, such as utilizing renewable energy and recycling more. Supply Chain 5.0 will also focus on customer-centricity in addition to making supply chains more transparent and effective by utilizing technologies such as blockchain, artificial intelligence, and the IoT (*Supply Chain 4.0 — The Next-Generation Digital Supply Chain*, 2020).

As the world continues to change, supply chains must continue to evolve and adapt. This is why we believe that the future of supply chains is Supply Chain 5.0, which will be defined by three key elements: **Customer-Centricity, Sustainability and Human Rights, and Advanced Digitalization.**

The first element, customer-centricity, involves evolving supply chain operations to better serve customers and provide more tailored products and personalized experiences. Supply Chain 4.0 refers to the adaptation of supply chains to meet the needs of customers. However, the new archetype takes things a step further by creating processes, systems, and value chain models that are centered around the customer. In other words, the focus shifts from simply adapting to the customer's needs to creating a model that prioritizes customer personalization above all else.

This represents a significant change from the previous approach and emphasizes the importance of putting the customer at the center of everything. There will therefore be a greater focus on customer-centricity, with companies using advanced analytics and real-time data to anticipate customer needs and preferences. This will require a greater level of collaboration between suppliers, manufacturers, and retailers, as they work together to create a seamless and responsive supply chain. This book discusses customer-centricity in detail as to why this is becoming increasingly important and how companies can innovate to create a more efficient and effective supply chain that meets their customers' needs.

The second element, Sustainability and Human Rights, is increasingly becoming a critical component of a successful supply chain. Sustainability is all about decreasing waste and emissions, ensuring ethical work practices, and making supply chains more socially responsible, which naturally leads to Human Rights. No business can thrive if these two elements are not fulfilled. The book provides insights into how organizations can incorporate Sustainability and Human Rights into their supply chain operations to create a more socially and ecologically responsible supply chain. The consumers of today, with the acceleration of connectivity fueled by the recent pandemic, are more aware of the issues and are taking a tough stance toward these elements. In many cases, brands have been boycotted if there were deviations found, making sustainability and human rights the basic hygiene factors of successful supply chains. There is enough evidence to show the new shoppers, the Gen Zs, gravitating towards companies that have purpose in their brands and take Sustainability and Human Rights as their priority.

Finally, the third element of Supply Chain 5.0, advanced digitalization, involves the use of digital technology to optimize operations achieve business objectives and create transparency to stakeholders and end users. The goal of digitalization will be to make supply chains embrace more visibility, openness and effectiveness. This book explores some elements of the technology breakthroughs we see in the world today. We discuss the evolution and usage of AI and Blockchain in supply chain management, the evolving metaverse, the digitalization of procurement, the evolving facets of healthcare and the future of cold supply chains which have become predominant with the recent outbreak of the pandemic. We also discuss resilience and agility, which the supply chain needs badly, and how, in the new era of Supply Chain 5.0, these elements will become complementary and supplementary to each other. Lastly, data protection and cyber-security will be important to establish trust with partners and consumers, which links us back to the first element of customer-centricity.

Many companies are already implementing these three components into their supply chains. For example, Adidas has introduced a "speed factory" that uses automation and 3D printing to produce customized shoes on demand, reducing waste and inventory costs. Coca-Cola has set a goal to be carbon-neutral by 2040, and has implemented a sustainable packaging strategy that includes using recycled materials and reducing plastic waste. Online retailer Zappos has become famous for its customer-centric approach, offering free and easy returns, and even allowing customers to customize their shoes with personal messages. In time, this will increase and become an essential ingredient for supply chains.

Some examples of Supply Chain 5.0 in action include the development of circular supply chains, which aim to reduce waste by reusing and recycling materials, and the implementation of ethical and fair labor practices to improve the social impact of supply chains. Companies such as Patagonia, Zara, and Levi's have implemented sustainable practices in their supply chains, such as using organic cotton and recycled polyester in their products (Corner, 2023).

The evolution of supply chains has been a dramatic story, full of innovation and challenges. From Henry Ford's assembly line to the introduction of Supply Chain 4.0 and beyond, supply chains have become more efficient and agile than ever before. But as we look to the future, we believe that Supply Chain 5.0 will usher in a new era of supply chain management defined by customer-centricity, sustainability and human rights, and advanced digitalization, in turn, creating a more efficient, responsive, and environmentally friendly supply chain for the future. Companies that embrace these three components will be fit for the future and will continue to transform their industries for years to come.

In writing this book, our primary objective is to explore the emerging global trends and identify the gaps that exist in meeting evolving consumer expectations. This exploration led us to develop the foundational principles of Supply Chain 5.0, which represent the next frontier in business performance. Each chapter in this book delves deep into these essential components, revealing the immense potential for transforming the end-to-end value delivery process into the era of Supply Chain 5.0.

Within these pages, readers will find a comprehensive examination of the future of supply chain management, viewed through the lens of Supply Chain 5.0. We shed light on three fundamental elements that form the bedrock of this holistic approach, with a core focus on fostering a sustainable planet, enhancing business efficiency, and ultimately elevating customer satisfaction. By connecting these vital dots, this book paints a clear picture of the path ahead, where supply chains evolve and thrive in the era of Supply Chain 5.0.

We hope you will enjoy reading this book as much as we enjoyed discussing and evolving it within ourselves and with fellow supply chain colleagues across industry and academia.

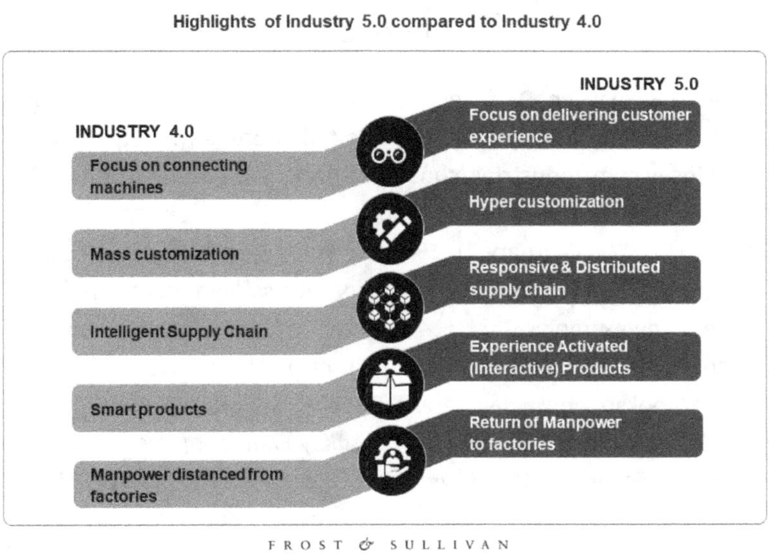

Figure 2.

Source: https://www.frost.com/frost-perspectives/industry-5-0-bringing-empowered-humans-back-to-the-shop-floor/.

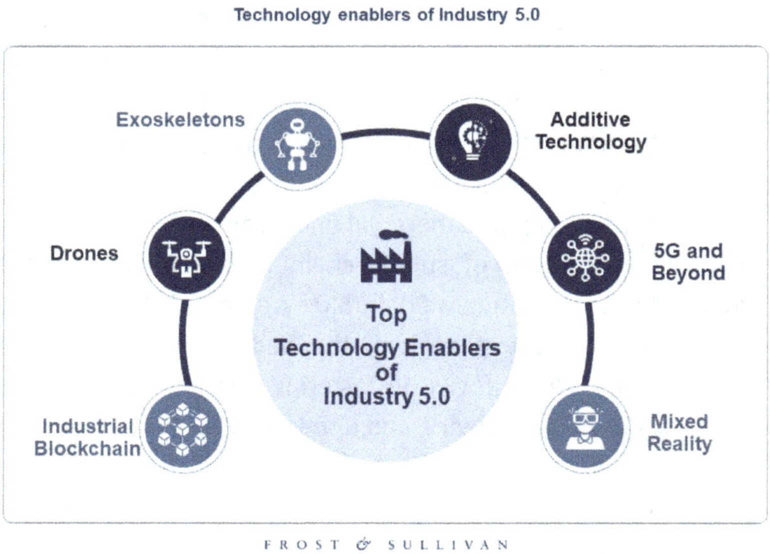

Figure 3.

Source: https://www.frost.com/frost-perspectives/industry-5-0-bringing-empowered-humans-back-to-the-shop-floor/.

References

Alicke, K., Rexhausen, D., & Seyfert, A. (2019, January 14). *Supply Chain 4.0 in Consumer Goods*. McKinsey & Company. https://www.mckinsey.com/industries/consumer-packaged-goods/our-insights/supply-chain-4-0-in-consumer-goods.

Corner, A. (2023, February 7). *15+ Case Study Examples, Design Tips & Templates — Venngage*. Venngage. https://venngage.com/blog/case-study-examples/.

Ferrantino, M. J. & Koten, E. E. (2019). https://www.wto.org/english/res_e/booksp_e/gvc_dev_report_2019_e_ch5.pdf.

Hero, F. (2021, April 12). *Industry 4.0: A Key Enabler of Resilient Supply Chains*. Forbes. https://www.forbes.com/sites/sap/2021/04/12/industrial-i0t-the-key-component-to-a-resilient-supply-chain/.

Hadavi, C. (2021, December 15). *Supply Chain 4.0: Why and How?* Forbes. https://www.forbes.com/sites/forbestechcouncil/2021/12/15/supply-chain-40-why-and-how/.

How the COVID-19 Pandemic Has Changed Supply Chain Practices. (2022, May 20). World Economic Forum. https://www.weforum.org/agenda/2022/01/5-ways-the-covid-19-pandemic-has-changed-the-supply-chain/.

Industry 4.0 and Supply Chain Sustainability: Framework and Future Research Directions. (2018, December 20). Emerald Insight. https://www.emerald.com/insight/content/doi/10.1108/BIJ-03-2018-0056/full/html.

Supply Chain 4.0 — The Next-Generation Digital Supply Chain. (2020, October 20). McKinsey & Company. https://www.mckinsey.com/capabilities/operations/our-insights/supply-chain-40--the-next-generation-digital-supply-chain.

Supply Chain 4.0: A Luxury or a Necessity? (2023, February 9). Social Innovation. https://social-innovation.hitachi/en-us/think-ahead/manufacturing/supply-chain-4-0/.

CONTENTS

INTRODUCTION

Amidst the dynamic currents of supply chain management, a new era has emerged, setting the stage for a transformative shift in how businesses operate and deliver value. Welcome to Supply Chain 5.0, a paradigm that goes beyond the boundaries of its predecessor, Supply Chain 4.0, by placing customer experience and sustainable value creation at its core. Gone are the days when meeting customer requirements in the most cost-effective and expedient manner was the sole focus. Supply Chain 5.0 introduces a new dimension that addresses the personalized needs of customers, while emphasizing sustainability, human rights and social responsibility.

In the era of Supply Chain 4.0, the mantra was clear: better, faster, and cheaper. Businesses leveraged advanced technologies, such as the Internet of Things (IoT), big data analytics, and artificial intelligence (AI), to optimize processes, enhance efficiency, and streamline operations. The goal was to meet customer demands swiftly and economically, prioritizing speed and cost above all else. However, as society evolved and became increasingly aware of environmental concerns, labor rights, and ethical practices, a new set of expectations emerged.

Supply Chain 5.0 recognizes that customers now seek more than just affordable and expedited products and services. They also demand sustainability, transparency, and ethical practices throughout the value chain. In this new era, the customer's voice resonates louder than ever, with an emphasis on personalized experiences and a genuine connection to the values and mission of the brands they engage with.

Imagine a customer who seeks not only a high-quality and affordable product but also assurance that it was produced in an environmentally responsible manner, with respect for human rights, and without compromising the well-being of communities. This new age of customer represents the shift from Supply Chain 4.0 to Supply Chain 5.0. In this new era, businesses must align their operations with these values and create value chains that are sustainable, ethical, and capable of meeting personalized customer needs.

In the era of Supply Chain 4.0, businesses focused on delivering products and services that met customer expectations. However, in Supply Chain 5.0, the emphasis is on creating meaningful relationships with customers, understanding their preferences, values, and feedback. It is about co-creating new solutions and business models with customers and suppliers that address social and environmental challenges.

Supply Chain 4.0 centered around optimizing existing supply chains for improved efficiency and meeting customer demand. However, the advent of Supply Chain 5.0 marks a transformative leap forward. It places the customer at the heart of the value delivery system, redefining how businesses operate and create value. Supply Chain 5.0 embodies a holistic approach that encompasses sustainability, human rights, and customer-centricity throughout the entire supply chain. It is no longer solely about achieving better, faster, and cheaper outcomes; it is about delivering products and services that are sustainable, ethical, and aligned with the personalized needs and values of the customer.

Supply Chain 5.0 breaks the traditional boundaries of supply chain management, fostering collaboration, innovation, and shared value creation among all stakeholders. It embraces a circular economy approach, minimizing waste and maximizing resource utilization. By leveraging advanced technologies, such as blockchain and data analytics, businesses can provide transparency, traceability, and information sharing throughout the supply chain, empowering customers to make informed choices and reinforcing trust.

As the table shows, Supply Chain 5.0 brings several new features and focus areas compared to Supply Chain 4.0. The new era of Supply Chain 5.0 represents a significant shift in the way businesses approach supply chain management. It is an era that recognizes the evolving demands of customers, the need for sustainability and ethical practices, and the importance of collaboration and innovation. By embracing Supply Chain 5.0, businesses can not only meet customer expectations but also contribute to a more sustainable and responsible future.

Feature/Focus Area	**Supply Chain 4.0**	**Supply Chain 5.0**
Goal	**To improve supply chain visibility and decision-making.**	**To enhance customer experience and revenue through sustainable value chains.**
Benefits	**Improved visibility, better efficiency, agility.**	**Improved visibility, efficiency, agility. Reduced environmental impact, improved working conditions, enhanced customer satisfaction, increased revenue, improved brand reputation.**

(*Continued*)

(*Continued*)

Feature/Focus Area	Supply Chain 4.0	Supply Chain 5.0
Customer Engagement	Focuses on delivering products and services that meet customer expectations.	Focuses on creating meaningful relationships with customers and understanding their preferences, values, and feedback.
Innovation	Adopting new technologies and processes to improve efficiency and performance.	Co-creating new solutions and business models with customers and suppliers that address social and environmental challenges.
Sustainability	Uses technology to reduce waste and optimize resources in the supply chain.	Uses technology to design products and services that minimize environmental impact and maximize social good throughout their life cycle.
Human Rights	Uses technology to comply with legal and ethical standards in the supply chain.	Uses technology to protect and promote the dignity, well-being, and empowerment of workers and communities in the supply chain.
Transparency	Uses technology to track and monitor the flow of goods and information in the supply chain.	Uses technology to share relevant information with customers and suppliers about the origin, quality, impact, and value of products and services.

(*Continued*)

Feature/Focus Area	Supply Chain 4.0	Supply Chain 5.0
Technology	**Uses advanced technologies such as the Internet of Things (IoT), big data analytics, blockchain and artificial intelligence (AI).**	**Builds on the foundations of Supply Chain 4.0 by incorporating sustainability, human rights, and customer-centricity into all aspects of the supply chain.**
Tools Used	**Just-In-Time (JIT), Kanban, supplier collaboration, Collaborative Planning, Forecasting & Replenishment (CPFR) are used to improve supply chain efficiency.** **Big data and cloud computing are used for optimization.**	**Personalization, specificity, availability of product next door or quickly online to customer are used to enhance customer experience.** **Collaboration with suppliers, partners, and customers through the use of technologies such as cloud computing and big data analytics.**
People	**Emphasizes the use of technology to automate tasks and improve efficiency.**	**Recognizes the significance of people in the supply chain and empowers them to make better holistic business decisions with the customer at its center.**

(*Continued*)

(*Continued*)

Feature/Focus Area	Supply Chain 4.0	Supply Chain 5.0
Culture	Cultivates a culture that values efficiency and performance.	Promotes a culture that embodies collaboration, responsibility, transparency, innovation, sustainability, and customer centricity.
Financials	Savings and bottom-line delivery in Profit and Loss Statement.	Sustainable revenue generation and bottom-line delivery in Profit and Loss Statement.
Economy	Linear economy	Circular economy
Resilience	Uses technology to anticipate and respond to disruptions in the supply chain.	Uses technology to adapt and transform the supply chain in response to changing customer needs and market conditions.
Supplier Relationship	Prioritizes effective negotiation of contracts and prices with suppliers.	Establishes and nurtures long-term partnerships with suppliers founded on trust, transparency, and shared values.
Risk Management	Places emphasis on the risks of disruption and lost sales.	Directs attention towards the risks of deforestation, use of non-renewable energy, human rights violation, loss of customers owing to reputation issues and lack of transparency, besides supply chain disruptions.

Now, let's explore the structure of this book and take a deeper dive into the subject of Supply Chain 5.0. The book is divided into nine sections, together covering the three key pillars of Supply Chain 5.0: customer-centricity, sustainability and human rights, and advanced digitalization. In the following, you will find a brief overview of the content covered in each section, providing a comprehensive understanding of the various aspects of Supply Chain 5.0.

Embracing a Customer-Centric Approach: How Supply Chains can Evolve

This is the first element of Supply Chain 5.0. The section emphasizes the importance of customer-centricity in modern supply chain management. With the rise of e-commerce and increasing customer demands for personalized experiences and quicker delivery times, a traditional focus on efficiency and cost savings is no longer enough. Establishing a customer-centric supply chain can help businesses enhance profits and long-term growth by identifying customer insights, increasing sales, and re-creating the supply chain to provide customers with a better experience. However, restrictions on data sharing and insufficient employee customer service awareness and empowerment can impede this strategy, so companies need to prioritize customer needs and continuously use data and digital technology to better understand and serve them.

Making Sustainability and Human Rights Hygiene Factors in Supply Chains

In the not-so-distant future, when sustainability and human rights are going to be fundamental in supply chains, companies must make these values central to their strategies. However, monitoring and ensuring compliance with standards can be difficult due to the complexity of supply chains. Emerging technologies like blockchain and AI can help, but it's important to consider all elements of the chain, from raw materials to distribution. Making sustainability and human rights hygiene factors is not just the right thing to do but also necessary for staying competitive. Businesses must work together with organizations to create a more responsible and sustainable world. This is the second element of Supply Chain 5.0.

Digitalization of Procurement: Strategies to Optimize Business

This section discusses the benefits and challenges of digitalization in businesses and specifically focuses on the use of data visualization tools in digitizing, visualizing, and analyzing data. The benefits of digitalization include accelerating business processes with automation, improving customer experience, better decision-making with data, greater agility, flexibility, scalability, reliability and security, and enhanced ability for creating productive digital workplaces and cultures. The section also provides recommendations for optimizing procurement strategies by using digital procurement, which involves the use of artificial intelligence, automation tools, and data analysis for developing procurement strategies. Digital procurement allows for an integrated network of people, processes, and technologies to generate greater value by reducing costs and creating more effective utilization of resources. Digitalization will help create transparency and speed to meet the new age customer requirements while ensuring elements of sustainability and human rights are preserved right from the beginning to the end of the value chain.

A Major Shift: AI and Blockchain Redefine the Supply Chain

This section explains how artificial intelligence (AI) and blockchain technology can work together to revolutionize the supply chain industry. AI is a technology that can analyze large amounts of data and make predictions based on that analysis. Blockchain is a decentralized, immutable ledger that keeps track of transactions and tracks digital assets across a network. When combined, these two technologies can create a supply chain that is more efficient, transparent, secure, and accurate than ever before. The chapter highlights three ways that blockchain and AI can revolutionize the supply chain industry. The global market for both technologies is predicted to expand significantly in the coming years, with organizations expected to spend billions of dollars on blockchain and AI. In summary, these cutting-edge technologies will become an integral part of how businesses operate in the future, and supply chain managers can increase the transparency and efficiency of their operations by utilizing them.

Metaverse — An Emerging Concept and Technology in Supply Chain Management

This section discusses the potential impact of metaverse technology on supply chain management. The metaverse is still in its early stages, but as it develops, it could lead to significant benefits, such as faster time-to-market, innovative planning strategies, and increased collaboration. By reducing obstacles and physical limitations, businesses can reduce costs, increase efficiency, and respond to customers more quickly. The metaverse could also revolutionize how we define supply chains by moving from a linear model to a collaborative supply network that is more interconnected and data-driven. Overall, the metaverse has boundless possibilities and the potential to transform the business landscape.

Innovating the Health System: A Look into the Future of Healthcare Supply Chains

This section discusses the importance of supply chain resilience and optimization in the healthcare industry, especially in the wake of the COVID-19 pandemic. It highlights the need for healthcare organizations to invest in technology and systems that enable better visibility, traceability, and data management. The section also presents tips for optimizing healthcare supply chains, including improving visibility, consolidating the supplier base, focusing on performance, and putting standardization into action. The optimization of the healthcare supply chain can result in cost savings for organizations and lower costs for patients, ultimately improving the quality of care. In the future, when healthcare will gain impetus, it is important to recognize this supply chain evolution in the context of Supply Chain 5.0.

Cold Supply Chain — The Future of Logistics and Supply Chain

The cold chain sector is expected to grow to a value of $340.3 billion by 2025 due to increased demand for specialized handling of personalized drugs and changing food distribution trends. Advancements in technology such as Blockchain, IoT, and AI are making it easier for suppliers to track their products and ensure they are kept at the correct temperature. As technology continues to progress, companies can manage their cold supply chains in a more efficient and sustainable way, reducing waste and energy consumption. Predictive analytics will allow companies to anticipate problems before they occur in the future. Innovations such as solar-powered refrigerated trucks are reducing emissions during transportation and assisting in the long-term viability of these cold supply chains. Overall, the future looks promising for the cold chain sector as a part of Supply Chain 5.0 with increased consumer demands and subsequent efficient and effective supply chains.

Harnessing the Power of Resilience to Create an Agile Supply Chain

The recent disruptions and pandemic have highlighted the importance of resilience and agility in supply chain management. According to a global study by Gartner, 87% of respondents plan to invest in supply chain resilience in the next two years, while 98% are looking to invest in agility. Supply chains need both agility and resilience to succeed, but which one should be prioritized depends on the business and industry. Companies can create a resilient and agile supply chain by analyzing their current processes, establishing a resilient and agile framework, strengthening supply chain relationships, embracing digital technologies, leveraging data and analytics, and mitigating risks. By doing so, they can reduce costs, mitigate risks associated with disruptions, and increase their competitive advantage.

Digital Defense: Protecting Supply Chains in the Cyber Age

As supply chains advance into the new era, the success of global supply chains relies heavily on effective cybersecurity strategies that address the complexity of cyber risks. Organizations must embed a culture of supply chain cyber risk, educate their staff on cybersecurity, implement effective policies, use advanced technologies, and increase collaboration with suppliers and partners. Ensuring the safety and integrity of the supply chain is essential to building confidence among business partners and customers, and protecting their data enables them to do business with the organization with peace of mind.

Welcome to the world of Supply Chain 5.0! This book is meant to be a guide to exploring the three essential elements of this exciting new era in supply chain management. We have meticulously crafted this book to provide you with comprehensive insights into the latest trends and developments in supply chain technology, logistics, and procurement. From blockchain to AI, we cover it all. As you read through these pages, you'll gain a deep understanding of how these crucial elements work together to form the backbone of Supply Chain 5.0. We hope this book will empower you to navigate the changing business landscape and prepare your organization for success in the era of evolving consumer demands and globalized economies.

Enjoy the read, and let's embark on this journey together to discover the exciting world of Supply Chain 5.0!

THE PATH TO SUPPLY CHAIN EXCELLENCE: EMBRACING THE CUSTOMER-CENTRIC PARADIGM

I

EMBRACING A CUSTOMER-CENTRIC APPROACH

HOW SUPPLY CHAINS CAN EVOLVE

Imagine you are browsing an online store to buy a pair of shoes. You find the perfect pair, select the right size, and proceed to the checkout page. But wait, there's an additional shipping charge that wasn't mentioned earlier, and the estimated delivery date is a week later than you expected. Frustrated, you abandon your shopping cart and begin your search again.

Imagine now if the online store had a customer-centric supply chain that anticipated your needs and delivered a seamless shopping experience. Your desired shoe size would be in stock, and the shipping charges would be transparent upfront, with an estimated delivery date that matched your expectations. This would make you more likely to return to the store and make future purchases.

In the era of supply chain 4.0, a clothing retailer might use technology to track and monitor the flow of goods and information in the supply chain, negotiate contracts and prices with suppliers, automate tasks and improve efficiency, and deliver products that meet customer expectations in terms of quality, price, and availability. However, in the era of supply chain 5.0, the same retailer might improve further to use technology to share relevant information with customers and suppliers about the origin, quality, impact, and value of products, build long-term partnerships with suppliers based on trust, transparency, and shared values, empower workers and communities in the supply chain to make better and holistic business decisions with the customer at its center, and co-create new solutions and business models with customers and suppliers that address social and environmental challenges.

This is the power of a customer-centric supply chain. In today's evolving business environment, it's essential to create a supply chain that revolves around your customers' needs. Supply chain managers are starting to realize that the traditional model of focusing solely on efficiency and cost savings or even adapting processes and systems to become more efficient in meeting customer demands is no longer sufficient. Customers demand personalized experiences, quicker delivery times, and a seamless shopping experience.

For businesses to succeed in this new era of e-commerce, they need to adopt a customer-centric approach to supply chain management. This means not only understanding the needs and wants of your customers but also creating a supply chain that can cater to those needs. From the initial product design to the final delivery, every step should be taken with the customer in mind.

In a customer-centric supply chain, the focus is not only on delivering products but also on delivering an experience. This requires collaboration across all departments, from design to sales and marketing, to ensure that the customer's needs are met at every step. By creating a supply chain that revolves around the customer, businesses can build brand loyalty and increase customer retention, leading to long-term success.

As the e-commerce industry continues to grow and evolve, businesses that fail to adapt to a customer-centric approach risk being left behind. A supply chain that puts the customer first is no longer a luxury but a necessity in today's competitive market. This becomes the key element of the new era in Supply Chain 5.0. So, let's dive into the world of customer-centric supply chain management and explore the strategies that companies can use to meet the needs of their customers and build a successful business.

What is a Customer-Centric Supply Chain?

A customer-centric supply chain is focused on delivering both profit and a high-value customer experience and is deeply knowledgeable of and responsive to customer needs (Gartner, n.d.). To meet customer requirements, all supply chain-related parties must operate in coordination and value the customer experience.

In other words, manufacturers focus on how they present their goods and services to the ever-changing market in addition to operational efficiency. They must be able to timely obtain, correlate, and act upon demand requests to make planning, routing, and scheduling decisions throughout the supply chain (Figure 1). This, in return, leads to an increase in customer lifetime value, customer satisfaction, and profitability while reducing churn (Sorgun, 2022).

Traditionally, the supply chain is an end-to-end chain consisting of raw materials, suppliers, manufacturing, distribution, and customers. In customer-centric supply chains, customers influence every component of the supply chain.

Customer-centric supply chains enable companies to develop longer-term relationships with consumers than just a sale. Providing connected customer experiences or product-as-a-service model are good examples of this — the aim is to provide

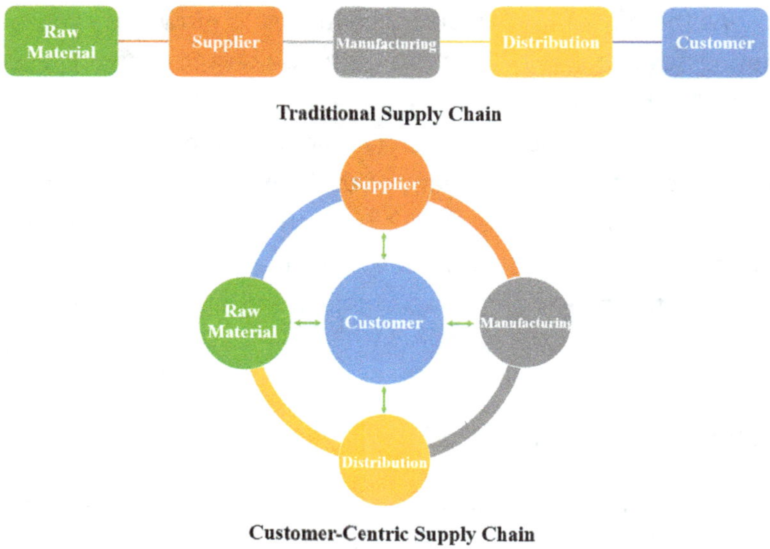

Figure 1. Traditional and Customer-Centric Supply Chain.

products as managed services, which enables greater control and monitoring of the consequences for the companies and better service and experience for their customers (Consultancy.asia, 2020).

Meeting Customers' Needs with Individual Customization

Today's customers no longer need standard products but expect products and services to be as tailored as possible. Mass customization and personalization are becoming trends in digital strategies for businesses and manufacturing in Industry 4.0 (Pech & Vrchota, 2022).

Companies must adopt a more flexible and responsive model to achieve a customer-centric supply chain. This model should be designed to meet the changing needs of consumers, including faster delivery times, greater product customization, and more personalized experiences. By adopting a customer-centric approach, companies can increase customer satisfaction and loyalty, which will help drive long-term growth and success.

Customer-centricity is the first essential and key element of Supply Chain 5.0, as supply chains will evolve from a support function to a critical partner in serving customers. All participants in the supply chain must collaborate to identify customer demands, meet customer requirements, and provide a satisfying customer experience. The future of supply chain management is about creating a customer-centric supply chain that is flexible, responsive, and sustainable. The use of big data and advanced technologies will play a crucial role in the evolution of supply chains and in delivering a better customer experience.

Trends Driving the Evolution of Supply Chains

E-commerce and Last-Mile Delivery

One of the key trends driving the evolution of supply chains is the rise of e-commerce and the growing importance of last-mile delivery. With the increasing popularity of online shopping, consumers are demanding faster and more convenient delivery options.

According to the EY future customer index, 44% of customers say the availability of delivery has become more important in guiding their purchases; 60% of customers are currently visiting brick-and-mortar stores less than before the pandemic; and 43% of customers shop more often online for products that they would have previously bought in stores (Alexander, 2021). To meet these needs, companies are investing in technology and logistics solutions to improve last-mile delivery and provide an impeccable experience for consumers.

The last or final mile is when an item is shipped to the consumer from a local warehouse or fulfillment center. Every stage of the supply chain process is essential, but the final mile impacts the customer experience. If a product is delivered late, damaged, or not delivered at all, there is a high likelihood that the customer will purchase from a competitor in the future. The last mile is where a business has its values, brand, and promise at the customer's door.

The last-mile delivery inefficiencies are referred to as the last-mile problem. The last mile is often the most expensive and time-consuming part of shipping, and the last mile often accounts for 53% of the total costs of shipments (Bell, n.d.).

The company progressively pays more attention to the customer's requirements in the delivery process, such as by implementing a customer-centric delivery system that includes delivery options, such as same-day or two-day delivery, and choosing delivery-to-door time — notifications via instant message, vehicle tracking, automated order import, and customer self-service (Figure 2).

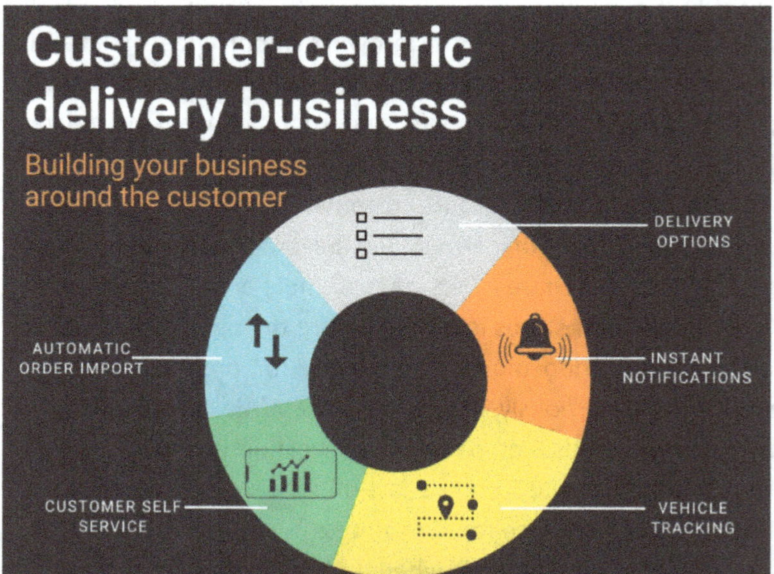

Figure 2. Customer-Centric Delivery Business (Miashkova, 2021).

The Rise of Data and Analytics

Another trend driving the evolution of supply chains is the rise of data and analytics. With the increasing amount of data generated by consumers and companies, big data and analytics are becoming an essential part of supply chain management. By analyzing these data, companies can gain insights into consumer behavior, demand patterns, and delivery times, which can help them make better decisions about inventory management, production planning, and supply chain optimization. Data processing functions like big data and AI can extract valuable insights from data, helping to identify market trends and understand customer needs for improved customer service.

Carrier is the maker of indoor air quality systems. Its systems relied on manual processes that caused inefficiencies in many parts of the supply chain. They used a database management system and EY technologists to correct this outdated strategy to integrate multiple ERP systems worldwide. This allowed all data to be in the cloud, which let Carrier and its customers quickly access needed information to make better-informed decisions. By developing this solid data foundation, Carrier now has a holistic view of its customer's needs, which it can use to identify new opportunities to add value and drive growth (Balis & Moore, 2021).

The Rise of Sustainability and Corporate Social Responsibility

The increase in sustainability and corporate social responsibility is also driving the evolution of supply chains. As consumers become more conscious of the environmental impact of their purchasing decisions, companies are looking for ways to reduce their carbon footprint and create more sustainable

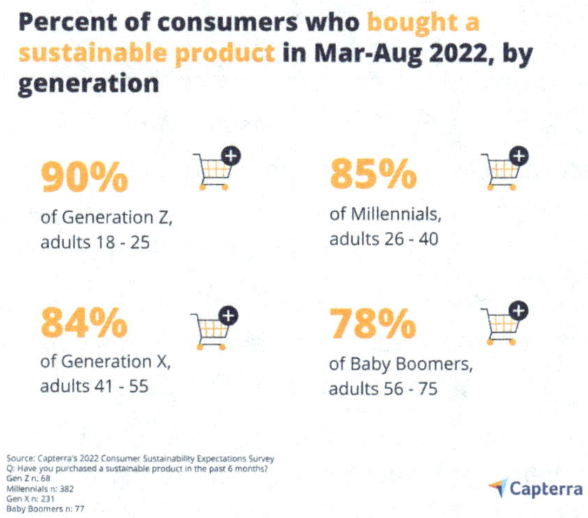

Figure 3. The Preference of All Age Groups for Buying Sustainable Products (Montgomery, 2023).

supply chains. This is achieved using renewable energy, more efficient transportation methods, and reduced waste and emissions.

Consumers want sustainable and ethically made products. 84% of the consumers purchased a sustainable product in the second half of 2022, up from 67% in 2021. Furthermore, studies have shown that on average, customers are willing to pay approximately 8% more for sustainable products (Montgomery, 2023). The preference of all age groups for buying sustainable products is shown in Figure 3, which shows that Generation Z adults are more inclined to purchase sustainable products.

In Germany, DHL runs 20,000 electric vehicles [EVs] daily — out of 60,000 total vehicles — to deliver parcels and letters. The delivery bicycle fleet has been transformed into 19,000 e-bikes and e-trikes. Delivery sites will also become greener. They are investing €600 million in EVs and carbon-neutral delivery sites, which leverage and store solar power and use heat pumps to achieve fossil-free heating (Hempsch, 2022).

Consumers pay close attention to food safety, requesting high-quality food with information transparency and safety assurances. Food traceability systems can reduce information asymmetry, implement safety governance across geographical boundaries, and help increase consumer faith in food safety to achieve sustainable agricultural development (Anastasiadis *et al.*, 2021).

Benefits and Challenges of a Customer-Centric Approach

How Does a Customer-Centric Approach Increase Long-Term Growth and Success?

The customer-centric approach is an effective strategy for long-term growth and success. It is a model that captures the relationship between customers and sales organizations in the Internet era. It incorporates three key factors (Palmatier, 2019): customer experience management, customer insights, and customer-centric marketing.

Companies that take a customer-centric approach focus on providing a positive customer experience and gaining insights into customer needs and wants. This helps them understand their customers better, anticipate their needs, and create tailored marketing messages. By understanding their customers and providing them with a positive customer experience, companies can build customer loyalty, increase customer satisfaction, and increase long-term growth and success.

Sephora is the world's leading specialty beauty retailer and a pioneer in predictive analytics. Sephora tracks trends related to your product consumption; the site homepage showcases products "recommended for you," a selection based on a mix of past purchases and browsing activity.

Besides, Sephora sends a message saying, "your goods are due for replenishment soon," and gives you options to renew in-store or online based on inventory detail. This is an excellent example of personalization, from a brand and customer experience perspective, while also connecting the supply chain ideally (Liddell & Bora, 2021). These efforts have garnered success, with 80% of surveyed Beauty Insiders professing complete loyalty to Sephora (Cah, 2018).

Similar to how Sephora predicts customer preferences and increases customer loyalty through data analytics, Walmart raises the purchasing experience for its customers.

In a growing yet underdeveloped e-commerce landscape, Walmart partnered with Publicis Sapient to develop the experience across all touchpoints, including a launched mobile app that is available on both iOS and Android. They provide customer-centric service, including a real-time slot booking engine for grocery pickup, a fixed grocery-list style shopping cart, and the ability to save customers' carts across devices and channels (Figure 4). The new experience results in a 98% increase in mobile orders (Publicis Sapient, n.d.).

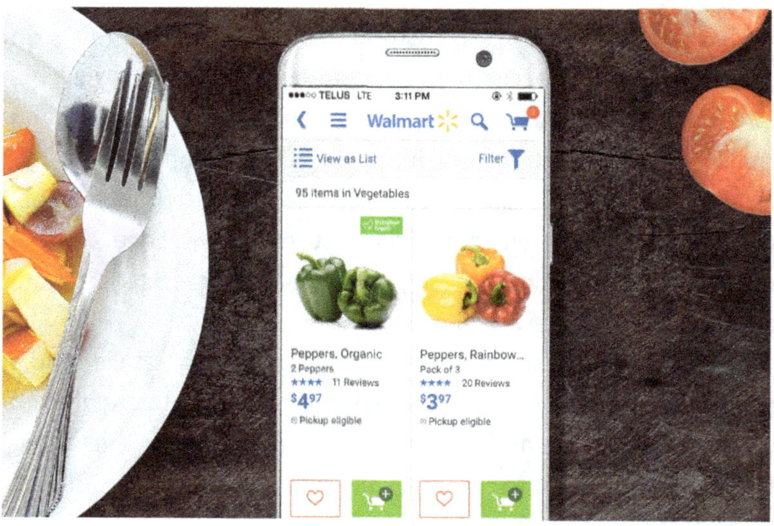

Figure 4. Walmart Mobile App (Publicis Sapient, n.d.).

Customer-centric marketing allows companies to target potential customers more effectively, as they can tailor their messages to their target audience. This helps attract more customers and increase the company's customer base, leading to increased sales and profits. Ultimately, the customer-centric approach is a compelling long-term growth and success strategy.

Meeting Customers' Needs with Individual Customization by Aligning Supply Chain with Customers

As businesses recognize the importance of meeting customers' needs with individual customization, they increasingly turn to customer-driven and customer-centric supply chains (Martinelli & Tunisini, 2019). The marketing function will gradually shift from mass marketing to segmented marketing and eventually toward customer-centric marketing in the 21st century. Customer-centric marketing seeks to fulfill the needs and wants of each customer (Sheth, 2000).

It is important to recognize that incorporating design-centric approaches into supply chain management can yield significant benefits. These approaches enable better alignment between product design and customer needs, leading to improved outcomes. Designers should employ outside-in thinking when designing services for industrial companies, aiming to gain insights into customer needs and achieve a Customer-Centric Supply Chain (Miettinen, 2016). Not only is the alignment of product design with the supply chain important for improving competitive advantage, but it also has a significant impact on improving supply chain responsiveness and resilience (Khan *et al.*, 2012).

Some Barriers to Customer-Centricity

1. **Organizational silos prevent customer data sharing (Alburger, 2020)**: Even though data silos have long been the

enemy of all organizations and their marketing departments, businesses confront new challenges. The distinctions between marketing, sales, and customer service are less distinct. Customer insights and data are no longer solely the responsibility of marketing departments but extend beyond them into upstream supply chains and their suppliers. The consumer necessitates that these teams share data to obtain a comprehensive view of the consumer experience.

2. **Employees are not empowered to focus on high-value experiences (Alburger, 2020)**: Customer support employees are frequently inundated with monotonous and repetitive tasks. This hinders their ability to handle complex issues, provide exceptional customer service, and provide corrective feedback to the upstream processes and supply chain.
3. **Products and services are not designed with data collection in mind (Alburger, 2020)**: To deliver personalized, customer-centric experiences, brands need access to customer information. However, services and activities must be designed to collect this information on the front end.

How to Build a Customer-Centric Supply Chain?

Use Customer Data to Gain Insights into Customer Needs

As data about consumers increase in value, customers are increasingly concerned about how their information is used. Data protection is slowly becoming more critical.

Even to be willing to share their data with a company, customers need to trust that the company will not re-purpose or re-sell the data downstream in ways they might find inscrutable or objectionable (Ucuzoglu & Hagel III, 2020). How do you convince customers to share data? There is no doubt that data sharing can increase customer value. The time has come for many organizations to ask the following question: How is customer data used to benefit customers?

One example of this is seen in recommender algorithms. Companies that utilize consumer data to benefit the customer have a valuable opportunity to stand out by targeting not only what customers will click on, but also what resonates with them on a deeper level. This deeper utility to the customer is why the integration of human-centric AI becomes crucial, impacting not just design but also unexpected areas such as social science, psychology, art and the humanities (Ucuzoglu & Hagel III, 2020).

To begin, start by leveraging the data you already have to benefit the customer. By adopting a customer-centric approach and applying human-centric AI disciplines to your existing data, new opportunities to satisfy your customers will undoubtedly emerge. Additionally, consider the customer throughout their entire lifecycle. To harness the full potential of data, businesses should shift away from a narrow transactional focus and explore ways to enhance value within a broader context, both before and after the sale. Furthermore, it is essential to realign the company's operations. Drawing insights from data, businesses need to reassess their emphasis on standardized processes and instead prioritize customized customer interactions that adapt to each individual customer's unique and evolving needs.

Corporations must use data to make data-driven decisions in order to build efficient supply chains. Effective management strategies, process enhancements, and improved chain cohesion can all be aided by accurate and thorough supply chain data. In this situation, it is crucial to gather and share real-time data from various sources, such as vendors and customers, which can be done efficiently using a business intelligence platform. Analytics tools can aid in accurate trend forecasting and preparation for supply chain shocks (Jain, 2023a).

Use Digitalization and Technology Readiness for Product Customization in the Supply Chain

As the demand for personalized goods and services rises, an increasing number of manufacturing businesses are transitioning to a customer-centric business model. Although this strategy can generate new sales opportunities, it can also increase production costs and complexity. By implementing digital technology like digital twins and machine learning, operating costs can be decreased, and production efficiency improved to better complete customized products for customers.

StarGrup, one of the leading manufacturers of custom glass products for shopping malls, etc., develops and delivers products that meet customers' needs and expectations (Figure 5). StarGrup's production facility in Hadımköy, which has around 350 employees, must handle orders for approximately 100 new products daily, a complicated task given the degree of customization required for each order. Besides, customers typically expect delivery in 7–10 days after their product specifications are set. ICRON devised a software platform solution for StarGrup to optimize its production process and resource utilization to solve this dilemma. Consisting of Planning and Scheduling

Figure 5. StarGrup (StarGrup Homepage, 2023).

Solutions, Capacity Planning Solutions, and Data Collection, it gives StarGrup's planners complete visibility and control over real-time operations and the capability to produce accurate, optimal daily production schedules as well as long-term capacity plans (ICRON, 2022).

Another important component was a Scenario Management Tool, a visual decision support environment through which planners can generate alternative production plans utilizing different machine loads and shifts to avoid bottlenecks. Overall, the implementation of ICRON's solution greatly improved the flexibility and efficiency of StarGrup's production process with a 200% increase in net profit, a 60% increase in sales, a 40% increase in on-time delivery, an 80% decrease in production planning time, and a 10% decrease in raw material safety stock (ICRON, 2022).

Amazon, for instance, created the Dynamic Delivery Planner (DDP) to solve the final-mile problems for faster delivery, reduced costs, and a better customer experience. DDP provides the best route sequence, delivery time window, and real-time routing using machine learning and is capable of real-time rerouting that handles constantly changing traffic conditions and customer time windows when drivers are already on the move. AWS developed the DDP solution jointly with Aramex Australia. As an outcome, Aramex Australia observed a 29% improvement in delivery efficiency during their simulation studies. Aramex Australia Chief Information Officer Ruby Wolff shares his feedback as follows: "The way the solution is able to balance travel time with delivery efficiency is making a big difference for our drivers" (Wu & Baeuml, 2023).

Prioritize Customer-Centricity in the Supply Chain

When starting a new project, seeking improvement, or implementing changes, it is crucial to prioritize the experience of the consumer. The strategies employed by supply chains must

Figure 6. Customer-Centricity Factors (Jain, 2023b).

continuously evolve to be customer-centric. Companies should also train their employees to think in this way, grant them more autonomy, and emphasize the importance of customer care. Understanding the customer and valuing their feedback is vital.

To foster loyalty, it is essential to adopt a customer-centric approach (Figure 6). Apart from making adjustments at the front-end, supply chains should establish connections with customer feedback systems. This enables them to provide maximum value by ensuring an end-to-end value chain that revolves around meeting customer needs.

Conclusion

With the rise of e-commerce, rising consumer demand for personalized experiences and product customization, faster delivery, and the growing influence of environmental and safety concerns on consumer purchasing decisions, the traditional emphasis on efficiency and cost savings is inadequate.

As businesses continue to grapple with the ever-changing demands of consumers, one thing is clear: customer-centricity is no longer just an option, it is a necessity. In the fast-paced world of supply chain management, the need for a customer-centric approach has never been more urgent.

Gone are the days when the supply chain was just a support function for a business. Today, it has evolved into a vital partner that can make or break a company's success. With the advent of Supply Chain 5.0, customer-centricity will become even more critical.

Establishing a customer-centric supply chain can assist businesses in enhancing their profits and long-term growth. Customer-centricity is the essential component of Supply Chain 5.0, as the supply chain has shifted from a support function to a vital partner. Applying customer-centricity to the supply chain requires the company to prioritize customer needs, use data and digital technology to continuously understand customer desires, and then tailor the supply chain, remove restrictions on data sharing, and raise employees' customer-focused awareness and empowerment to create a more socially responsible and sustainable supply chain.

To create a truly customer-centric supply chain, companies must first prioritize the needs of their customers. This means understanding the desires and preferences of customers and then creating the supply chain around those needs. But it's not just about using data and digital technology to understand customer demands; it's also about removing restrictions on data sharing and raising employee awareness and empowerment to create a socially responsible and sustainable supply chain.

In this new era of supply chain management, businesses that prioritize customer-centricity will be the ones that thrive. The companies that focus on delivering personalized experiences and faster delivery times while also prioritizing environmental and safety concerns will be the ones that capture the hearts and minds of consumers.

As the world continues to change at a breakneck pace, the need for a customer-centric supply chain will only become more critical. Businesses that embrace this approach will not only enhance their profits and long-term growth but also create a better world for everyone. The future of supply chain management is here, and it's all about putting the customer first.

References

Alburger, J. (2020, December 9). *5 Barriers to Customer-Centricity (And How to Overcome Them).* Hubtype. https://www.hubtype.com/blog/customer-centricity.

Alexander, H. (2021, September 8). *How Could Last-Mile Strategy Be Your Biggest Competitive Advantage*? EY. https://www.ey.com/en_us/strategy-transactions/supply-chain-last-mile-strategy.

Anastasiadis, F., Apostolidou, I., & Michailidis, A. (2021, March 5). Food traceability: A consumer-centric supply chain approach on sustainable Tomato. *Challenging the Status Quo to Shape Food Systems Transformation from a Nutritional and Food Security Perspective*, 10(3), 543. https://doi.org/10.3390/foods10030543.

Balis, J. & Moore, B. (2021, October 28). How data analytics is used to support a customer-centric strategy. EY. https://www.ey.com/en_us/cio/how-data-analytics-is-used-to-support-a-customer-centric-strategy.

Bell, R. (n.d.). *Last Mile Delivery Explained: Trends, Challenges, Costs & More.* Merchants Fleet. Retrieved March 2023, from https://www.merchantsfleet.com/industry-insights/what-is-last-mile-delivery/.

Cah. (2018, November 13). *Beauty in the Age of Individualism: Sephora's Data-Driven Approach.* Technology and operations management MBA student perspectives. https://d3.harvard.edu/platform-rctom/submission/beauty-in-the-age-of-individualism-sephoras-data-driven-approach/.

Consultancy.asia. (2020, August 10). *Redesign Chinese Supply Chains with Customers at the Core*. https://www.consultancy.asia/news/3448/redesign-chinese-supply-chains-with-customers-at-the-core.

Gartner. (n.d.). *Four Steps to Become a Customer-Centric Supply Chain.* Retrieved March 2023, from https://www.gartner.com/en/supply-chain/trends/customer-centric-supply-chain.

Hempsch, C. (2022, August 2). *DHL on Sustainable, Customer-Centric Delivery in the Last Mile.* McKinsey & Company. https://www.mckinsey.com/capabilities/operations/our-insights/global-infrastructure-initiative/voices/dhl-on-sustainable-customer-centric-delivery-in-the-last-mile.

ICRON. (2022, September 8). *Glass Manufacturer Increases Net Profit by 200% with ICRON.* https://www.icrontech.com/blog_item/glass-manufacturer-increases-net-profit-by-200-percent-with-icron/.

Jain, P. (2023a, February 22). *Building Customer-Centric Supply Chains — A Critical Aspect in Organizational Performance.* LinkedIn. https://www.linkedin.com/pulse/building-customer-centric-supply-chains-critical-aspect-jain%3FtrackingId=cyiZOSU9Teyb8KbN4l%252Fsfg%253D%253D/?trackingId=cyiZOSU9Teyb8KbN4l%2Fsfg%3D%3D.

Jain, P. (2023b, February). *What Does It Mean to Be Customer Centric.* LinkedIn. https://www.linkedin.com/posts/prateekjain01_branding-customercentric-supplychain-activity-7029343129862381568-NOA8/?utm_source=share&utm_medium=member_desktop.

Khan, O., Christopher, M., & Creazza, A. (2012, April 27). *Aligning Product Design with the Supply Chain: A Case Study.* Emerald Insight. https://www.emerald.com/insight/content/doi/10.1108/13598541211227144/full/html.

Liddell, P. & Bora, L. (2021, February 15). *Transforming to a Customer Centric Supply Chain.* KPMG. https://kpmg.com/au/en/home/insights/2020/03/transforming-to-customer-centric-supply-chain.html.

Martinelli, E. M. & Tunisini, A. (2019, March 1). Customer integration into supply chains: Literature review and research propositions. *Journal of Business & Industrial Marketing.* ISSN: 0885-8624. https://www.emerald.com/insight/content/doi/10.1108/JBIM-07-2017-0162/full/html.

Miashkova, Y. (2021, June 8). *How to Build a Customer-Centric Delivery Business.* Track-POD. https://www.track-pod.com/blog/customer-centric-delivery/.

Miettinen, S. (2016). *Introduction to Industrial Service Design.* Routledge.

Montgomery, O. (2023, January 24). *A Customer-Centric Supply Chain Strategy Evolves As 80% of SMBs Invest in Sustainability.* Capterra.

https://www.capterra.com/resources/customer-centric-supply-chain-strategy-evolves-as-eighty-percent-of-small-businesses-invest-in-sustainability/.

Palmatier, R. W., Moorman, C., & Lee, J.-Y. (2019, August 30). Handbook on Customer Centricity. *Business 2019,* 133–155. https://doi.org/10.4337/9781788113601.00012.

Pech, M. & Vrchota, J. (2022, March 9). The product customization process in relation to industry 4.0 and digitalization. *Manufacturing Industry 4.0: Trends and Perspectives,* 10(3), 539. https://doi.org/10.3390/pr10030539.

Publicis Sapient. (n.d.). *How Customer-Centricity Drives a Reimagined Multichannel Shopping Experience*. Retrieved March 2023, from https://www.publicissapient.com/work/walmart.

StarGrup. (2023). StarGrup Homepage. Retrieved June 26, 2023, from https://stargrup.com.tr/

Sheth, J. N., Sisodia, R. S., & Sharma, A. (2000, December). The antecedents and consequences of customer-centric marketing. *Journal of the Academy of Marketing Science* 28, 55–66.

Sorgun, Ö. (2022, September 9*). Customer Centric Supply Chain: What is It, Why is It Important Now?* ICRON. https://www.icrontech.com/blog_item/customer-centric-supply-chain-what-is-it-why-is-it-important-now/.

Ucuzoglu, J. & Hagel III, J. (2020, April 24). *Use Your Customer Data Actually to Help Your Customers.* Harvard Business Review. https://hbr.org/2020/04/use-your-customer-data-to-actually-help-your-customers.

Wu, C. & Baeuml, M. (2023, March 1). *AWS Last Mile Solution for Faster Delivery, Lower Costs, and a Better Customer Experience.* AWS. https://aws.amazon.com/blogs/supply-chain/aws-last-mile-solution-for-faster-delivery-lower-costs-and-a-better-customer-experience/.

NAVIGATING THE ETHICAL LANDSCAPE BEYOND PROFIT

2

MAKING SUSTAINABILITY AND HUMAN RIGHTS HYGIENE FACTORS IN THE SUPPLY CHAIN

Imagine a future in which sustainability and human rights preservation are as essential as hygiene factors in our supply chains. What would that look like?

Sustainability and human rights are critical issues that are rapidly gaining attention in today's global economy. Consumers are becoming increasingly conscious of the impact their purchases have on the environment and society, and they expect companies to take responsibility for their impact. As consumers, we want to buy products that are made responsibly without harming people or the planet. This has led to a growing demand for products that are both environmentally friendly and ethically sourced. And companies are responding by making sustainability and human rights central to their supply chain management strategies (Figure 1).

However, ensuring that supply chains are sustainable and human rights compliant is not without its challenges. Supply

Figure 1. Brief Introduction of Supplier Code of Conduct (Five Key Points) (CKPower, n.d.).

chains can be long and complex, spanning multiple countries and involving many different actors. It can be difficult to monitor and control the environmental and social impact of all the activities that take place within a supply chain and to ensure that all suppliers are adhering to the same standards.

Unfortunately, there have been instances where many large companies have prioritized profits over environmental or human rights concerns, choosing to engage in harmful practices that result in waste, pollution, deforestation (see Figure 2), or violations of human rights. For example, in 2015, Volkswagen acknowledged deceiving emissions tests in the US, which had severe environmental implications. Similarly, FMCG companies pledging to use responsibly sourced palm oil were implicated in palm oil abuse in Papa New Guinea (Figure 3), leading to deforestation and displacement of indigenous communities (Hotten, 2015). Furthermore, allegations of labor rights violations have plagued

Figure 2. Aerial view of a large burned area in the city of Candeiras do Jamari in the state of Rondônia (Greenpeace, 2019).

Figure 3. Rainforest Damage Caused by Palm Oil Operation (Global Witness, 2021). https://www.globalwitness.org/en/campaigns/forests/true-price-palm-oil/#conclusions

a leading AI company, to develop super-efficient servers for data center cooling. Together, they have achieved a remarkable 40% reduction in cooling energy consumption by creating a more efficient framework for understanding data center dynamics and optimizing efficiency (Sanu, 2022).

When thinking about how to make sustainability and human rights hygiene factors in the supply chain, it is important to consider all elements of the chain. This includes the sourcing of materials, production processes, transport, storage, and distribution.

Ultimately, it's not just about following the law; it's about creating a culture of respect and dignity by taking the necessary steps to make sure that everyone involved in the supply chain is being treated fairly and ethically.

Why Sustainability and Human Rights Matter

Around the world, 1.4 billion workers endure appalling working conditions. Slavery and forced labor are affecting an increasing number of people. The International Labor Organization (ILO) has recently estimated that there are currently 28 million people in this category. Additionally, more and more children are being made to work against their will because their parents' incomes are insufficient. Examples of this include Burkinabe goldmines, Bangladeshi textile factories, and the Republic of Côte d'Ivoire cocoa plantations. The COVID-19 pandemic has made the situation even worse, and as a result, the ILO estimates that there are currently about 160 million children working — of which, more than half are under the age of twelve (BMWK — Federal Ministry for Economic Affairs and Climate Action, 2022).

International supply chains also exacerbate global environmental problems. The extent of greenhouse gas emissions and air pollution, which vary by industry, can be up to 90% attributable to supply chain activities rather than the day-to-day business companies like Nike, with accusations of exploiting workers through low wages, excessive overtime, and unsafe conditions in factories across countries like China, Vietnam, and Indonesia (Dhaka Tribune, 2023). Zara has also faced allegations of using slave labor and sweatshops in multiple countries, forcing workers to endure long hours, wage withholding, and hazardous environments. These examples underscore the critical importance of holding companies accountable for their actions and fostering sustainable practices that respect both the environment and human rights (Westervelt, 2015).

Sustainability and human rights are absolutely paramount when it comes to any supply chain. Sustainability refers to business operations that do not harm the environment, animal welfare, or human rights, which encompass the right to freedom, fair labor practices, and an adequate standard of living.

One of the biggest drivers of sustainability and human rights in supply chains is technology. Emerging technologies like blockchain and artificial intelligence are helping companies better track and monitor the environmental and social impacts of their supply chains and ensure that suppliers are adhering to the right standards. For example, AI-powered systems are utilized to optimize the routing of delivery trucks, which in turn reduces fuel consumption and greenhouse gas emissions (Alansari, 2021), while block-chain technology helps with the complete traceability of the raw material right up to its source. These technologies will continue to play a key role in promoting sustainability and human rights in supply chains and will shape the future of the industry. However, if not properly managed, technology such as Google data centers can lead to a substantial increase in power consumption. In the past year alone, data centers globally accounted for approximately 3% (equivalent to around 416 terawatts) of the world's total electricity usage, which is nearly 40% higher than the entire electricity consumption of the United Kingdom. Consequently, Google has collaborated with Deepmind,

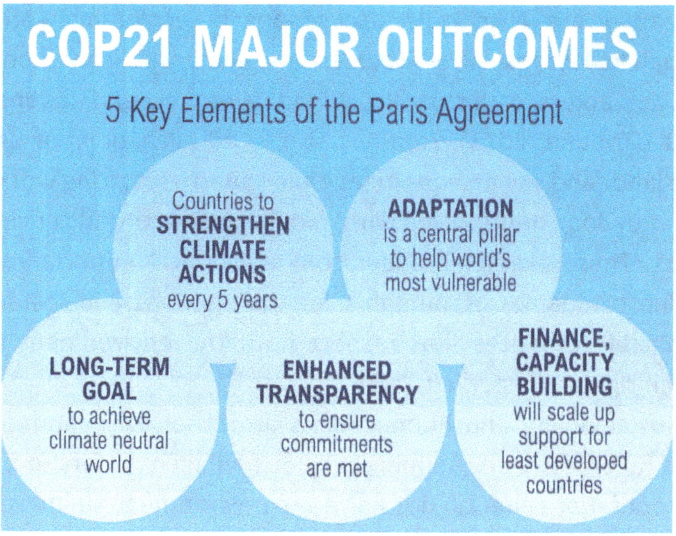

Figure 4. Five Key Elements of the Paris Agreement (Designed by World Resources Institute).

operations of multinational corporations. For instance, the food and textile industries almost entirely consume land and water at the supplier level (BMWK — Federal Ministry for Economic Affairs and Climate Action, 2022).

It's not just about avoiding bad publicity, though; it's also about ensuring that we meet global targets for sustainability. The Paris Agreement is a recent example of this from 2015, when countries came together to agree on measures to reduce greenhouse gas emissions in order to prevent dangerous levels of climate change (Figure 4). Achieving these targets will require businesses to adopt sustainable practices throughout their supply chains.

Outdoor apparel and gear retailers provide models for supply chain sustainability, such as making clothes from recycled plastic bottles or repairing used garments.

- Patagonia runs a green distribution facility that has won awards, and it created a "zero waste" program by using sustainable packaging materials and minimizing the weight of its packaging. The Sustainable Apparel Coalition is an industry collaboration with the mission of creating "an apparel industry with no needless environmental harm and a positive impact on the people and communities associated with its activities" (Luther, 2020).

- According to stories from publisher SustainCase, sustainable practices are universal and can cross all industries. For example, one road builder reduced shipping distance and associated carbon emissions by 40% and achieved a lower total landed cost by purchasing local supplies, as opposed to previously purchasing asphalt based solely on price (Luther, 2020).
- Tons of waste were eliminated when a fast-food chain redesigned its packaging to prevent repacking in the supply chain (Luther, 2020).
- The "code of conduct compliance declaration" that an electronics company requires suppliers to sign emphasizes integrity and governance (Luther, 2020).

Businesses are increasingly waking up to the realization that they need to factor in sustainability and human rights preservation into their supply chains if they want to maintain a good reputation and stay in business. The Impact of Sustainability and Human Rights on Customers, a report by the Business & Human Rights Resource Center, states that: "When companies do not respect human rights throughout their operations, it can lead to boycotts, protests, and regulatory action. In some cases, it has also led to the withdrawal of investment, legal action, and the loss of contracts. The damage to a company's reputation can be significant" (Govindan *et al.*, 2021).

As consumers become increasingly aware of ethical business practices, sustainability and human rights preservation are becoming critical components for businesses to sustain and thrive. According to Opentext, companies with ethical sourcing strategies in place are prioritized by 90% of consumers, and 83% of consumers are willing to spend more on products from such companies. Therefore, incorporating ethical and sustainable practices is no longer just a nice thing to do; it is essential for the survival of businesses (OpenText, 2021). Therefore, companies, especially their supply chains, should make sustainability a priority and ensure strict adherence to human rights policies. This is crucial to maintaining competitiveness in the market and safeguarding their reputation.

Consumer engagement is a critical aspect of the sustainability journey, as highlighted in Prateek Jain's diagram (Figure 5). To accelerate the achievement of carbon-neutral targets by 2050, it is essential to actively involve consumers. While organizations and governments are beginning to prioritize sustainability, the role of consumers will become increasingly important in the future. Supply chains must recognize this and adopt sustainable practices earlier to maintain their competitiveness.

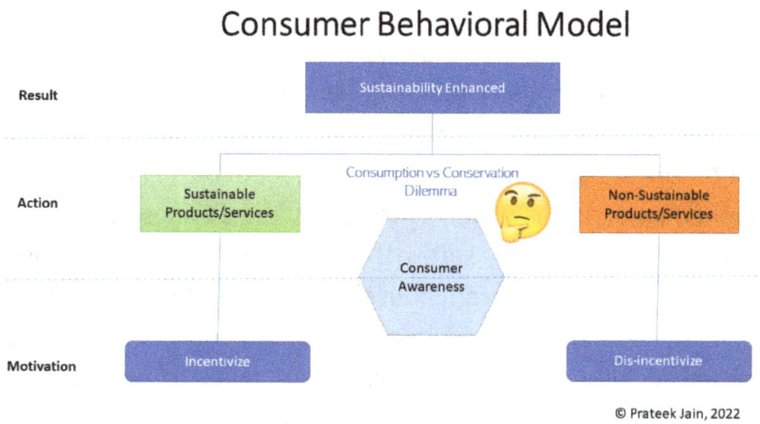

Figure 5. Consumer Behavioral Model to Engage and Involve Consumers in a Sustainability Drive. Without Consumer's Involvement the Acceleration Toward Achievement will be Slow [Prateek Jain, 2022]. This was designed by Prateek Jain and was delivered at a keynote address to European Chamber of .Commerce, Singapore Members.

Failing to engage consumers in this sustainability journey can hinder progress towards a sustainable future. By actively involving consumers and making them a part of the solution, supply chains can have a significant impact. This requires creating awareness, providing information, and encouraging sustainable choices among consumers.

Collaboration between supply chains and consumers is crucial to driving the adoption of sustainable practices. It not only helps in meeting carbon-neutral targets but also protects the environment, preserves resources, and safeguards the well-being of future generations. By prioritizing consumer engagement and integrating sustainable practices, companies can not only remain competitive in the market but also protect their reputation as responsible and environmentally conscious entities.

Emphasizing the Importance of Human Rights in Supply Chains

The consideration of human rights in supply chains is of utmost importance for several reasons. Firstly, it is a matter of ethical responsibility for businesses to ensure that the goods and services they provide are not associated with human rights violations. Companies have a duty to respect the rights of workers, communities, and other stakeholders involved in their supply chains (NAPs on Business and Human Rights, n.d). This means taking proactive steps to prevent and address any human rights abuses that may occur throughout the supply chain. By prioritizing human rights, businesses can demonstrate their commitment to social responsibility and contribute to a more equitable and sustainable global economy (Goldman, 2020).

Human rights violations in supply chains can have significant negative impacts, both for the individuals directly affected and for the companies involved. Consumers are becoming increasingly aware of the importance of ethical sourcing and are more likely to support businesses that prioritize human rights (Angotti & Will, 2022). Companies that fail to address human rights issues in their supply chains may face reputational damage, loss of consumer trust, and potential legal consequences (Smith *et al.*, 2021). Additionally, the exploitation of workers and disregard for human rights can lead to labour unrest, strikes, and disruptions in the supply chain, ultimately affecting the productivity and profitability of the business (World Favor, 2023). Therefore, it is in the best interest of companies to ensure that human rights are respected throughout their supply chains.

In 2013, the Rana Plaza building in Bangladesh tragically collapsed, resulting in the death of 1,134 workers and many injuries (Figure 6). The incident revealed the harsh working conditions faced by the employees. Despite authorities' warnings about structural problems, the textile factory owners ignored them and forced the workers to return to work on that tragic day. This

Figure 6. The Collapsed Rana Plaza, April 2013 (Dhaka Tribune, 2023).

sparked widespread public anger, media attention, and a strong demand for change and transparency in the fast fashion industry (Westervelt, 2015).

Similarly, in 2016, surf brand Rip Curl faced significant backlash after it was revealed that their clothes were being manufactured in North Korea under exploitative working conditions. Factory workers endured long hours, low pay, and even the threat of imprisonment and torture for disobedience. Rip Curl admitted their knowledge of the issue after the products had already been sold, leading to public backlash and calls for transparency from consumers (McKenzie, N., & Baker, R., 2016).

To effectively address human rights issues in supply chains, companies need to implement robust human rights due diligence processes. This involves:

- Identifying and assessing risks associated with human rights violations (Bovis *et al.*, 2023).
- Taking appropriate actions to prevent and mitigate harm, such as implementing policies, procedures, and monitoring systems (Bovis *et al.*, 2023).
- Providing remedies for any adverse impacts that occur, including establishing mechanisms for reporting and addressing grievances (Bovis *et al.*, 2023).
- Working closely with suppliers to ensure they also adhere to human rights standards and practices (World Favor, 2023).
- Consulting with communities and workers on the ground to understand their perspectives and concerns (World Favor, 2023).
- Establishing transparent and accountable mechanisms for monitoring and addressing human rights violations, such as conducting regular audits and assessments (World Favor, 2023).
- Integrating human rights considerations into supply chain management practices to contribute to the protection and promotion of human rights globally (House, 2022).

- Recognizing that respecting human rights is not only a legal and moral obligation but also a crucial factor in building a resilient and responsible supply chain (Bovis *et al.*, 2023).

In today's globalized world, it is imperative for companies to prioritize human rights in their supply chains. As customers become increasingly demanding and conscious of fair and ethical practices, brands must understand that meeting these expectations is crucial for their reputation and customer loyalty. By implementing robust due diligence processes, collaborating closely with suppliers, and establishing transparent monitoring mechanisms, companies can protect and promote human rights while building resilient and responsible supply chains.

Respecting human rights is not just a legal and moral obligation; it is a fundamental pillar of sustainable and ethical business practices. By taking proactive measures, companies can not only contribute to a more equitable and just world but also maintain the trust and support of their customers, who are willing to hold brands accountable and even boycott them if they fail to meet these ethical standards.

Strategies for Integrating Human Rights into Supply Chains

Supply chains play a critical role in global business operations, but they also face increasing scrutiny when it comes to human rights. The ethical treatment of workers, the prevention of labor abuse, and overall respect for human rights are becoming essential factors for sustainable and responsible supply chain management. In the following, we explore key strategies that companies can adopt to integrate human rights into their supply chains, fostering a culture of respect and responsibility.

Human Rights Due Diligence: Mitigating Risks and Upholding Standards

To effectively address human rights issues, companies need to:

- Conduct comprehensive assessments: Thoroughly assess the supply chain to identify and address human rights risks, such as forced labor and child labor (Bovis *et al.*, 2023).
- Mitigate risks effectively: This process involves identifying and assessing actual and potential human rights risks within the supply chain and taking appropriate measures to prevent and mitigate those risks. All to ensure that human rights are respected and upheld (Human Rights Watch, 2016).
- Ensure accountability: Implement robust due diligence processes to identify, prevent, and account for the organization's approach to human rights in the supply chain (Toolbox Human Rights, n.d).

Collaboration with Suppliers and Stakeholders: Building Responsible Partnerships

Building Responsible Partnerships Collaboration is key to integrating human rights into supply chains. Companies need to work closely with suppliers and partners to:

- Map the supply chain: Work closely with suppliers to map the supply chain, assess risks, and implement necessary measures to protect human rights (Bovis *et al.*, 2023).
- Build trust and commitment: Foster strong partnerships with suppliers and business partners based on trust, commitment, and complementary resources and capabilities (Brun, 2020).
- Share responsibility: Collaboration minimizes risks throughout the supply chain and develops shared responsibility among stakeholders for upholding human rights, and enabling

effective risk minimization throughout the supply chain (Audi, 2023).

Transparency and Reporting: Driving Accountability and Improvement

Transparency and reporting play a crucial role in integrating human rights into supply chains. Companies need to:

- Create transparency and accountability: Enhance transparency and accountability to address issues in global supply chains and ensure better visibility (Bovis *et al.*, 2023).
- Identify and minimize risks: Transparency helps identify and minimize human rights risks, improve conditions on the ground, and inform stakeholders about the status of human rights in the supply chain (Bateman & Bonanni, 2019; Gardner *et al.*, 2019).
- Collaborate and share information: By working closely with suppliers, consulting with communities and workers, and sharing information, companies can address human rights issues effectively (World Favor, 2023).
- Report on progress: Regular reporting on human rights efforts and progress allows for greater visibility, encourages accountability, and drives continuous improvement in supply chain practices.

Environmental Impact Assessment

To ensure that their products are ethically and environmentally sound, many companies are turning to the CSRD, or Cooperative Social Responsibility Directive, which provides guidelines specifically devoted to the ethical and sustainable production of goods and is rapidly gaining momentum in the European Union.

The European Union (EU) Taxonomy is a classification system that came into effect in 2021 and assists businesses in mapping their supply chains to identify areas where they may have an environmental impact. The draft EU Supply Chain Act imposes a requirement on EU companies to responsibly manage social and environmental impacts throughout their entire value chain, promoting sustainable and ethical production in Europe. Compliance with the specific regulations outlined in the act is necessary for companies to conduct business in Europe. Additionally, this legislation applies not only to EU entities but also to companies and indirect suppliers that conduct business in Europe, making adherence to the act mandatory for their entire supply chain. The draft EU supply chain act, as outlined by the European Commission, also includes a ban on imported products linked to forced labor and imposes fines and civil liabilities on suppliers found to violate or breach due diligence. The act is scheduled to take effect in 2025, while the broader goal is to achieve Climate Neutrality by 2050.

If any company wants to be sure that it is ready for the impending changes in European law, it is important to conduct a comprehensive Environmental Impact Assessment. This will help identify any weak points in the supply chain and take corrective action before the new laws go into effect.

Similarly, the German Supply Chain Due Diligence Act (LkSG), which came into effect on January 1, 2023, marks a significant milestone in the realm of corporate due diligence (Figure 7). This act represents the first comprehensive international regulation that addresses the responsibility of businesses to uphold human rights and protect the environment.

Under the LkSG, businesses are required to implement effective risk management practices to identify, prevent, and minimize the risk of human rights violations and specific forms of environmental degradation. This includes conducting thorough assessments of their supply chains and taking proactive measures to ensure compliance with human rights standards and environmental protections.

By implementing robust risk management systems, businesses can play a crucial role in mitigating potential harm and promoting responsible practices throughout their supply chains. The LkSG serves as a framework to encourage businesses to prioritize human rights and environmental sustainability, thereby contributing to a more ethical and sustainable global business landscape. The Act mandates that businesses establish a complaints procedure and regular reporting in addition to outlining the preventative and corrective measures required within their own operations and throughout their supply chains (BMWK — Federal Ministry of Economic Affairs and Climate Action, 2022) The European directive, similar in nature to the German Supply Chain Act, seeks to promote sustainable and responsible corporate behavior across global value chains. This directive primarily affects companies operating within the European Union, expanding their social and environmental due diligence obligations to encompass their global supply chains. The objective is to ensure that companies uphold high standards of social and environmental responsibility throughout their entire supply chain, regardless of geographical location. By extending the scope of due diligence requirements, the directive aims to address potential human rights violations, environmental harm, and other negative impacts associated with global business operations. This broader approach emphasizes the importance of transparency, accountability, and ethical practices in global supply chains. It calls upon companies to assess and mitigate risks, implement measures to protect human rights and the environment, and collaborate with their suppliers to drive positive change. Overall, the European directive aligns with the growing global focus on responsible and sustainable business practices, seeking to create a more inclusive and environmentally conscious economy (Certainty, 2022).

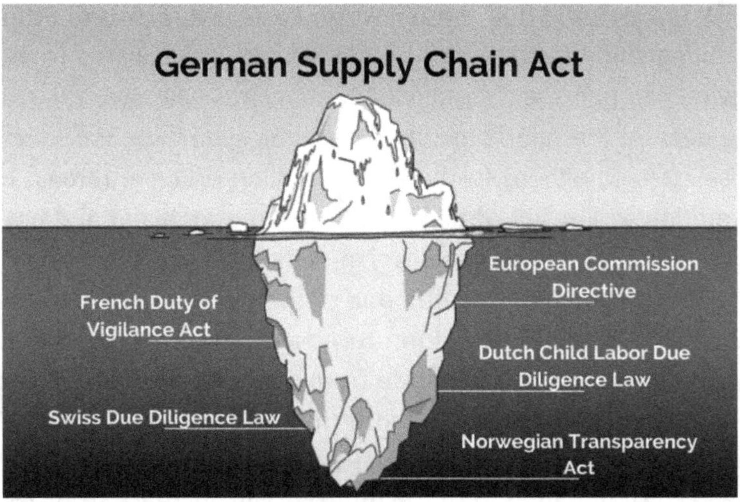

Figure 7. German Supply Chain Act is the Tip of the Social and Ethical Regulatory Iceberg (Certainty, 2022).

The Supply Chain Act increases the transparency of businesses' sustainable practices while also increasing the visibility of a product's environmental impact. The private sector has a strategic interest in environmental protection. Particularly, multinational corporations cannot continue to turn a blind eye and they will now be held more accountable for how their supply chains impact people and the environment around the world (BMWK — Federal Ministry for Economic Affairs and Climate Action, 2022).

Raising due diligence standards in extended global supply chains is a key business, social, and governance responsibility. The EU is taking the lead on this, but a principle-based approach that encourages public–private partnerships and multi-stakeholder approaches is as important as legislation. Other complementary building blocks include sectoral taskforces, which bring together governments and private organizations; geo-tagging of upstream sectors; local stakeholder involvement; engagement in traceability efforts; regular third-party audits; and whistle-blowing programs (Koepel *et al.*, 2020).

It is inevitable that these laws and acts will spread to other continents and nations, and businesses will be obligated to follow human rights and sustainability standards wherever they do business. At the same time, it will become even more crucial for businesses to adhere to these standards in order to remain in operation as a result of decreased consumer demand and boycotts of brands and companies that do not follow them.

According to Reed Smith, due to the series of policies, the number of employees and net turnover generated worldwide by EU companies will decrease from over 500 employees and 150 million net turnover to more than 250 employees and 40 million net turnover. Similarly, the net turnover generated in the EU by companies in third-countries will decrease from 150 million to about 40 million due to these policies (Melin *et al.*, 2022).

Another factor contributing to the need for regulations is that companies' voluntary actions are insufficient to address human rights and environmental impacts. This is evidenced by reports of employees working under dangerous and unsafe conditions, as well as being forced to work long hours for minimal or no pay. Unfortunate events have never ceased, just as the 2013 Rana Plaza collapse and the 2016 Rip Curl worker exploitation demonstrate. It is inevitable that the entire value chain, from sourcing to selling, will uphold human values and sustainability, either through voluntary actions or through pressure from consumers and legal requirements.

Sustainable Product Design

Designers have always been at the forefront of change, and as pressure mounts to create more sustainable products, they are rising to the challenge. In order to reduce the environmental impact of their work, with an increasing number of designers turning to sustainable design principles.

Sustainable product design is about more than just using recycled materials or opting for biodegradable packaging. It's about creating products that meet the needs of the present without compromising the ability of future generations to meet their own needs. It's about looking at the whole life cycle of a product and finding ways to reduce waste and minimize negative environmental impacts.

Some progressive companies have already begun moving in this direction. For instance, Patagonia has created a design philosophy called "Cradle to Cradle" that aims to make products that are secure for both people and the environment. Similarly, Interface, a major carpet producer, has incorporated sustainability into the core of its business strategy and set a target of having no environmental impact by 2020 (Capgemini, n.d.). Another example is the company Kiehl's, which launched the "Recycle and Be Rewarded" program in 2009 and further improved it in 2020 (see Figure 8). This program helped Kiehl's collect over 13 million empty bottles, as well as reconstruct their packaging so that 80% of it contained post-consumer recycled material. (Kiehl's, n.d.a).

As consumers become increasingly aware of the importance of sustainability, we can expect to see more brands follow suit.

Design decisions are responsible for about 80% of the environmental effects linked to products. The significance of sustainable product design is increasing due to its potential to bring about positive changes in the environment, society, and economy. Sustainable design aims to maximize the benefits for the environment, society, and economy throughout the entire lifecycle of a product while minimizing any associated social and environmental costs. This definition aligns with the "triple-bottom-line" accounting philosophy, which emphasizes that the success of a system should be measured by how it treats its users and the environment, not just its profitability (Capgemini, n.d.).

Figure 8. The Procedures of "Recycle and Be Rewarded" Designed by Kiehl's (n.d.b).

Designing for flexibility in the use of a product is an approach to addressing sustainability. A well-designed product that serves a multitude of functions is more sustainable due to reduced material use and waste and less energy consumption. It is also ideal to design in such a way that all components are manufactured and assembled at a single location. Designing for an increased lifespan of the product is also important, as it implies that it needs to be replaced less frequently (for example, Ben & Jerry's has partnered with farmers since 2018 to achieve progressive change in the dairy and agriculture sectors. This progressive change includes helping farms install new, renewable energy and improve their pastures to support biodiversity, collaborating with and investing in farmers to adopt new

Figure 9. Brief Introduction to Sustainable Design (Acaroglu, 2020).

technology, and aiming to decrease dairy emissions by 15,000 metric tonnes) (Fast Company, 2022).

There are usually four stages of the product life cycle, which are defined as production, delivery, use, and disposal. The typical workflow in a linear economy is to use the product once and then discard it. The Cradle-to-Cradle philosophy of William McDonough and Dr. Micahel Braungart envisions a new life for the product and its components after the present one has come to an end (Mandalay, 2020). In this approach, products integrate with the concept of a circular economy, and the practice that facilitates this is known as circular systems design (Figure 9).

Here are the sustainable design principles which include the ability to:

- optimize site potential;
- minimize non-renewable energy consumption;
- use environmentally preferable products;
- protect and conserve water;
- enhance indoor environmental quality; and
- optimize operational and maintenance practices (U.S. General Services Administration, n.d.).

Recycle, Repair, and Reuse are key components of sustainable design that aim to minimize waste (Figure 10). It is easier to recycle and reuse homogeneous products or products that can

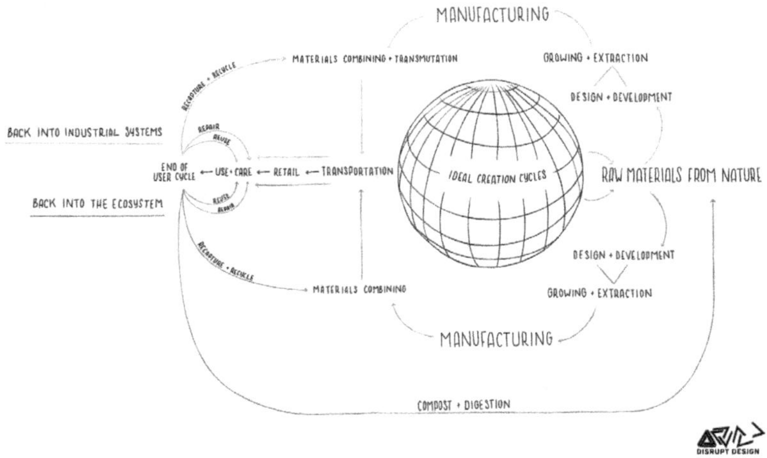

Figure 10. Summary of the Life Cycle Stages of a Sustainable Product (Acaroglu, 2020).

easily be dismantled into their components. Products that can either be recycled easily or biodegrade quickly are ideal, as their environmental impact is significantly lower. Product packaging generates a large amount of waste, which usually ends up in a landfill. Packaging design is essential for designing sustainable products, as it can be upcycled, reused, or refilled. It should also be designed to convey important information about its sustainability, encouraging buyers to make sustainable choices (Mandalay, 2020).

Designing products that appeal to consumers and support a sustainable way of life can have a profound effect. Integrating sustainable design principles into the education system cultivates a community of designers capable of developing responsible strategies. Embracing sustainability as designers has positive effects on our processes, including reduced environmental impact, social benefits, and driving innovation. It also enhances our reputation and appeals to an increasingly eco-conscious market, opening up new opportunities for growth (Mandalay, 2020).

According to research, businesses that prioritize sustainable product design stand to gain from increased compliance, decreased emissions, and decreased resource scarcity concerns, as well as from improved customer and employee relations and revenue growth (Capgemini, n.d.).

Developing a Green Supply Chain

Developing a Green Supply Chain is key for any business looking to promote sustainability and human rights in their supply chain. Emerging technologies can be used to monitor the environmental and social aspects of the supply chain while at the same time facilitating collaboration and communication with suppliers, customers, and other stakeholders. This will enable companies to identify potential risks and opportunities early on so that solutions can be implemented before they become too costly or difficult to handle.

To enhance green supply chain management within an organization, the utilization of various software applications and advanced technologies at different stages of the process can be beneficial. These tools encompass warehouse management systems (WHS) to improve warehouse efficiency, innovative manufacturing technologies that minimize energy consumption and reduce the use of hazardous materials in production. The effective integration of such technologies relies on employee receptiveness and proficiency in utilizing them. Conversely, implementing lasting changes becomes challenging in the face of employee resistance or limited adoption (Agility, 2021). This clearly shows that having a culture of sustainability within an organization is paramount before embarking on the journey to sustainability.

According to studies, a company's supply chain is largely responsible for its environmental impact. The most significant impact that organizations can have is by altering their supply chains, as the intricacy of supplier connections and cross-border operations can make it challenging to sustain the supply chain. Additionally, it is also difficult to see critical operational aspects such as working conditions at a supplier's distant factory or the intensive production and transportation as goods are produced and shipped around the world (Luther, 2020). (To illustrate, roughly 50% of worldwide trade takes place between locations that are over 3,000 km apart. As a result of this geographical distance, most international transportation of goods involves multiple modes of transportation, as it is not feasible to maintain a physical flow of freight over long distances) (Anderson & Rodrigue, n.d.).

Companies should start using data to anticipate customer expectations for sustainability and human rights, collect environmental data regularly, and ensure transparency on human rights and sustainability to build trust with customers and other stakeholders.

Understanding of their supply chain to ensure sustainability and human rights are taken seriously. This should be done through a thorough due diligence process and careful supplier selection. Checking against lists of sanctioned companies, monitoring and tracking supplier practices, and obtaining certifications can help identify potential human rights issues and ensure labor standards are met.

While there could be different methodologies, there is quite an exhaustive set of steps proposed by Sarah Roberts that can help provide good guidance on setting up the Green Supply Chain (Nastu, 2008).

1. **Redesign the product, even with modest adjustments to its design**: Friesland Coberico Dairy Foods in the Netherlands reduced their transportation needs by 127,000 miles per year by adjusting recipes and production processes. Innovation or new technologies may make it possible to eliminate

components or ingredients entirely and shorten the supply chain.

2. **Reconfigure manufacturing**: Canadian pulp and paper company Catalyst Paper Corporation reduced greenhouse gas emissions by 70% and saved $4.4 million by reusing waste products and switching to natural gas.
3. **Shift to green suppliers**: Green suppliers can have a big impact on the carbon implications of bringing products to market, providing potential benefits such as meeting regulations or appealing to new consumers. For example, the Sony Corporation faced a setback in 2001 when the Dutch government blocked over 1.3 million boxes of Playstation 2 game consoles due to an excessive amount of the toxic element Cadmium discovered in the cables of the game controls. The incident resulted in losses exceeding $130 million and indirectly prompted the re-inspection of more than 6,000 factories and the implementation of a new supplier management system (Villanueva-Ponce *et al.*, 2015).
4. **Shorten distances**: Travel distances and associated fuel use can be decreased by rationalizing sourcing, assembly, and distribution in relation to markets. Working with suppliers who are located geographically close to important markets can significantly reduce energy use for some products. By moving its warehouses, an American manufacturer of bath and kitchen products was able to reduce carbon emissions by 34% without incurring additional costs.
5. **Alter service-level agreements**: Add carbon to the conventional metrics of cost, quality, and service when gauging the efficiency of your supply chain. Check service-level agreements for obtrusive requirements that hinder productivity. For instance, just-in-time and min-max clauses may compel suppliers to make hurried, small deliveries that significantly increase energy consumption.

6. **Shrink packaging**: Smaller and lighter packages made possible by new technologies and designs enable businesses to increase the volume of goods that can be transported in a truck or shipping container. The burden of recycling or eliminating packaging materials at the end of the supply chain can also be lessened by improved package designs. Tesco, a UK retailer, asked suppliers to provide lighter-weight wine bottles, cutting its yearly glass consumption by 2,600 tons and transportation-related carbon emissions by 4,100 tons.
7. **Plan for reverse supply chain activity**: Reverse supply chains are becoming increasingly important due to government regulation and the need to reduce waste and energy costs. How products are originally designed, assembled, labeled, and packaged can have a profound effect on the efficiency of any reverse supply chain.
8. **Consolidate shipments**: Amazon charges less for shipping if customers consolidate their orders, but it requires careful analysis to determine which suppliers to use, where to locate facilities, and what inventory levels to maintain.
9. **Plan smarter routes**: UPS used a software planning tool to cut 28.5 million miles off its delivery routes, saving three million gallons of gas and reducing CO2 emissions by 31,000 metric tons per year. Factoring in costs and carbon implications can lead to more rational routes.
10. **Coordinate with partners**: Many opportunities to make your supply chain greener or more transparent will depend on careful coordination with allies both upstream and downstream. British retailer Marks & Spencer worked with suppliers to create a new level of transparency in their supply chain, with meat sourced back to the cow and traceability for clothing reaching as far as dye houses and spinning mills.
11. **Take a life-cycle view**: To understand where energy is being used and where opportunities exist, consider the entire life cycle of the product. A product may use a lot of energy

while it is in use. For example, a life cycle analysis conducted by Unilever revealed that just 2% of the carbon emissions generated in the production of Ben and Jerry's ice cream was attributed to the manufacturing process. The largest share of emissions, amounting to 46%, was traced back to retail operations such as refrigeration.

12. **Start now!** The ability to reduce waste and pollution is a requirement that buyers are placing more weight on. Making progress gives your brand more credibility and gives employees a sense of accomplishment. Mandatory changes are an unavoidable reality for many businesses. Begin by determining which opportunities necessitate immediate investment and which can be postponed. Reach out to the opportunities upstream and downstream in your supply chain after concentrating on the opportunities an organization can control.

It's critical to keep in mind that respect for human rights and sustainability extends beyond supplier compliance, fostering an environment where everyone working on the supply chain is treated with dignity and respect. This entails making certain that workers receive proper health and safety protections, a fair wage, and fair treatment. Responsible production and ethical sourcing should also be given careful consideration, which calls for the use of only sustainably and ethically sourced raw materials and the creation of production methods that have the least possible detrimental effects on the environment.

Benefits of Creating a Sustainable Supply Chain

Making sustainability and human rights efforts as essential as hygiene factors in supply chain strategies means companies can gain more trust and loyalty from their customers. Here are some of the benefits that come with implementing sustainability and human rights initiatives in the supply chain:

- Case studies have shown that companies with sustainable supply chains tend to have better customer loyalty, higher customer satisfaction ratings, and an improved public image.
- Creating a sustainable supply chain can be a differentiating factor for any brand, setting it apart from competitors. In today's world, consumers are more likely to buy from ethical and sustainable businesses than from ones that don't take those initiatives seriously.
- Having a sustainable supply chain is also great for employee morale — it creates a sense of pride in the company and encourages workers to take ownership over their roles in making the company better.

Supply chain sustainability benefits not only companies' own interests and those of their stakeholders but also society and the planet at large. Companies have realized, for example, that climate change can put their business continuity at risk with extreme weather disruptions and growing resource scarcities. (Since the onset of the pandemic, social media has contributed to a 30% increase in awareness regarding human rights and climate change issues. Consequently, companies that are driven by a deeper societal purpose are expected to be more robust and successful in the long term.) (Soroka *et al.*, 2019).

Building upon these initial advantages, a comprehensive study has detailed ten additional benefits that arise from the implementation of sustainability and human rights in the supply chain.

1. **Supply chain operations**: Recent examples demonstrate how, for instance, setting emission targets with suppliers and assisting them in identifying potential improvement areas can reduce energy costs (Luther, 2020).

2. **Branding**: Where products come from and how they are made are issues that consumers are becoming increasingly concerned with. Consumers are willing to pay 2–10% more for goods that offer supply chain transparency, according to research from MIT's Sloan School of Management (Luther, 2020).
3. **Investor relations**: Institutional investors are aware of the reputational risk of unsustainable supply chain operations, which have hurt companies' stock prices. A recent Gallup poll found that nearly half of investors are interested in sustainable investment funds (Luther, 2020).
4. **Corporate culture**: Demographers claim that Millennials in particular seek a greater sense of meaning in their work. The corporate culture and values of an organization play a big part in successfully hiring and keeping employees, and sustainability is one of those values (Luther, 2020).
5. **Compliance:** Governments are mandating greater supply chain sustainability to meet the 2030 Sustainable Development Goals, including traceability of pharmaceuticals, disposal of electronics, and avoidance of conflict minerals (Luther, 2020).
6. **Reduced environmental impact**: Reducing environmental impact can lead to big savings by reducing waste and increasing the efficiency of buildings, vehicles, and machinery.

   John Mitchell Ltd. achieved savings exceeding £650,000 by providing driver training to its haulage fleet. Meanwhile, Nike restructured its trainer manufacturing process, resulting in a reduction of labor costs by up to 50% and material usage by 20%, thereby generating a 0.25% increase in profit margins (Supply Management, 2019).
7. **Improve supply continuity**: Diversify supply chains to avoid over-reliance on a single link, which can have ramifications for other businesses.

Having multiple suppliers in different parts of the world can help ensure the continuity of products or services, preventing downtime and reputation damage. In 2011, a harsh monsoon season in Thailand caused global prices of hard drives to rise, leading to delays, shortages, and steep costs (Supply Management, 2019).

8. **Protecting against reputational damage**: Since information is easily accessible online, the supply chain has an impact on the reputation of your brand. To promote the expansion of any business, it is crucial to safeguard your reputation.

   Companies need to make sure that their sustainability plan improves the quality of life for every employee along the supply chain. Fair working conditions, pay, and minimizing environmental impact are all part of this. They should also not be putting employees and associates in unnecessary danger.

   Apple has suffered due to scrutiny of the working conditions at their Chinese factory, resulting in a 27-spot drop in the Reputational Quotient Poll and a decline in market share in China and Japan (Supply Management, 2019).

9. **Potential for new partnerships**: A sustainable supply chain makes a company a compelling partner candidate for other businesses, as it is compatible with their principles and creates the possibility of new business partnerships.

   Sainsbury's is a good illustration. To support its dairy farmers, the company collaborated with veterinarians, training them on how to identify and manage common health concerns. As a result, the 55,000 cows under its care yielded 140 liters more milk per cow than the national average. This has led to a reduction in the number of cows required to meet the demand as healthier cows are happier cows (Supply Management, 2019).

10. **Win more business**: ISO 14001 is a management system that helps businesses identify gaps in their supply chains and make green efficiency savings (Supply Management, 2019).

By obtaining accreditation to support their environmental efforts, businesses demonstrate to potential clients that they are taking crucial measures to minimize their impact on the world. This accreditation serves as evidence of their commitment to sustainability and can enhance their credibility and attract environmentally conscious clients.

When a business reviews its supply chain and proactively makes changes, it reaps plentiful rewards. By taking positive action the company can achieve significant cost savings, improved profit margins, and simultaneously contribute to mitigating environmental harm.

The Future of Sustainability and Human Rights in Supply Chains

The future of sustainability and human rights in supply chains is an encouraging one. Consumers have become increasingly educated and aware of the importance of buying from responsible, ethical businesses. In turn, companies have made every effort to comply with human rights standards and sustainability regulations in order to create a positive image.

Data suggest that consumers are more likely to purchase from companies that they perceive as ethical, sustainable, and responsible. It is evident that any company that neglects and fails to comply with the laws and regulations that safeguard people and the environment will be susceptible to penalties and the possibility of being blacklisted.

Due to this wave of awareness, we can expect that in the near future, supply chains will be much more mindful when it comes to respecting human beings and nature because they will no longer be able to ignore or disregard these issues. This is a massive step forward in terms of improving global awareness, standards, laws, and regulations on these matters.

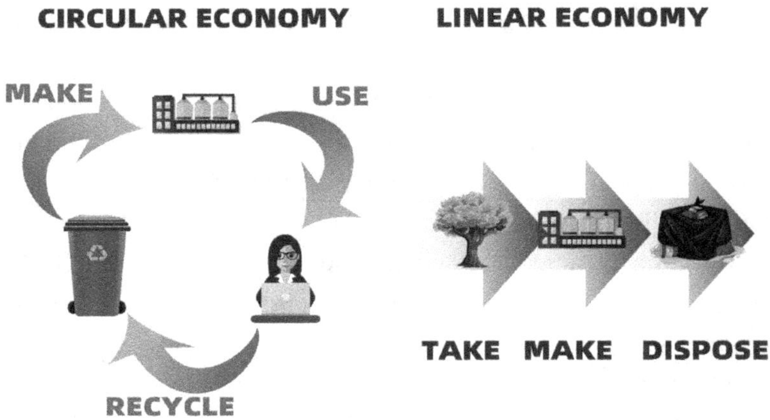

Figure 11. The Difference Between Linear Economy and Circular Economy.

Innovation has and will drive supply chain sustainability in the years to come. Two trends that will keep the momentum going in this area are the **Circular Economy** and **data-driven supply chains** (Luther, 2020).

A **circular economy** (Figure 11) is an alternative to a traditional linear economy (take, make, waste). It seeks to reduce waste, recover resources at the end of a product's life, and channel them back into production, thereby significantly reducing pressure on the environment (Nutburn, n.d.). The goal of a **circular economy** is to design pollution and waste out of products and systems like supply chains. In this system, products are built to have a light environmental footprint, last longer, and be easily disassembled and remade or transformed for reuse.

In **data-driven supply chains**, companies leverage cloud-based supply chain execution systems that provide detailed analytics and may even pull data from equipment sensors and other Internet of Things (IoT) devices (Figure 12). This gives businesses deeper visibility into their operations, and they can then find, implement, and monitor strategies to become more sustainable.

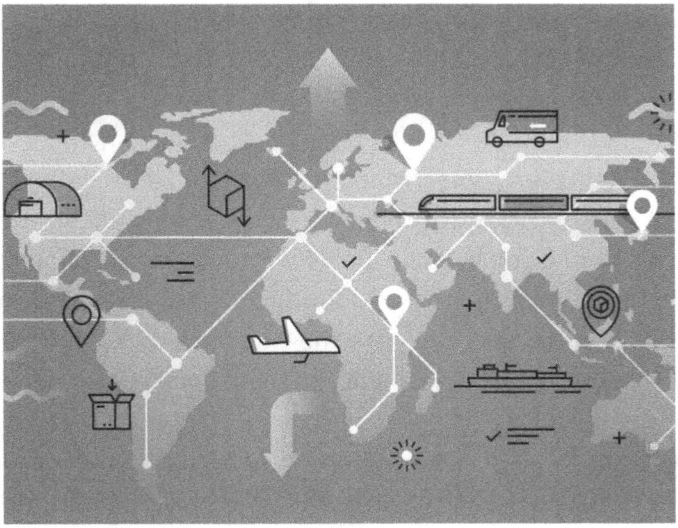

Figure 12. TheBriefGraphofData-DrivenSupplyChainsintheWholeWorld(LogiSYM,2020).

Conclusions

In conclusion, making sustainability and human rights hygiene factors in the supply chain is not only the right thing to do from a moral and ethical perspective, it is also critical for staying competitive in today's market. Consumers are becoming more conscious of the impact of their purchases, and they expect companies to take responsibility for their impact on the environment and society. By incorporating sustainability and human rights into their supply chain strategies, conducting due diligence, collaborating with suppliers, and leveraging technology, companies can create sustainable and responsible supply chains that benefit everyone.

As sustainability, human rights preservation, and the principles of Supply Chain 5.0 become integral components of future supply chains, businesses will need to ensure that necessary precautions are taken to protect these fundamental aspects. Consumers are becoming more aware of the importance of sustainability and are voiding their demand for it, so businesses that want to stay competitive will need to find a way to include these values in their operations.

We, as authors, firmly believe that sustainability and human rights are intertwined dimensions that define the responsible and forward-thinking supply chains of the future in the era of Supply Chain 5.0. By embracing sustainability, respecting human rights, and adopting the principles of Supply Chain 5,0, businesses can pave the way for a thriving and harmonious society while enhancing their own resilience, efficiency, and profitability.

Intriguingly, there is an interplay between customer centricity and sustainability. Sustainability demands a shift towards conservatively reusing and avoiding excess production, seemingly at odds with customer-centric practices. However, the shared economy offers an ingenious solution. Through sharing, customers gain access to a multitude of choices that are not only affordable but also provide the opportunity to use and experience different products and then switch to another after use. This connection between sustainability and customer centricity becomes more apparent as we delve into the role of Advanced Automation in enabling such experiences within a shared economy through digitalization. We will explore this further in the Afterword, once the reader has grasped the significance of Advanced Automation's role in shaping the future of supply chains in the era of Supply Chain 5.0.

Fortunately, businesses embarking on the transition to a more sustainable and ethical supply chain have access to a wide array of solutions. Numerous organizations specialize in assisting businesses in adopting sustainable practices, providing valuable guidance and expertise. Additionally, there is a wealth of resources available to help businesses comprehend the significance of human rights preservation in their operations. By embracing sustainability and human rights as interconnected and mutually reinforcing principles, businesses can chart a course towards a thriving and harmonious society.

Simultaneously, they can unlock the advantages of a responsible and profitable supply chain, capitalizing on the rewards that come from ethical business practices.

It is imperative that the Supply Chains take the lead in embracing the Sustainability and Human Rights elements as they redesign the network, configure themselves to serve the future needs of consumers, and provide the necessary edge to their organizations. By prioritizing sustainability and human rights, businesses can not only do their part in creating a better world but also contribute to their own long-term success. This conscious integration of sustainability and human rights not only aligns with our moral compass but also serves as a strategic imperative, enhancing brand reputation, fostering customer loyalty, and mitigating risks associated with environmental degradation and human rights violations. Let us strive together towards a future where sustainability and human rights are at the core of every supply chain, creating a world that thrives on ethical practices and a deep respect for our planet and fellow human beings.

References

Acaroglu, L. (2020, May 27). *Quick Guide to Sustainable Design Strategies*. Medium. https://medium.com/disruptive-design/quick-guide-to-sustainable-design-strategies-641765a86fb8.

Agility. (2021, April 28). *Guide to Sustainable and Green Supply Chain Practices*. https://www.agility.com/en/blog/what-are-green-supply-chain-practices-your-guide-to-supply-chain-sustainability/.

Alansari, M. (2021, April 4). *Global Technology Governance Summit*. World Economic Forum. https://www.weforum.org/agenda/2021/04/4-steps-to-using-ai-in-an-environmentally-responsible-way-artificial-intelligence-bcg-code-carbon/.

Anderson, W. & Rodrigue, J. P. (n.d.). *Transborder and Crossborder Transportation*. The Geography of Transport Systems. https://transportgeography.org/contents/chapter7/transborder-cross border-transportation/.

Angotti, A., & Will, A. (2022, January 26). *Human Rights in Your Supply Chain Isn't Just Good Business—Regulations are Coming. Guidehouse.* https://guidehouse.com/insights/financial-services/2022/esg/human-rights-supply-chains

Audi. (2023, March 16). *Respecting human rights — protecting the environment.* https://www.audi.com/en/company/sustainability/core-topics/value-creation-and-production/sustainability-supply-chain.html

Bateman, A., & Bonanni, L. (2019, August 20). *What Supply Chain Transparency Really Means*. Harvard Business Review. www.hbr.org/2019/08/what-supply-chain-transparency-really-means

BMWK — Federal Ministry for Economic Affairs and Climate Action. (2022, December 29). *Better Protection of Human Rights and the Environment along Global Supply chains.* https://www.bmwk.de/Redaktion/EN/Pressemitteilungen/2022/12/20221229-better-protection-of-human-rights-and-the-environment-along-global-supply-chains.html.

Bovis, B., Kancherla, S., & Molino, A. (2023, April 21). *Why you need to be more proactive with human rights to have a resilient supply chain.* Kearny. https://www.kearney.com/service/sustainability/article/-/insights/why-you-need-to-be-more-proactive-with-human-rights-to-have-a-resilient-supply-chain

Brun, A., Karaosman, H., & Barresi, T. (2020). Supply Chain Collaboration for Transparency. *Sustainability*, 12(11), 4420. https://doi.org/10.3390/su12114429

Capgemini. (n.d.). *Why Sustainable Product Design is the Need of the Hour*. Retrieved February 5, 2023, from https://www.capgemini.com/insights/research-library/sustainable-product-design/.

Certainty. (2022, June 22). *Why the German Supply Chain Act Will Change How Thousands of Companies Around the Globe Manage Social & Environmental Compliance — For Good!* https://www.certaintysoftware.com/why-the-german-supply-chain-act-will-change-how-thousands-of-companies-around-the-globe-manage-social-environmental-compliance-for-good/.

CKPower. (n.d). *Supply Chain Management.* https://www.ckpower.co.th/en/sustainability/stakeholder-engagement/supply-chain-management#.

Dhaka Tribune. (2023, April 6). *Rana Plaza owner secures bail in murder case.* https://www.dhakatribune.com/court/2023/04/06/rana-plaza-owner-secures-bail-in-murder-case

Fast Company. (2022, May 10). *Ben & Jerry's is Cutting the Carbon Footprint of Your Ice Cream.* https://www.fastcompany.com/90750457/ben-jerrys-is-cutting-the-carbon-footprint-of-your-ice-cream.

Gardner, T., Benzie, M., Börner, J., Dawkins, E., Fick, S., Garrett, R., Godar, J., Grimard, A., Lake, S., Larsen, R., Mardas, N., McDermott, C., Meyfroidt, P., Osbeck, M., Persson, M., Sembres, T., Suavet, C., Strassburg, B., Trevisan, A., . . . Wolvekamp, P. (2019). Transparency and sustainability in global commodity supply chains. *World Development, 121,* 163-177. https://doi.org/10.1016/j.worlddev.2018.05.025

Global Witness. (2021, October 7). *The True Price of Palm Oil.* https://www.globalwitness.org/en/campaigns/forests/true-price-palm-oil/.

Goldman, S. (2020, January 22). *The Ethical Supply Chain: Definition, Examples, Stats.* The Future of Commerce. https://www.the-future-of-commerce.com/2020/01/22/ethical-supply-chain-definition-stats/

Govindan, K., Shaw, M., & Majumdar, A. (2021). Social sustainability tensions in multi-tier supply chain: A systematic literature review towards conceptual framework development. *Journal of Cleaner Production,* 279, 123075. https://doi.org/10.1016/j.jclepro.2020.123075.

Greenpeace. (2019). *Greenpeace captures images of fires in the Amazon.* https://www.greenpeace.org/international/press-release/23958/greenpeace-captures-images-forest-fires-amazon/

Hotten, R. (2015, December 10). *What is Volkswagen Accused of?* BBC News. https://www.bbc.com/news/business-34324772.

House, D. (2022, July 11). *Why Ethics in Supply Chain Management Must Be a Priority.* Shyft. https://www.shyftservices.com/resources/ethics-in-supply-chain-management

Human Rights Watch. *Human Rights in Supply Chains.* (2016, May 30). Retrieved June 29, 2023, from https://www.hrw.org/report/2016/05/30/human-rights-supply-chains/call-binding-global-standard-due-diligence

Kiehl's. (n.d.a). https://www.kiehls.com.sg/en_SG/future-made-better.html#how-gives.

Kiehl's. (n.d.b). Facebook. https://www.facebook.com/KiehlsUKI/photos/we-are-so-excited-to-announce-our-new-improved-%EF%B8%8Frecycle-be-rewarded%EF%B8%8F-scheme-here/3252120424902695.

Koepel, A., Deo, A. S., Okhumale, I., & Doneva, M. (2020, July 8). *Human Rights Due Diligence and Sustainable Supply Chains.* Best in Brussels. Retrieved February 5, 2023, from https://www.bestinbrussels.eu/human-rights-due-diligence-and-sustainable-supply-chains/.

LogiSYM. (2020). *Digitalizing the Supply Chain: How Unlocking Data Fast Tracks Logistics Transformation — LogiSYM May/June 2020.* https://logisym.org/digitalizing-the-supply-chain-how-unlocking-data-fast-tracks-logistics-transformation-logisym-may-june-2020/.

Luther, D. (2020, October 2). *Creating a Sustainable Supply Chain*. Oracle NetSuite. Retrieved February 5, 2023, from https://www.netsuite.com/portal/resource/articles/erp/supply-chain-sustainability.shtml.

Mandalay, A. (2020, June 17). *Sustainable Practices in Industrial Design — Rethinking the Future*. RTF. Rethinking the Future. Retrieved February 5, 2023, from https://www.re-thinkingthefuture.com/rtf-fresh-perspectives/a1058-sustainable-practices-in-industrial-design/.

Mckenzie, N. & Baker, R. (2016, March 13). *North Korea: Rip Curl Reportedly Produces Surf Clothing in North Korean Factory with Exploited Workers, Company Says Factory Was Unauthorized*. Business & Human Rights Resource Centre. https://www.business-humanrights.org/en/latest-news/north-korea-rip-curl-reportedly-produces-surf-clothing-in-north-korean-factory-with-exploited-workers-company-says-factory-was-unauthorized/.

McKenzie, N., & Baker, R. (2016, February 21). Surf clothing label Rip Curl using 'slave labour' to manufacture clothes in North Korea. *The Sydney Morning Herald.* https://www.smh.com.au/business/surf-clothing-label-rip-curl-using-slave-labour-to-manufacture-clothes-in-north-korea-20160220-gmz375.html

Melin, Y., Kim, W. J., Fressynet, I., & Golouchko, A. (2022, November 21). *The EU Aims to Introduce Mandatory Supply Chain Due Diligence Obligations*. Reed Smith. https://www.reedsmith.com/en/perspectives/2022/11/the-eu-aims-to-introduce-mandatory-supply-chain-due-diligence-obligations.

NAPs on Business and Human Rights. (n.d). *Supply chains*. Globalnaps. www.globalnaps.org/issue/supply-chains/

Nastu, J. (2008, November 30). *12 Steps to Creating a Greener and More Efficient Supply Chain*. Environment + Energy Leader. Retrieved February 5, 2023, from https://www.environmentalleader.com/2008/11/12-steps-to-a-greener-supply-chain/.

Nutburn, M. (n.d.). *Reducing Waste and Adopting a Circular Economy Approach Will Benefit the Environment and Create Economic Opportunities.* Towards Zero Waste. https://www.towardszerowaste.gov.sg/circular-economy/.

OpenText. (2021, September 29). *OpenText Survey Shows Increase in Demand for Ethically Sourced Goods.* https://investors.opentext.com/press-releases/press-releases-details/2021/OpenText-Survey-Shows-Increase-in-Demand-for-Ethically-Sourced-Goods/default.aspx.

Sanu, M. (2022, August 22). *5 Examples of How AI Is Helping Companies Become More Sustainable*. Winnow. https://blog.winnowsolutions.com/5-examples-of-how-ai-is-helping-companies-become-more-sustainable.

Smith, N.C., Scholz, M., & Williams, J. (2021, December 2). *Does Your Business Need a Human Rights Strategy?*. MIT Sloan. https://sloanreview.mit.edu/article/does-your-business-need-a-human-rights-strategy/

Soroka, S., Fournier, P., & Nir, L. (2019). Cross-national evidence of a negativity bias in psychophysiological reactions to news. *Proceedings of the National Academy of Sciences*, 116(38), 18888–18892. https://doi.org/10.1073/pnas.1908369116.

Supply Management. (2019, July 29). *Five Benefits of a Sustainable Supply Chain.* https://www.cips.org/supply-management/opinion/2019/july/five-benefits-of-a-sustainable-supply-chain/.

Toolbox Human Rights. (n.d). *Human rights due diligence — How.* Retrieved July 10, 2023, from www.business-humanrights.be/tool/8/how

U.S. General Services Administration. (n.d.). *Sustainable Design.* https://www.gsa.gov/real-estate/design-and-construction/design-excellence-program-overview/sustainability/sustainable-design.

Villanueva-Ponce, R., Avelar-Sosa, L., Alvarado-Iniesta, A., & Cruz-Sanchez, V. (2015). The green supplier selection as a key element in a supply chain: A review of cases studies. *DYNA*, 82(194), 36. https://doi.org/10.15446/dyna.v82n194.54466.

Westervelt, A. (2015, April 24). *Two Years after Rana Plaza, Have Conditions Improved in Bangladesh's Factories?* The Guardian. https://www.theguardian.com/sustainable-business/2015/apr/24/bangladesh-factories-building-collapse-garment-dhaka-rana-plaza-brands-hm-gap-workers-construction.

World Favor. (2023, February). *How to address human rights issues in your supply chain.* https://blog.worldfavor.com/how-to-address-human-rights-issues-in-your-supply-chain

Further Reading

Apple. (n.d.). People and Environment in Our Supply Chain. https://www.apple.com/supplier-responsibility/pdf/Apple_SR_2021_Progress_Report.pdf.

Beuchelt, T. D., Schneider, R., & Gamba, L. (2022). Integrating the right to food in sustainability standards: A theory of change to move global supply chains from responsibilities to impacts. *Applied Economic Perspectives and Policy*, *44*(4), 1864–1889. https://doi.org/10.1002/aepp.13308.

Bové, A., & Swartz, S. (2019, May 11). *Starting at the Source: Sustainability in Supply Chains*. McKinsey & Company. https://www.mckinsey.com/capabilities/sustainability/our-insights/starting-at-the-source-sustainability-in-supply-chains.

Global Supply Chains Are Focusing More on Ethics, Human Rights, and Sustainability. (n.d.). Diversity Plus. https://diversityplus.com/web/Article?id=Global-Supply-Chains-are-Focusing-More-on-Ethics-Human-Rights-and-Sustainability-5858.

Hayat, K., JianJun, Z., Ali, S., & Khan, M. A. (2021). Exploring factors of the sustainable supply chain in the post-COVID-19 pandemic: SWARA approach. *Environmental Science and Pollution Research*, 1–19. https://doi.org/10.1007/s11356-021-16908-6.

Mukarji, S. (2022, November 1). *How Will Your Organisation Demonstrate Commitment to Ethical Supply Chains and Human Rights through ESG Activity?* Economist Impact. https://impact.economist.com/sustainability/social-sustainability/big-question-human-rights.

Schilling-Vacaflor, A. (2021). Integrating human rights and the environment in supply chain regulations. *Sustainability, 13*(17), 9666. https://doi.org/10.3390/su13179666.

Suhi, S. A., Enayet, R., Haque, T., Ali, S. M., Moktadir, M. A., & Paul, S. K. (2019). Environmental sustainability assessment in supply chain: An emerging economy context. *Environmental Impact Assessment Review*, *79*, 106306. https://doi.org/10.1016/j.eiar.2019.106306.

Villena, H. V. & Gioia, A. D. (2020, November 16). *A More Sustainable Supply Chain*. Harvard Business Review. https://hbr.org/2020/03/a-more-sustainable-supply-chain.

REVOLUTIONIZING SUPPLY CHAINS: ADVANCED DIGITALIZATION

3

ADVANCED DIGITALIZATION — THE 3RD CRITICAL ELEMENT OF SUPPLY CHAIN 5.0

Welcome to the third element of Supply Chain 5.0, where we explore the cutting-edge technologies revolutionizing the supply chain industry. In this chapter, we dive into Advanced Digitalization, which includes a groundbreaking array of technologies such as Big Data, AI, Blockchain, Metaverse, and Cybersecurity. These innovative technologies play a vital role not just in improving decision-making and efficiencies, but also in ensuring transparency, trust, and confidence among business partners and consumers.

By leveraging advanced digitalization, businesses can optimize their procurement process and reduce the time and effort spent on manual tasks. Through the use of cutting-edge technologies such as AI, businesses can automate their procurement process, improving accuracy and reducing the risk of errors. Blockchain technology can also play a significant role in procurement, creating a secure and transparent system for tracking and verifying transactions.

The benefits of advanced digitalization in procurement are numerous and far-reaching. Businesses can achieve greater efficiency, improve their supplier relationships, and make better-informed decisions based on real-time data. These advancements create new opportunities for businesses to succeed in an increasingly competitive market.

As we explore this element, we will focus on several key topics that highlight the major evolving scenarios and supply chains in the industry. Our first stop is Procurement, a crucial aspect of any business that involves connecting with extended value chain partners. In today's fast-paced and ever-changing market, businesses need to embrace advanced digital technologies to streamline their procurement process, increase efficiency, and gain a competitive edge.

Let's take a deeper dive into how advanced digitalization is transforming the procurement landscape and creating new opportunities for businesses to succeed.

3.1

DIGITALIZATION OF PROCUREMENT:

STRATEGIES TO OPTIMIZE BUSINESS

Procurement has always been a critical component of any business's operations, ensuring the organization receives the goods and services necessary to function effectively. In today's digital era, the process of procurement has undergone significant changes with the emergence of new technologies and the growing influence of automation. This transformation has given rise to what we call "digital procurement," which leverages technology to streamline the buying process, reduce costs, and increase efficiency. Digital procurement involves not only the adoption of new tools and systems but also the development of a strategic plan that takes into account the impact of technology on the procurement process. In this section, we will explore the different aspects of digital procurement, its impact on businesses, the key technologies driving its evolution and how it would link into the concept of Supply Chain 5.0 for delivering overall business success.

Introduction

The procurement process involves acquiring goods, products, or services from external sources. This process includes purchase planning, supply management, supply-chain handling, sourcing techniques, logistics, price negotiation, inventory control, risk management, legal analysis, and value analysis, as described by Chakraborty (2022).

Digital procurement is a strategic approach to sourcing goods and services that leverages technology to enhance the buying experience, decrease costs, and accelerate the process. The primary objective is to simplify the procurement process for both buyers and suppliers. Specifically, a digital procurement strategy is a plan that outlines how to use technology to enhance the purchasing of products and services, as highlighted by BizVibe (2022). Procurement involves evaluating and managing risks to obtain the best deal from suppliers and improve the organization's performance. It is a crucial contributor to fostering innovation and supporting business growth. Procurement also adds value to the supply chain by cultivating relationships with key stakeholders. The cost of products and operating expenses for a company can be significantly influenced by procurement.

Procurement professionals must possess a comprehensive understanding of daily operational tools like SAP, Ariba, or Blue Prism, as these digital solutions play a crucial role in product delivery, control, and bidding processes. Leveraging technology in procurement can streamline and enhance the often lengthy and intricate procurement procedures. With their expertise, procurement departments can collaborate with specialized suppliers to successfully implement efficient digital procurement strategies and achieve their goals effectively (Schweitzer, 2017).

The rise of digital technologies, including drones, self-driving cars, robots, artificial intelligence (AI), the Internet of Things (IoT), 3D printing, and augmented reality, is revolutionizing the way businesses leverage their purchasing capabilities.

These advancements facilitate the automation or utilization of cognitive technologies to replace humans in repetitive and mundane tasks, leading to increased efficiency and productivity in procurement processes.

This impact of digitalization on procurement is not limited to tangible aspects such as product delivery and bidding, it also extends to intangible aspects like supplier negotiations. With the integration of digital tools, businesses can enhance their ability to negotiate with suppliers, optimize contract terms, and improve relationship management, thereby transforming the entire procurement landscape (Schweitzer, 2017).

To understand the significance of digital procurement, it is crucial to analyze how automation can drastically change a business's value proposition and organizational structure, while also having a positive impact on the business ecosystem.

Procurement Digitalization

Let's start with the basics. The term "procurement" can be ambiguous, and defining "digital procurement" can be even more challenging. Procurement involves managing the entire product life cycle, from identifying needs and selecting suppliers to acquisition and management. It is often confused with purchasing or sourcing, despite the fact that the three have different roles. Purchasing is a straightforward practice that focuses on money spent and goods acquired, while procurement is a much broader responsibility. Digital procurement software simplifies the procurement process by offering an electronic platform (Chakraborty, 2022).

Digital procurement involves the use of active digital processes and the conversion of analog processes into digital ones. It starts with a basic switch to digitalization, where organizations can invest in software from vendors such as Coupa, Ariba, or

Sunsmart Global to incorporate automation. The most significant advantage of digitalization is that it increases the speed of procurement processes, resulting in faster and more efficient transactions (Chakraborty, 2022).

Digitalization allows companies to stay competitive by adapting to changing customer needs and business environments quickly. With digital procurement, businesses can reduce costs, improve efficiency, and gain greater visibility over their procurement process.

In recent years, the world has experienced significant disruptions, including the COVID-19 pandemic, conflicts, and energy crises, which have fundamentally reshaped the way we live and work. These events have highlighted the critical importance of sustainability, human rights, and customer-centricity in business operations. To thrive in the new era, these elements, previously overlooked in Procurement 4.0, will become integral components of Supply Chain 5.0. While digitalization will continue to play a crucial role, there will be a renewed focus on incorporating sustainability, human rights, and customer-centric approaches into supply chain practices. In the following, we will delve deeper into the significance of these missing elements and their evolving role in shaping the future of supply chain management.

Overview of Procurement Strategies

A procurement strategy is a comprehensive plan designed to build strategic partnerships with competitive suppliers, obtain high-quality goods and services within a specified cost range, and ensure timely delivery. It covers various processes involved in the procurement cycle (Golobrodska, 2022). Vodafone, for example, has implemented a digital procurement strategy to optimize its processes by fostering synergies between its HR department and procurement team. The company has combined workers from different generations to create a pool of digital expertise and experience, transforming its organizational culture and expanding collaboration opportunities (Schweitzer, 2017).

Procurement strategies are adaptable and applicable to organizations of all sizes (Figure 1). Common types of procurement strategies include:

- **Cost reduction**: This is one of the most popular methods used by companies worldwide. Businesses can reduce costs by negotiating better terms with suppliers or switching to less expensive options.
- **Risk management**: This strategy helps lower the risks associated with acquiring goods and services from external sources. Prior to engaging with a supplier, this process involves researching their financial standing, reputation, and history.
- **Supplier management and optimization**: This strategy enables companies to maximize their relationships with external suppliers while safeguarding their resources. It involves evaluating potential suppliers, negotiating prices and contracts, and fostering supplier loyalty.
- **Green purchasing**: This refers to the practice of acquiring goods and services that promote environmental protection. For example, companies can choose to purchase electricity from renewable sources or use recycled paper for printing documents (BizVibe, 2022).
- **Global sourcing**: This involves purchasing products or services from foreign suppliers, which can help organizations reduce costs as there are no import taxes or duties to pay on imported goods (BizVibe, 2022).

"Green purchasing" and "global sourcing" are two procurement practices that organizations can adopt to achieve environmental benefits and cost savings. While green purchasing involves

Figure 1. The Five Common Procurement Strategies.

selecting environmentally friendly products and services, global sourcing involves procuring goods and services from global suppliers to capitalize on cost advantages. By implementing both practices, organizations can not only contribute to sustainability efforts but also optimize their supply chain operations.

In today's business environment, a digital procurement strategy is essential for procurement professionals to succeed. To maximize the benefits, it's important to implement it intelligently. By leveraging digital technologies, procurement experts can enhance collaboration, analytics, and engagement at various stages of the procurement value chain. These stages include planning, sourcing, contract management, order delivery, payment control, and supplier management (Schweitzer, 2017).

As the business landscape continues to evolve, organizations must recognize the importance of these elements and embrace a comprehensive approach to procurement. By doing so, they can stay ahead of the curve, build strategic partnerships, obtain high-quality goods and services, and ensure timely delivery, all while aligning with the changing demands of the new era.

In today's dynamic business landscape, the adoption of a digital procurement strategy is crucial for organizations to thrive. However, to fully leverage its benefits, it is essential to align this strategy with the evolving context of Supply Chain 5.0. By incorporating sustainability, human rights, and customer-centricity, organizations can unlock new opportunities for success.

Benefits of Digitalization for Procurement Strategies

Digital procurement transformation offers numerous benefits that justify the initial investment of time and resources. Some of the key advantages include:

Cost Savings

A digital procurement transformation enables organizations to consolidate their budget information in one centralized location, providing a comprehensive overview of spending across departments. This enhanced visibility allows businesses to exercise greater control over their expenses and receive timely alerts if a particular department exceeds its allocated budget (Portt, 2021). By leveraging digital technologies, organizations can optimize their procurement processes and achieve better financial outcomes.

Automated procurement systems offer significant cost efficiency and savings for organizations. By streamlining procurement processes, these systems optimize overhead costs and enhance productivity, resulting in reduced processing time. Furthermore, they enable organizations to negotiate more effectively with suppliers, leveraging techniques such as multiple rounds of bidding or e-auctions (Abdellaoui, 2021).

By managing supplier relationships and procurement through a single portal, organizations can prevent duplicate purchases and benefit from economies of scale. They can also gain insights into their project and departmental workflows, enabling them to identify areas where staffing may be unnecessary (Portt, 2021).

For example, Maersk, a global logistics giant, partnered with Coupa to leverage the e-auctions system, enabling them to achieve agility and cost savings in times of change. By adopting this technology, Maersk has achieved double-digit returns and generated incremental savings of 5–7% compared to traditional negotiations for over 50% of procurement events. Over the past decade, Maersk has conducted thousands of e-auctions, delivering impressive results and demonstrating the benefits of this approach (Figure 2). By embracing digital procurement technologies, organizations can unlock new opportunities for cost optimization and performance improvement.

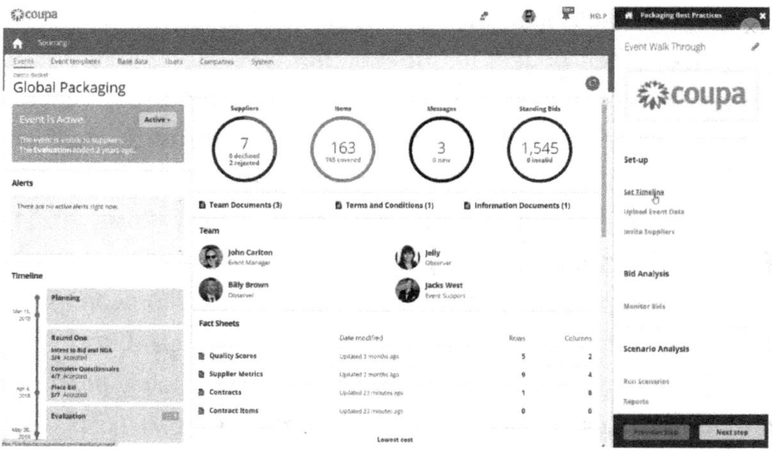

Figure 2. Maersk E-Auction System (Coupa, n.d.).

Increased Efficiency

Digital procurement transformation enables organizations to integrate all customer and distributor data into a single system, optimizing supply chain performance and capturing production data (if applicable). This approach leads to reduced inventory costs, shorter lead times, and improved customer experiences, while also enhancing supplier performance (Portt, 2021). Workflows are streamlined by eliminating unnecessary steps, and system functionalities are utilized to comply with regulations and enhance control. Additionally, online bidding tools facilitate better competition among suppliers and provide greater negotiation leverage (Abdellaoui, 2021). By embracing digital procurement technologies, organizations can drive operational efficiency and achieve strategic goals while delivering greater value to customers and suppliers alike.

Another key advantage of digital procurement is the simplification of processes through automation. By automating tasks such as collaborations, negotiations, sourcing, and service management, digital procurement eliminates the manual interference that often hinders staff productivity. This approach allows organizations to create a more sustainable workforce that is free from the burden of tedious tasks and can instead focus on value-added activities (Portt, 2021). With digital procurement, businesses can unlock new levels of efficiency and productivity while reducing the risk of errors and delays associated with manual processes.

Improved Visibility

Digital procurement can serve as a valuable business advisor, providing powerful analytical insights to help organizations make informed decisions. With data reporting features available in procurement systems, organizations can efficiently analyze large volumes of information from multiple sources to identify areas for improvement and new opportunities with clarity and precision (Portt, 2021).

In contrast to traditional paper-based procurement processes, digital procurement provides greater control and visibility. Access to the system is granted based on role-based permissions, ensuring that only authorized personnel can access sensitive information. The system also enables clear accountability and well-defined responsibilities for each user, and it facilitates easy audits of buyer and user activities, tendering processes, and technical and commercial evaluation results (Abdellaoui, 2021).

Value Creation

Digital procurement leverages artificial intelligence and robotic process automation to automate repetitive and operational tasks, freeing up employees' time to focus on long-term initiatives and strategic activities. By doing so, it can help organizations achieve new levels of cost savings and market competitiveness (Portt, 2021). Procurement automation systems enable procurement employees to utilize their time for more value-added activities, while the system handles the repetitive and operational tasks. This allows procurement to focus its efforts on more strategic activities, enhancing its ability to drive business growth and competitive advantage (Abdellaoui, 2021).

A procurement team that is adept at digital technologies can facilitate faster collaboration with top suppliers and drive change by re-evaluating operating models and partnerships. By eliminating the need for manual processes, employees can redirect their time and energy to analyzing the organization's bigger picture (Portt, 2021).

Risk Control

Utilizing the information available in the digital procurement system, organizations can easily identify and assess the risks associated with procurement. Detailed reports can be accessed instantly, allowing for easy monitoring of the entire procurement process. This enables organizations to quickly identify and mitigate potential threats. Furthermore, tools such as supplier prequalification information and performance evaluation reports can be utilized to analyze the risks posed by suppliers, ensuring that organizations are working with trustworthy and reliable partners (Abdellaoui, 2021).

Environment Protection

Traditionally, procurement relied heavily on paper-based materials, such as contracts and orders, and any changes to these documents required the printing of new copies, resulting in significant paper consumption. However, by implementing an eSourcing system, both buying companies and suppliers can save on paper and printing costs. Automation of procurement activities also eliminates the need for suppliers to physically submit their bids in-person, reducing gas emissions associated with transportation (Abdellaoui, 2021).

Furthermore, digital procurement makes it easier to track various sustainability measures along the entire supply chain, enabling companies to monitor their environmental impact and take steps towards a more sustainable future.

In conclusion, digitizing procurement brings numerous benefits that align with Supply Chain 5.0. It enables organizations to save costs, streamline workflows, and improve customer experiences. With enhanced visibility and analytics, informed decision-making becomes easier. Automation frees up time for strategic activities, while risk control and environmental protection are strengthened. By embracing digital procurement within the framework of Supply Chain 5.0, organizations can optimize processes, achieve goals, and shape a sustainable and customer-centric future.

Challenges of Digitizing Procurement Strategies

As organizations embrace the concept of Supply Chain 5.0, digitizing procurement strategies becomes essential. However, several challenges (Figure 3) need to be addressed to ensure successful implementation and maximize the benefits of digitalization. Digital transformation is causing widespread change and disruption across industries. While this presents many opportunities, it also poses challenges, particularly for procurement teams, which are at the forefront of these changes.

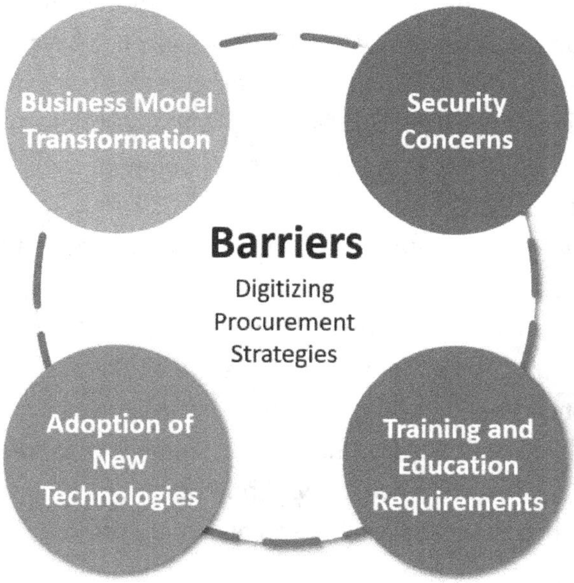

Figure 3. Challenges of Digitizing Procurement Strategies.

It's essential to distinguish between digitization and digitalization in procurement. Most companies are already utilizing digital procurement processes, which are referred to as "digitization". In contrast, digitalization is the active use of digital tools throughout the entire procurement process. This includes the incorporation of data management and e-procurement tools with a measurable impact on the organization's bottom line (Scoutbee, 2019).

Budget constraints are typically the most significant obstacle to digitalization. Organizations have finite resources, and every expenditure must be carefully justified. While digitalization has a clear potential for returns, several factors make it challenging to secure buy-in from stakeholders. Therefore, it is crucial to provide a straightforward return on investment (ROI) calculation to demonstrate the project's value (Scoutbee, 2019). The following are some of the barriers:

Business Model Transformation

While some leading companies have successfully integrated procurement into their core enterprise strategy, many procurement groups are still facing challenges gaining influence within their organizations. These challenges often stem from outdated paradigms that limit their potential impact. The biggest obstacle to digitalization is often the mindset that it is difficult to achieve or not worth the effort. Procurement organizations have traditionally prioritized cost-related metrics and performance indicators, resulting in limited supplier management resources being focused on suppliers with the highest spending levels.

The ultimate objective is to encourage procurement organizations to adopt an entrepreneurial mindset (ProcureCon Event, 2023). Procurement departments are transforming from clerical back-office functions to strategic business units that manage supply networks, drive innovation and growth, align operations with corporate ethical and social values, and mitigate risks amidst constant market and technological changes (SAP ARIBA, 2019).

Adoption of New Technologies

While many procurement leaders acknowledge that emerging technologies such as artificial intelligence (AI), big data, and robotic process automation (RPA) can yield exceptional outcomes, only half of them recognize their significance in achieving success. This is akin to boarding a train simply out of habit without comprehending its final destination (Scoutbee, 2019).

Procurement leaders must recognize technology as a valuable partner in an organization's value creation and realize the potential of digital procurement solutions in cutting costs and promoting innovation. However, Chief Procurement Officers (CPOs) need to go beyond this and acknowledge that they are not just leaders in procurement but also experts in data usage and digital innovation. This additional step places greater demands on leadership and expertise, posing a significant challenge for current procurement leaders (Scoutbee, 2019).

Security Concerns

One legitimate concern when transitioning to a fully digital model is the security of organizational data. This includes security of not only the organization's own data but also the data of its clients, suppliers, and customers, which could be put at risk.

To overcome this obstacle, organizations pursuing digitalization need to collaborate with trustworthy partners who can help establish secure workflows and prioritize data security. When selecting a supplier, it's important to inquire about their security certifications to ensure they meet the necessary standards.

While cloud services usually have high-security standards, it is essential to have strong endpoint security. Therefore, the best approach is a two-pronged strategy that involves a reliable supplier and robust internal security measures (Cloudia, 2020).

Integrating Cybersecurity Measures for a Resilient Future

In the era of rising cybercrime, it is imperative for companies to safeguard themselves, their customers, and their partners. Procurement professionals play a crucial role in this endeavor, as they are responsible for onboarding new suppliers and connecting them with their organization's systems.

As we move towards the next generation of Supply Chain 5.0, it is essential that cybersecurity becomes an integral part of supplier induction processes. Procurement professionals need to proactively build aspects of cybersecurity into their supplier evaluation and selection criteria. By doing so, organizations can mitigate the risks associated with cyber threats and ensure the protection of sensitive data.

By prioritizing cybersecurity and adopting robust measures, organizations can establish a resilient supply chain ecosystem that not only embraces technological advancements but also safeguard against potential threats, setting the stage for a secure and successful future.

To delve deeper into the intricacies of cybersecurity in supply chain management, we invite you to refer to Section 3.7. This section provides comprehensive insights and detailed guidelines on how organizations can fortify their cybersecurity measures and navigate the evolving landscape of digitalization and data protection.

Training and Education Requirements

The successful implementation of digital procurement requires an efficient organizational structure that spans across departments. However, the success of this implementation heavily relies on the full support of top management (Ang, 2021).

Therefore, to ensure the successful adoption of this strategy, organizations must prioritize training and education for all employees involved. This will help to equip employees with the necessary skills and knowledge to effectively implement and utilize digital procurement solutions.

A well-planned and systematic training program is crucial to ensuring that employees have a comprehensive understanding of the procurement process when implementing a new system. Sufficient knowledge of the new system will enhance work efficiency and minimize errors. Proper communication at all stages of the project is crucial to preventing misunderstandings. To ensure a successful implementation, proper financial resources should also be allocated to the project, enabling it to be completed smoothly and on time (Ang, 2021).

To thrive in the era of Supply Chain 5.0, organizations must not only digitize their procurement strategies but also ensure that they align with the core principles of human rights, fair trade, sustainability, and ethical practices. Overcoming the challenges of digitalization becomes essential to providing customers with personalized services that are deeply rooted in ethics and values.

By shifting mindsets, adopting innovative technologies, and prioritizing data security, organizations can navigate the digitalization journey while upholding the principles of Supply Chain 5.0. Investing in comprehensive training and education programs enables procurement teams to become strategic business units that drive innovation, achieve cost savings, and foster sustainable growth. Through effective supply network management and risk mitigation, organizations can deliver personalized services to customers, ensuring their needs are met while upholding ethical standards.

A well-planned and holistic approach to digital procurement empowers organizations to unlock its full potential within the framework of Supply Chain 5.0.

By embedding human rights, fair trade, sustainability, and a commitment to combating greenwashing into their procurement strategies, organizations can offer personalized services that align with customers' values. In this evolving landscape, organizations that embrace digitalization while upholding ethics and values position themselves for long-term success and contribute to a sustainable and customer-centric future.

Digitalization Strategies to Optimize Procurement Strategies

In today's ever-evolving world of Supply Chain 5.0, where human rights, fair trade, and sustainability take center stage, organizations are on a mission to revolutionize their procurement processes. They're embracing digitalization strategies like never before, harnessing the power of cutting-edge technologies, data analytics and intelligent automation. Why? because they know that by doing so, they can supercharge their efficiency, slash costs, and go above and beyond to provide personalized services that are infused with unwavering ethics and core values. It's a journey towards a brighter future, where procurement becomes a force for good, leaving no room for greenwashing or compromise.

The impact of digital disruption is widespread and not limited to specific sectors or company sizes. It has created new opportunities for businesses to engage with partners and clients, disrupting traditional business models and industry dynamics. Digital procurement is a solution that aims to automate repetitive tasks, enhance efficiency, and potentially reduce costs. By utilizing artificial intelligence (AI), user-friendly tools, and real-time analytics, digital procurement delivers valuable information to stakeholders (ProcurePort Blog, 2021).

By utilizing advanced data analytics, digital procurement solutions provide businesses with unprecedented insights that were once out of reach. This empowers businesses to make more informed decisions, leading to competitive advantage, increased efficiency and productivity, reduced costs, and improved customer service.

Microsoft's supply chain team successfully optimized its operations and reduced carbon dioxide emissions by 40% using Coupa's Supply Chain Design and Planning tool. With approximately 500 GB of supply chain data, the team was able to make real-time decisions and improve demand forecasting during peak periods. This data-driven approach not only enabled them to make informed and sustainable spending decisions, but also highlighted the potential of AI in driving Environmental, Social, and Governance (ESG) initiatives.

Procurement Policy and Systems

An effective procurement policy can serve as a roadmap for an organization to allocate its spending in a manner that maximizes the value obtained from its vendors and suppliers. A well-designed procurement policy should have long-term objectives, goals, and key performance indicators (KPIs) that help the organization monitor and measure its procurement performance over time (BizVibe, 2022).

A well-functioning procurement system should have well-defined roles and responsibilities, backed by streamlined processes and procedures. The objectives and goals of the organization should be closely linked to its procurement policy to ensure that the procurement process supports the overall organizational strategy.

Establishing effective supply chain management systems is a critical element of a successful digital procurement strategy. One of these systems is purchase order management, which involves tracking all purchase orders, regardless of how they were entered (manually, electronically, or on paper). With a well-managed e-PO system, every purchase order can be traced from creation to approval and receipt from the vendor. This approach ensures a completely foolproof, standard, and documented process that is followed consistently as the organization begins to digitize its procurement procedures.

Implement Technology

Procurement software is an essential component of any digital procurement strategy. It helps manage spending limits, saves time, and reduces costs associated with manual bookkeeping. These tools automate the process of finding and purchasing goods and services, making it easier for businesses to keep track of all their expenses (BizVibe, 2022).

The technology toolbox encompasses the various technologies that collect and utilize data, such as analytics, bots, artificial intelligence (AI), and natural language processing (NLP). By gathering relevant data and utilizing these advanced tools, companies can enhance and automate various processes beyond simple automation. It is essential to incorporate a technology toolkit that comprises various components such as automation and intelligence to implement a successful digital procurement strategy (ProcurePort Blog, 2021).

Companies have reported significant benefits by implementing an optimized cloud-based platform across their spending, which includes reductions in indirect spending and increased spend coverage, and across their procurement processes, which includes improvements in sourcing efficiency, procurement cycle time, processing time, safety, and regulatory compliance (EY Canada, 2021).

Intelligent automation is a powerful way that can be used to automate high-volume, complex, and multi-step data handling tasks. Chatbots, which are rule-based services powered by artificial intelligence, can carry out human-like conversations and provide essential information, intelligence, and online services that the organization requires. This technology can help organizations streamline their processes and improve their efficiency, making it an important component of a successful digital procurement strategy (EY Canada, 2021).

Developing an end-to-end source-to-pay (S2P) solution is an effective way to bridge the gap between supply chain planning and execution, as it helps to establish greater resilience and sustainability. This solution can connect disparate systems and ensure a seamless flow of data and information across the entire supply chain network. By doing so, it can help build a stronger S2P and enhance the overall efficiency of the procurement process (Zhong, 2022).

The distributed ledger technology called Blockchain performs the functions of receiving, validating, and permanently storing transactions. It is a secure means of sharing information, like the origin and authenticity of goods, creating a transparent and trustworthy public record that can be accessed by verified parties (EY Canada, 2021).

The procurement technology landscape is evolving, and according to a report by PWC, S2P solutions and data analytics are still receiving a considerable amount of interest, while the enthusiasm for robotics, AI, and blockchain is dwindling (Figure 4). The report highlights that investments are now being directed toward technologies that have already proven to provide tangible benefits with practical use cases, rather than just being hyped-up buzzwords (PWC, 2022).

Procurement software is an essential element of any digital procurement strategy, as it assists in managing spending limits, reduces time spent on manual bookkeeping, and minimizes associated costs. To successfully implement a digital procurement strategy, it is crucial to have a technology toolkit that

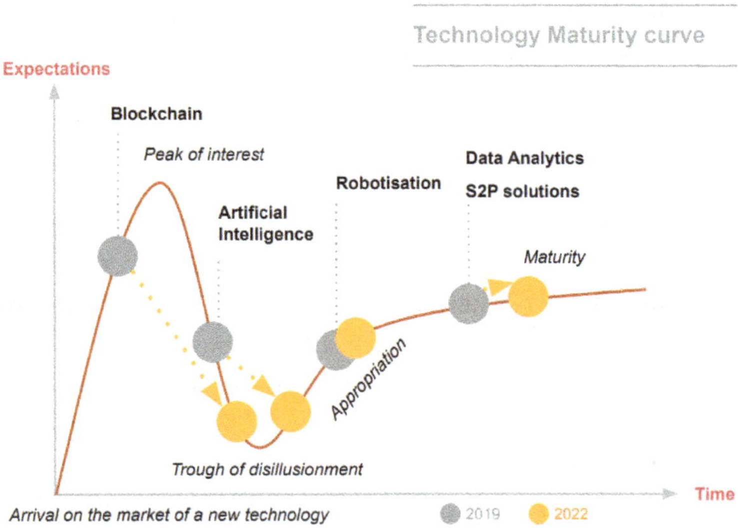

Figure 4. Technology Maturity Curve (PWC, 2022).

includes various components, such as automation and intelligence. Incorporating these tools can streamline procurement processes, increase efficiency, and drive better outcomes for the organization.

Data Analytics

To successfully forecast consumer needs, identify the best goods and services, and select optimal suppliers, businesses must leverage data. The development and execution of a digital procurement strategy demands that organizations take a deliberate approach to capture substantially more internal and external data than they currently do (ProcurePort Blog, 2021).

Data analytics plays a crucial role in automating and enhancing processes such as data cleansing, transformation, and classification in procurement. Adopting data visualization tools such as Power BI or Tableau brings a host of benefits, including a more robust sourcing process, compliance with organizational policies and contracts, data-driven communications to stakeholders, and increased negotiating power with suppliers (EY Canada, 2021).

Dynamic Monitoring and Refining

Thanks to advanced technologies and digital procurement systems, companies can now monitor their entire procurement process from selecting suppliers, placing orders, and transporting goods to the final entry of products into inventory. In case of any changes or disruptions, such as emergencies or policy changes, the procurement officers can be informed in real time through the system, allowing them to respond quickly and efficiently.

Moreover, by analyzing the data collected from the procurement process, which can be updated daily, companies can refine their procurement policies and make informed decisions based on current conditions. This allows them to continuously optimize their procurement strategy and achieve better results.

In the evolving world of Supply Chain 5.0, organizations have a powerful ally in their quest for success: digital procurement strategies. These strategies, in perfect harmony with the principles of Supply Chain 5.0, unlock a treasure trove of benefits.

Procurement professionals have to ensure that they create appropriate internal processes of asking suppliers to submit Sustainability and Human Rights related information, ask for relevant certifications and then have a system to verify and audit, before they are inducted into the eco-system of the operations. Coupa and Ariba can help with such fields in future, but the initiative has to be taken to embed such processes by the Supply Chain and Procurement Managers as their personal responsibility.

By fortifying their procurement policies, embracing cutting-edge technologies, and harnessing the power of data analytics, businesses can supercharge their procurement processes and propel themselves towards sustainable growth.

They become champions of personalized services, never compromising on human rights, fair trade, or environmental sustainability. With unwavering commitment, they continuously monitor and refine their strategies, adapting swiftly to market shifts, and delivering value infused with a profound sense of ethics and values.

Conclusions

Summary of Benefits and Challenges of Digitalization

Digital transformation is no longer just a trendy term but a reality that many companies have recognized. According to a recent survey, 70% of companies are now aware of the benefits of digital transformation and are in the process of developing or implementing a strategy. To facilitate this process, data visualization tools have proven to be a powerful means for organizations to digitize, visualize, and analyze their data. Mroczkowska (2020) aptly summarizes the key benefits of digital transformation, including:

1. Accelerating business processes through automation

Digital transformation enables organizations to automate tasks that previously consumed employees' time, resulting in improved accuracy, reduced error rates, and lower costs. This frees up employees to focus on crucial tasks that require advanced judgment and creativity.

2. Improving the customer experience

Automating tasks can significantly enhance both customer and employee experiences in several ways. For instance, automating the process of responding to support tickets can lead to much faster turnaround times for customers. Software solutions can provide truly omnichannel support, simplifying the process for customers to contact a company via phone, live chat, email, mobile app, or support forum. By providing customers with multiple touchpoints, the business can track interactions easily and gather feedback to provide even better service. Keeping all these channels digital ensures seamless communication and an improved customer experience. The organization can leverage the functionalities of these channels to provide personalized recommendations using the data attached to customer accounts.

In 2011, Target made a strategic move to bring its web presence back from Amazon and make it the main channel for its business. Target invested in store redesigns to create a seamless shopping experience that blurred the line between physical and e-commerce shopping. The company also introduced online ordering and in-store pick-up services and increased its social media presence to help customers discover new products and make purchases. This holistic digital strategy allowed Target to customize the different touchpoints of the customer experience, leading to steady revenue growth and plans to invest $7 billion in store remodeling.

According to Shelagh Dolan (2022), Target's online sales increased by nearly 188.6% from 2019 to 2021. However, recent trends show a turnaround. As Conley (2023) reports, Target's digital sales declined by 3.6% in Q4 2022, even though overall sales rose modestly. Nassauer and Seal (2023) note that Target's profit was hurt by slower sales growth and rising operating costs in the quarter ended January 28, 2023, due to cautious consumer spending and inflation affecting shoppers' budgets. While more shoppers visited Target stores in the fourth quarter, they spent differently than in the previous year. Chief Executive Brian Cornell attributes this to strong sales in food, beauty, and essentials, offsetting weaker consumer spending in other categories.

This recent turnaround highlights the importance of customer-centric strategies and improving consumer experiences, especially in an increasingly volatile and competitive business environment. Companies face unprecedented disruptions and crises like the COVID-19 pandemic and the Ukraine–Russia war, which not only pose risks and challenges to businesses' viability but also change consumers' purchasing choices and priorities. Therefore, companies must make better decisions using data to remain relevant and competitive in the market.

3. Better decision-making thanks to data

Digital tools enable managers to collect and process data in real time, allowing them to see what works well and what needs improvement. With software-driven processes, it is easier to recognize patterns and opportunities for improvement. For example, Hasbro, a toy and game company, invested in digital transformation and data strategies, which helped them understand customers better and meet their needs proactively. They created targeted marketing campaigns on multiple channels and recommended the most relevant products to parents, who made the purchases. This focus on data and digital marketing allowed Hasbro to face rapid changes in the industry during the last decade and stay ahead of the curve.

4. Greater agility, flexibility, and scalability

Modern software is simpler to integrate, allowing businesses to connect various aspects of their operations and avoid creating data silos by department or function. By linking data to advance a task without manual input, your solution can streamline processes and increase agility. Additionally, modern tools provide more flexibility and scalability, allowing businesses to adapt quickly to changes in the market and scale operations as needed.

5. Reliability and security

Legacy systems can be difficult and expensive to maintain and protect, making them more susceptible to malfunctions and cyber threats. By switching to modern tools, businesses have a wider selection of applications to choose from that are qualified to support their systems. Moreover, operating costs for risk-taking activities can be cut by 20–30% through creative digital risk initiatives.

6. Creating a productive digital workplace and culture

Digital transformation can benefit both customer and employee experiences. By implementing cutting-edge digital tools, businesses can encourage greater productivity and collaboration among employees. A productive digital workplace and culture also lead to higher employee satisfaction, retention, and motivation.

With the advent of Supply Chain 5.0, organizations need to recognize the tremendous benefits of digital transformation. By leveraging advanced technologies and data visualization tools, businesses must accelerate their processes, improve customer experiences, and make better-informed decisions. The power of digital transformation lies in its ability to foster agility, scalability, and reliability while creating a productive digital workplace and culture. With these advantages, organizations will be able to navigate through disruptions and changes in the market, deliver exceptional customer experiences, and stay ahead of the competition. Embracing digitalization is essential ammunition for companies in their procurement to embrace Supply Chain 5.0, as it forms the foundation of the value delivery system. Without a robust beginning in the procurement process, achieving transparency regarding human rights and sustainability will be challenging.

Recommendations for Optimizing Procurement Strategies

Digital procurement involves more than just the adoption of new technologies in the procurement process. It also incorporates artificial intelligence (AI) and automation tools, advanced data analysis, and data-driven optimization to aid in the company's strategy development. Digital procurement transforms how tasks are carried out, using automation to complete tasks efficiently while cutting costs. The system employs sophisticated methods of data model analysis to comprehend and execute operations, making strategic sourcing more predictable (Procurement Tactics, 2022).

Digital procurement facilitates collaboration among buyers, suppliers, and third parties, opening up new ways of working together. The system allows for information sharing among all stakeholders, promoting closer and mutually beneficial cooperation. This creates an integrated network of people, processes, and technologies that generates more value by reducing costs and making more efficient use of resources.

To thrive in today's fast-paced business environment, companies must be able to move quickly and efficiently. Digital procurement is a key component of this transformation. By implementing a framework for digital procurement, businesses can streamline their operations, making them more agile and efficient. This transformation can have a significant impact on the overall operation of a business, allowing it to adapt and thrive in a rapidly changing marketplace.

Digitalization isn't just a buzzword anymore in the new era of Supply Chain 5.0; it's a game-changer that unlocks a host of benefits for businesses. By embracing it, companies can improve their information exchange, promote standardization, and free up more time, ultimately leading to growth and cost savings. But that's not all. When a digitalization plan is implemented correctly, it gives professionals access to global information at their fingertips, streamlining the decision-making process and reducing risks. In fact, a survey by McKinsey and Company found that procurement departments implementing digitalization can anticipate staggering annual savings of 40%, a 30–50% reduction in transactional sourcing time, and a 50% drop in value leakage. It's clear that the future of procurement lies in being quick, transparent, and responsive — all of which are only possible through digitalization (Metalshub, n.d.).

The future of procurement hinges on the swift, transparent, and responsive processes made possible through digitalization. Embracing digital transformation in procurement is not just an option; it is an imperative for organizations in the era of Supply Chain 5.0. By implementing digital procurement strategies, businesses can optimize their operations, reduce costs, and deliver exceptional customer experiences. This transformative approach fosters collaboration, standardization, and efficiency across the entire procurement ecosystem, unlocking significant growth potential and cost savings. The ability to access global information in real-time empowers professionals to make informed decisions swiftly, mitigating risks and enhancing strategic sourcing.

The evidence is clear: organizations that embark on a digitalization journey in procurement can anticipate substantial savings, streamlined processes, and minimized value leakage. To succeed in the dynamic market landscape, companies must embrace digitalization as the key to agility, transparency, and responsiveness. It is the ammunition they need to excel in Supply Chain 5.0 and drive sustainable growth while upholding the principles of human rights, fair trade, and environmental sustainability.

References

Abdellaoui, S. (2021, November 3). *10 Benefits of Procurement Digital Transformation.* LinkedIn. https://www.linkedin.com/pulse/10-benefits-procurement-digital-transformation-sanae.

Ang, Y. (2021, October 9). *Major Issues for Digital Procurement and Supply Risks.* SIPMM Publications. https://publication.sipmm.edu.sg/major-issues-digital-procurement-supply-risks/.

BizVibe. (2022, September 26). *How to Build a Digital Procurement Strategy in 10 Steps: 2022 Guide*. https://blog.bizvibe.com/blog/business/digital-procurement-strategy.

Chakraborty, A. (2022, September 30). *What Is Digital Procurement? Definition, Benefits & Pitfalls*. SelectHub. https://www.selecthub.com/eprocurement/what-is-digital-procurement/.

Cloudia. (2020, June 3). *Top 5 Barriers to Procurement Digitalization*. https://cloudia.com/top-5-barriers-to-procurement-digitalization-and-how-to-overcome-them/.

Conley, P. (2023, February 28). *Target Overall Sales Rise Modestly in Q4, but Digital Sales Decline 3.6%*. Digital Commerce 360. https://www.digitalcommerce360.com/article/target-online-sales/.

Coupa. (n.d.). *Deliver More Value Across the Spend Lifecycle*. Retrieved December 17, 2022, from https://www.coupa.com/products/procurement/source-to-pay.

Dolan, S. (2022, April 26). *Target's Annual Revenue Crosses $100 Billion in 2021 — With Growth Expected to Continue*. Insider Intelligence. https://www.insiderintelligence.com/insights/target-annual-revenue-top-ecommerce-companies-2/.

EY Canada. (2021, June 2). *The Journey to Procurement Digitization*. https://www.ey.com/en_ca/supply-chain/the-journey-to-procurement-digitization.

Golobrodska, M. (2022, March 30). *Procurement Strategy. How to Get It Right? [Guide + Template]*. Precoro. https://precoro.com/blog/procurement-strategy/.

Metalshub. (n.d.). *Metalshub — Digital procurement — Advantages*. Retrieved December 17, 2022, from https://www.metals-hub.com/blog/advantages-of-digital-procurement.

Mroczkowska, A. (2020, February 2). *Digital Transformation Benefits and Challenges | What Do They Mean to Your Business?* Droids on Roids. https://www.thedroidsonroids.com/blog/digital-transformation-benefits-and-challenges.

Nassauer, S., & Seal, D. (2023, February 28). *Target's Slim Sales Growth, Rising Costs Weigh on Earnings*. The Wallstreet Journal. https://www.wsj.com/articles/target-tgt-q4-earnings-report-2022-f4d3d6cd.

Portt. (2021, July 7). *Top 5 Immediate Benefits of Digital Procurement*. https://www.portt.com/news/impacts-implementing-digital-procurement/.

ProcureCon Event. (2023, September 11–13). *Digitalization Challenges & Strategies in Procurement.* https://procureconeast.wbresearch.com/blog/procurement-organizations-digitalization-roadblocks-strategy-move-past.

Procurement Tactics. (2022, May 20). *Digital Procurement — The Ultimate Guide of 2023.* https://procurementtactics.com/digital-procurement/.

ProcurePort Blog. (2021, December 30). *5 Steps to a Successful Digital Procurement Strategy.* https://blog.procureport.com/digital-procurement-strategy/.

PWC. (2022, July). *Digital Procurement Transformation-Combining Human Ingenuity with Technology Innovation to Drive Sustained Procurement Outcomes.* https://www.pwc.com/gr/en/PwC%20Greece%20Digital%20Procurement%20survey.pdf.

SAP ARIBA. (2019, June 5). *Global Survey Confirms Digitalization Tops Chief Procurement Officers' Agendas*. Businesswire. https://www.businesswire.com/news/home/20190604006186/en/Global-Survey-Confirms-Digitalization-Tops-Chief-Procuremen.

Schweitzer, A. S. (2017, October 26). *How Does Digital Transformation Influence the Procurement Function?* Geneva Business New. https://www.gbnews.ch/how-does-digital-transformation-influence-the-procurement-function/.

Scoutbee. (2019, February 13). *3 Procurement Challenges Facing Digital Transformation in 2019 — Better Data. Better Decisions.* Better World. https://scoutbee.com/blog/procurement-challenges-2019/.

Zhong, A. (2022, July 11). *Digitalization in Procurement: Seizing the Opportunity Now*. GEP. https://www.gep.com/blog/technology/digitalization-in-procurement.

3.2

A MAJOR SHIFT

AI AND BLOCKCHAIN REDEFINE THE SUPPLY CHAIN

The supply chain has evolved significantly over the years. The rise of logistics technology and global manufacturing has made it easier for companies to distribute their goods all over the world, but it's also created challenges for them. Today's supply chains are more complex than ever, and they're under constant pressure from rising costs, changing consumer demands, and evolving regulations. This has forced companies to become more innovative when it comes to managing their supply chain operations.

Blockchain and artificial intelligence (AI) are pivotal technologies in Supply Chain 5.0, enabling more secure, efficient, and reliable operations. Many vendors and analysts have considered these technologies individually when it comes to the supply chain. However, the real value comes when you start combining some of these technologies together. Even though the word "autonomous" has been closely associated with Artificial intelligence (AI), from a supply chain point of view, we believe that when you combine AI with IoT and blockchain, you can develop a supply chain platform that is more intelligent, connected, and trusted in how it operates. The combination of these technologies drives the advancement of Supply Chain 5.0, fostering competitiveness and sustainability in the supply chain system.

Many companies will be leveraging all three of these technologies without realizing that they are, in effect, enabling their own autonomous supply chains. To maximize the return on investment of these technologies, it's important to have a digital foundation in place. No matter how appealing these technologies are, if you cannot exchange information electronically with an external digital ecosystem, then it is going to be difficult to obtain maximum ROI (Morley, 2022).

As a refresher, artificial intelligence is an area of technology that has been gaining momentum over the last few years, largely due to its ability to analyze large amounts of data and make predictions based on that analysis. This technology is unique in that it can learn from its mistakes as it goes along, meaning that AI systems get better every time they make a decision about something new.

The blockchain is a database system in which all transactions are recorded publicly, so no one person or company can alter any information without others being aware of it in real time. This distributed ledger allows for full transparency across all parties involved in any interaction with one another (so long as all parties agree on who those parties are).

From the time of product pickup to the time it reaches the end user, all of it can be tracked end-to-end through AI and blockchain. The latter, in fact, also has a permanently saved digital ledger, that is error-free and safe for holding transactions. Organizations can digitize physical assets and create a decentralized transactional record for greater visibility. SCM can thus eliminate shipping delays, reduce fraud and errors, and improve management.

With technological advancements changing the world rapidly, as we see, it is challenging to keep up with the market. Logistics companies might not be able to adopt new technologies quickly. In a nutshell, if supply chain companies want to reform the way they move around commodities and ensure timely delivery, blockchain and AI applications are the answer (R, 2021).

Stronger supply chains are essential for any business. The management of the production, distribution, and consumption of goods and services is handled by this vital logistics network. Blockchain and AI are transforming how companies run their supply chains. They are significantly improving the ease with which information, money, and goods are moved. They thereby contribute to the advancement of sectors like automotive, healthcare, and retail.

By digitizing largely paper-based processes, sharing and trusting data, and adding intelligence and automation to the execution of transactions, AI and blockchain are transforming how companies do business. For instance, SGX, the Singapore Exchange, has implemented Amazon Managed Blockchain to streamline its operations and enhance efficiency. As an electronic marketplace for financial products, SGX faced challenges with manual paperwork, complex transaction workflows, and reliance on heavy data-center infrastructure. By leveraging Amazon Managed Blockchain, SGX eliminates the need for managing complex API integrations across different banking systems and improves the efficiency of data and transaction transfers. Blockchain technology enables transaction transparency through a shared ledger, reducing settlement time for trades by up to 60 percent. SGX sees this implementation as a significant step toward mainstream adoption of blockchain, and they anticipate it will not only enhance transaction models but also create a new digital asset class that can revolutionize fundraising and enable borderless transactions. SGX's collaboration with AWS reflects their commitment to harnessing emerging technologies for the growth and advancement of the ecosystem (Amazon Web Services, 2020).

They can even facilitate and expedite new product development within the supply chain. For instance, Moderna, a biotechnology company, partners with Amazon Web Services (AWS), a comprehensive cloud service provider that offers innovative business solutions, including machine learning (ML) and blockchain capabilities (Amazon Web Services, 2017). By harnessing the power of AWS, Moderna accelerates its research and development process in the medical field, focusing particularly on messenger RNA (mRNA) therapeutics. AI, specifically ML, is leveraged to uncover hidden discoveries and patterns within the vast amount of genetic data collected by Moderna. This allows for the swift exploration and design of mRNA sequences, thereby facilitating the identification of potential therapeutic options. Additionally, Moderna employs a combination of blockchain technology and AWS's cloud storage to securely store and ensure the integrity of their research data. This integration of AI and blockchain showcases the significant role these technologies play in advancing biotechnology research and development, paving the way for potential breakthroughs in medicine (Clifford, 2020).

Industry-specific researchers are developing solutions that can revolutionize the way data are stored and analyzed. The integration of blockchain and AI in the supply chain helps analyze big data and make better decisions. With their ability to process vast amounts of data, AI systems can provide insights and recommendations that surpass human capabilities.

Supply Chain 5.0 recognizes that customers and stakeholders demand transparency and accountability. Through the utilization of AI, companies can analyze vast amounts of data collected from IoT devices and various touchpoints within the supply chain. The integration of blockchain into Supply Chain 5.0 enables the creation of decentralized, immutable records. This distributed ledger technology enhances trust among participants by providing a transparent and tamper-proof platform for storing transactional information. With these technologies, companies can establish a customer-centric supply chain ecosystem that ensures end-to-end visibility, trust, and accountability. Customers and stakeholders can have confidence in the accuracy and authenticity of the data, fostering stronger relationships and collaboration throughout the supply chain network.

The Supply Chain is Getting a Much-Needed Upgrade

The supply chain is complex, and it's not just about cutting costs.

In fact, the supply chain is getting a much-needed upgrade. It's not just about cutting costs. Industry leaders prepare for change as blockchain technology enables a whole new level of transparency and integrity in the manufacturing space. Blockchain technology is revolutionizing the supply chain by providing secure and verifiable data that can be used to track shipments and ensure accurate payments. For example, Walmart is using blockchain technology to track the movement of mangoes from farms in Mexico to stores in the United States. This has helped Walmart reduce food waste and improve the traceability of its products.

Similarly, AI has a huge potential to improve efficiencies and customer experiences. AI can provide insight into customer behavior, inventory management, and supply chain operations by analyzing data. For example, Amazon is using AI to predict demand for products and optimize its supply chain accordingly. This has helped Amazon improve its customer service and reduce its costs.

With the help of AI and blockchain technology, industry leaders can develop better forecasting models, optimize their processes, and create a more sustainable supply chain. Thus promising opportunities for improvement are being presented by new technologies throughout the supply chain. Blockchain technology has the potential to decrease administrative costs while also increasing supply chain transparency and traceability.

Blockchain supply chains can help participants record price, date, location, quality, certification, and other relevant information, so as to manage the supply chain more effectively. It can improve material supply chain traceability, reduce losses from counterfeit and gray market products, and increase visibility and compliance for outsourced contract manufacturing.

Blockchain technology can help companies manage their supply chains more efficiently and reduce losses from gray market and counterfeit products. The availability of these data on the blockchain can improve visibility and compliance in outsourced contract manufacturing. It can increase material supply chain traceability and reduce costs associated with lost or intercepted goods (Deloitte, 2017).

One approach to addressing supply chain coordination issues is the development of next-generation blockchains, which combine blockchain and cloud technologies. Similar to how end users of a retailer like Amazon can track orders and shipments, businesses can use blockchain technology to track cargo. The value of blockchain is found in the opportunity it provides parties to quickly and securely share data in a decentralized manner.

They prioritize compliance, security, and privacy. Using straightforward permission mechanisms, next-generation blockchains and distributed ledgers provide out-of-the-box solutions for data privacy, making it simple for data producers to control who can view or update their data. Businesses must be able to enforce (and audit) who has access to their mission-critical business data because there are so many parties involved and so much real-time data about the supply chain being produced and consumed. These issues become even more urgent if antitrust or competition laws are involved (Deloitte, 2017).

It's Not Just About Technology

AI and Blockchain are about transforming the way we think about supply chain management.

AI can be used to track the movement of goods through supply chain, providing real-time data on everything from the origin of the materials to the working conditions of the person who made them. This data can be used to ensure that products are ethically sourced and that workers are treated fairly.

Blockchain can be used to create a tamper-proof record of all transactions in the supply chain. This can help prevent fraud and ensure that customers can be confident in the provenance of the products they are buying.

Even from a transactional viewpoint, they're so beneficial because they can help reduce errors in everything from inventory management to customer service. For example, one major retailer recently used AI to optimize its delivery routes by 15% that added up to 900 trucks' worth of efficiency saved over the course of a year! Similarly, blockchain technology has been used in supply chain management for years now, but it's only recently become popular among companies looking for ways to innovate their products or services for customers (i.e., Nike).

With all this potential at our fingertips, it's time we stopped seeing AI and blockchain as buzzwords or short-term solutions and started seeing them as tools we can use every day to build better business practices that improve lives across industries around the world.

Seven benefits of adopting AI and blockchain in the supply chain are as follows (Rupareliya, 2021):

1. *Greater geographic scalability of intelligence*: AI and blockchain are increasingly important in delivering high-value commodities, such as pharmaceutical drugs and diamonds. The technologies also advance the inventory management system, reduce courier costs, and build consumer trust faster.
2. *Data interoperability for extracting more supply value*: Blockchain and AI products allow data to be interoperable and easily shared among all stakeholders, such as manufacturers, wholesalers, retailers, and logistics service providers. It also prevents goods from getting stuck in the supply chain

because they can be tracked in real time, thus reducing misplacements.

3. *Fewer human errors result from increased automation*: Simply put, paperwork and bureaucracy are reduced by AI and blockchain. Up to 10% of freight invoices may have inaccurate information, which leads to disputes and other supply-chain process inefficiencies. This could be prevented. The two technologies guarantee an automated process that stores all the data in a digital format and tracks a commodity's pick-up and delivery timelines, creating a more direct relationship between each stakeholder, such as a wholesaler, logistics service provider, and consumer, as opposed to managing a long paper trail. When supply chain automation is guaranteed, there is less room for error, and everyone in the supply chain is responsible for their actions.
4. *Increased connectivity across supply chains*: An average logistics process is not free from manual processes and extensive paperwork. There is significant value in logistics that organizations cannot tap into due to the fragmented nature of the industry. AI and blockchain can facilitate data visibility among various stakeholders. Goods can be picked up and dropped off faster and without any delays or errors.
5. *Increased traceability and transparency in supply chains*: Businesses that use AI and blockchain in supply chain management can collect and analyze information about how products are made or sourced, what raw materials they contain, how they are managed, and other factors. A blockchain-based system can store all commodity-related information, making it accessible to all interested parties. The ability to track and trace the goods is now more powerful than ever for logistics partners, which is more important. Additionally, they can demonstrate legitimacy, particularly for expensive items like gold jewelry and medical supplies.

The end user, who is curious about the products, can also access the information (e.g., authenticity).

6. *Improved technical skills and knowledge*: Like every industry, the supply chain also evolves, requiring organizations to keep up with market changes. When new technologies enter the picture, it becomes crucial for partners and contributors to pull up their socks and learn them. In conclusion, AI and blockchain fasten the learning process, which otherwise gets slowed down or delayed due to manual and tedious supply chain networks.
7. *Enhanced culture of collaboration*: In SCM, the word "chain" immediately conjures up images of connectivity, alliances, and collaboration. Any process that is completed successfully is the result of strong collaboration between various stakeholders. To add logistical value, this cooperation is required. An organization commits to a closely related endeavor when it integrates AI and blockchain technologies into its SCM. The use of these technologies can promote internal and external collaboration between various stakeholders, increasing supply chain efficiency and transparency.

Industry Leaders Prepare for Change

As supply chain leaders brace for change, they're also taking steps to prepare. Among these are investments in new technology (AI and blockchain), staff training, new processes, systems, and partnerships.

In 2019 alone, Amazon purchased AI company Harvest Automation Inc., while Walmart acquired cloud robotics startup Spatialand Inc. Both companies are investing heavily in automation technology that can help reduce the costs associated with human labor and increase efficiency by reducing errors and speeding up processes. In addition to these internal investments, industry leaders like Accenture and IBM have partnered with retailers such as Adidas USA to develop solutions that improve the end-to-end experience for customers via digital operations management platforms.

It is estimated that by 2026, more than 75% of commercial supply chain management application vendors will deliver embedded advanced analytics (AA), Artificial Intelligence (AI), and data science (Hippold, 2022).

According to surveys conducted by Mckinsey (Balakrishnan et al., 2020; Chui et al., 2021; Chui et al., 2022), there has been a significant shift in the allocation of digital budget towards AI adoption over the past five years. Previously, only 40 percent of respondents from AI-utilizing organizations reported allocating more than 5 percent of their digital budgets to AI. However, the landscape has transformed, with over half of the respondents now indicating such levels of investment. Looking ahead, the trend is expected to continue, as 63 percent of respondents anticipate a further increase in their organizations' investment in AI over the next three years. This demonstrates a growing recognition of the value and potential that AI offers, prompting organizations to prioritize and expand their AI initiatives.

These investments, acquisitions, and partnerships all demonstrate that the industry is actively engaging with new technologies and systems to build up its competitive advantage. These also provide a glimpse into the future of retail, which is increasingly automated and driven by technology. It is becoming increasingly clear that retailers are investing in technology-driven automation as a way to lower their costs, increase efficiency, and provide customers with a better overall experience.

While blockchain can be used to verify the authenticity of goods, AI can automate the process of detecting counterfeit products. In this way, it's possible for companies to reduce time-to-market for new products and increase efficiency in manufacturing processes. A look into the future shows that blockchains and AI will continue to redefine supply chains as we know them today.

There are seven noteworthy applications of AI and Blockchain in supply chain management (Rupareliya, 2021):

1. *Machine Learning (ML) for supply planning*: Based on demand projections, raw material availability, and capacity restrictions, supply planning entails planning for the procurement, production, and distribution of goods and commodities. ML-powered systems assist organizations in more accurately forecasting inventory, consumer demand, and supply. They improve decision-making in the supply chain. Stakeholders can use big data to calculate intelligent algorithms and perform machine-to-machine analysis.
2. *NLP for smooth human-machine communication*: NLP, or "natural language processing," combines AL and ML to allow people to communicate naturally with machines via text or voice. Examples of NLP include email filters, intelligent assistants, and digital phone calls. NLP can be used in the supply chain to reduce administrative costs and effectively analyze data in other languages. Massive data sets can be produced, and compliance and auditing processes that were previously impractical because of specific language barriers between suppliers and buyers can now be streamlined.
3. *ML for inventory and warehouse management*: A successful supply chain is the result of a robust inventory and warehouse management system. This is especially important for any service-based or consumer-specific company. An ML-equipped forecasting tool can enable retailers to understand the combinations of data streams and algorithms and better forecast demand.

4. *Blockchain for automotive supplier payments*: Without engaging in any conventional banking transactions, the technology allows for fund transfers between the payer and the payee to take place anywhere in the world. In contrast to taking days, it is also swift and safe, taking only a few minutes. Because of this, blockchain development is effective.
5. *Smart contracts for quality shipment*: In logistics, the phrase "smart contract" refers to a digital contract that automatically executes when certain criteria are met. For instance, once it is documented on the blockchain that the former has shipped goods in accordance with the manufacturer's specifications, payment to the logistics service provider is made. It guarantees high-quality delivery.
6. *Blockchain-powered supply chain monitoring for food and pharmaceutical products*: Medicines and food items require specific storage conditions. These products have sensors that can measure environmental variables like humidity and temperature. Blockchain platforms can be used to store the readings. Additionally, nobody can tamper with that because the platform is secure and error-free. Before any harm is done to the food or medicines, a smart contract can alert stakeholders whenever a storage condition changes. For instance, the blockchain system may deem certain food items unfit for use if they pass their "use-by dates."
7. *RFID-driven contractual bidding for cartons*: Despite being an older technology, SCM uses RFID tags primarily to store product information that IT systems can automatically tag and process. Information about the time and place of delivery is stored on RFID tags for cartons. For example, logistics service providers use apps to locate these tags and submit bids for delivery contracts based on the locations. Naturally, the company that provides the best price and delivery timeframe wins the contract. By doing this, a quicker and more affordable delivery cycle is guaranteed.

AI Will Never Replace Humans in the Supply Chain

We firmly believe that AI serves as an invaluable tool in supply chain management, empowering organizations with faster, more accurate, and consistent decision-making capabilities. However, it is crucial to acknowledge that we firmly believe AI cannot and will not completely replace humans in businesses in the near future. Instead, the optimal approach lies in harnessing the immense potential of AI alongside transformative technologies.

AI-based machines are fast, more accurate, and consistently rational, but they aren't intuitive, emotional, or culturally sensitive. And it is precisely these abilities that humans possess that enable us to be effective (De Cremer & Kasparov, 2021).

Some of the interesting debates in the industry have been around machine intelligence vs. human intelligence.

In its simplest form, AI is a computer that acts and decides in ways that seem intelligent. In line with Alan Turing's philosophy, AI imitates how humans act, feel, speak, and decide. Because of its imitation abilities, AI has the ability to identify patterns that optimize trends relevant to the job.

Humans represent a different kind of AI or what we would call authentic intelligence; they are able to think, act, and judge in a different way from AI. When open systems are in place, this kind of intelligence is required. These skills are specific to humans, unlike AI, which depends on data from outside the body to function. In an open management system, the team or organization interacts with the outside world and must thus manage external influences. Such a setting at work necessitates the use of artificial intelligence (AI1) and human intelligence (AI2). In the context of organizations, both types of intelligence offer a range of specific talents.

Augmented intelligence, the third type of AI, is a significant leap towards the future of intelligent work. The term "the future of work" refers to the development of workers and their ability to perform tasks more effectively. However, the debate on this subject has started to take on some unclear intentions. Businesses are currently in a stage where machines are frequently introduced as the new "super employee," which may ultimately place humans in an inferior role to serve machines because of cost-cutting strategies and narratives. The expansion of the workforce, which will include both humans and machines, is a necessary component of a truly intelligent type of future work, but with the goal of enhancing humanity and well-being while doing so (De Cremer & Kasparov, 2021).

In the new era of Supply Chain 5.0, where the customer is at the center and sustainability and human rights are prioritized, the integration of machines and augmented intelligence becomes even more crucial. By incorporating elements of Supply Chain 5.0, businesses can harness the power of machines and AI to generate transparency and ensure ethical practices throughout the supply chain. This enables businesses to make better-informed decisions and empowers stakeholders, including customers, to have complete visibility into the processes and practices involved in the production and delivery of goods and services. Embracing Supply Chain 5.0 principles alongside augmented intelligence not only enhances efficiency and productivity but also strengthens the commitment to creating a responsible and sustainable future of work. By leveraging the capabilities of machines and AI in a way that aligns with the values of Supply Chain 5.0, businesses can strike a balance between technological advancements and human well-being, driving positive outcomes for all stakeholders involved.

AI and Blockchain Technologies have the Potential to Completely Revolutionize A Business

AI and blockchain are two different technologies, but they can work together to revolutionize the supply chain. Together, both of these technologies have the potential to completely revolutionize any business.

Blockchain and AI: The combination of these two technologies can create a supply chain that is more efficient, transparent, secure, and accurate than ever before.

According to a new Facts and Factors market research analysis, the global AI market size and share revenue are predicted to expand from $29.86 billion in 2020 to $299.64 billion in 2026, representing a 35.6% compound annual growth rate (CAGR). Similarly, the worldwide blockchain market is predicted to increase at a CAGR of 67.3%, from $3 billion in 2020 to $39.7 billion in 2025. Organizations are predicted to spend upwards of $4.4 billion on blockchain in 2020, with worldwide investments expected to reach $19 billion by 2024 (Deloitte, 2017).

AI is a field of study in computer science that focuses on building intelligent machines that can carry out tasks that typically require human reasoning. AI has been hailed as one of the best technological developments to date, with applications in everything from business organizations to financial institutions. Blockchain is a decentralized, immutable ledger that keeps track of transactions and tracks digital assets across a network. A blockchain architecture makes it possible to trace and exchange almost anything of value, which lowers costs and risks all around.

In addition to developing new data-driven businesses for the future, the objective is to boost the profitability and efficiency of the current products. Numerous companies have already made significant investments in the massive amounts of data and the technologies needed to extract true value from them. We are generating more data than we can possibly process or even use for decision-making, which is the problem. AI programs can handle this issue by learning about and associating relevant items to the task. The data passing through a machine learning decision, which is essentially a centralized process, can be recorded by linking a distributed, decentralized, and immutable ledger. Then there is blockchain, which can help with the identification, understanding, and defense of those actions and outcomes (Deloitte, 2017).

The integration of AI and blockchain in the supply chain offers significant potential for businesses. The combination of these technologies enables a more efficient, transparent, and secure supply chain ecosystem. With AI's data processing capabilities and blockchain's transparency and traceability, businesses can optimize operations, reduce costs, mitigate risks, and enhance customer satisfaction. As the global market for AI and blockchain continues to grow, businesses are recognizing the value they bring. The future of the supply chain lies in leveraging the seamless integration of AI and blockchain to drive innovation and transform operations in a data-driven world.

There are many interesting AI and blockchain applications. For example, Netflix leverages artificial intelligence (AI) and big data to drive business performance and enhance the user experience. They employ AI to better understand their customers by analyzing viewer behavior, such as stopping a movie before it ends, and providing insights into individual preferences. Additionally, Netflix uses algorithms and machine learning to deliver personalized content recommendations based on user data, including viewing history and genre preferences. Furthermore, they utilize AI to auto-generate thumbnails, selecting the most enticing images to capture viewers' attention within the limited time they spend browsing for their next watch. By harnessing AI, Netflix optimizes user satisfaction, engagement, and business performance in the competitive streaming industry (Parker, 2021)

The manufacturing industry is also harnessing the power of AI to optimize operations and improve outcomes. One example is intelligent maintenance, where AI analyzes data to identify the root causes and drivers of machine downtime. General Motors utilizes image analysis from cameras mounted on assembly robots to detect signs of failing components, collaborating with suppliers to proactively prevent breakdowns. In a pilot test, the system identified 72 instances of component failure, averting unplanned outages that can cost up to $20,000 per minute of production-line downtime. Similarly, Audi has implemented an image recognition system based on deep learning in its press shop (Figure 1). Cameras capture images of pressed sheet metal, and AI analyzes these images to identify even the finest cracks, achieving high accuracy through training on millions of test images. These applications showcase how AI enhances maintenance and product quality inspection in the manufacturing sector, leading to increased efficiency and cost savings (Brosset et al., 2020).

Figure 1. AI-Optimized Quality Inspections: Audi Press Shop (Audi MediaCenter)

One interesting blockchain application is how Voatz is revolutionizing the voting process by leveraging blockchain technology to ensure secure voting and protect sensitive personal information. They offer a service for jurisdiction administrators, enabling citizens within a specific jurisdiction to vote conveniently using the Voatz mobile application. To create a Voatz account, voters provide their phone number or email and submit a picture of themselves, a photo ID, and a biometric identity such as a fingerprint or retinal scan. The system guarantees voter anonymity and privacy by storing personally identifiable information off-chain and employing a hash table to create an encrypted online identity. Importantly, voters retain control of their encryption key. Beyond public elections, Voatz's blockchain-based voting system can be applied to college elections, shareholder meetings, or any context that requires vote tallying. Voatz has already achieved successful deployments with leading universities, labor unions, state political parties, church groups, and non-profits. Currently, the company is actively implementing its technology for town meeting voting in Massachusetts (Marian, 2018).

Conclusions

For many supply chain managers, AI and blockchain technologies are still new concepts. But as the world becomes more digitalized, these cutting-edge technologies will become an integral part of how businesses operate.

AI and blockchain have proven to be formidable duos, enhancing nearly every industry in which they are used. AI and blockchain collaborate to enhance everything from food supply chain logistics to healthcare record sharing to media royalties and financial security (Zabolotnyy, n.d.).

The supply chain industry has been witnessing a technological uprising with the advent of AI and blockchain. These two game-changing technologies have combined forces to usher in a new era of supply chain management. But, there's more to come. The dawn of Supply Chain 5.0 will introduce a new level of intelligence that will enable a more autonomous, interconnected, and sustainable supply chain.

AI and blockchain will not just enhance the supply chain but revolutionize it. Imagine a supply chain that can self-optimize, self-configure, and self-heal. A supply chain that uses AI to predict potential disruptions and blockchain to create a secure and transparent system of record-keeping. The integration of these technologies will allow for a more efficient and sustainable supply chain, one that is capable of adapting to dynamic and ever-changing business environments.

As we move forward into the future, Supply Chain 5.0 will enable businesses to operate with greater agility, speed, and accuracy. By leveraging AI and blockchain in a comprehensive and strategic manner, companies will be able to streamline their supply chain operations, minimize waste, and improve the overall customer experience. Supply Chain 5.0 is not just the next step in supply chain evolution; it's a paradigm shift that will redefine the industry and pave the way for a more sustainable future.

References

Amazon Web Services. (2017). *Moderna Therapeutics Delivers mRNA Drugs Faster, at Lower Cost Using AWS.* https://aws.amazon.com/solutions/case-studies/moderna-therapeutics/?nc1=h_ls

Amazon Web Services. (2020). *SGX Uses Amazon Managed Blockchain to Build Innovate Payment Solution.* https://aws.amazon.com/solutions/case-studies/singapore-exchange-case-study/

Audi MediaCenter. (2018, October 15). *Audi optimizes quality inspections in the press shop with artificial intelligence.* https://www.audi-mediacenter.com/en/press-releases/audi-optimizes-quality-inspections-in-the-press-shop-with-artificial-intelligence-10847

Balakrishnan, T., Chui, M., Hall, B., & Henke, N. (2020, November 17). *The state of AI in 2020*. McKinsey & Company. https://www.mckinsey.com/capabilities/quantumblack/our-insights/global-survey-the-state-of-ai-in-2020

Brosset, P., Thieullent, A. L., Patsko, S., Buvat, J., Khemka, Y., Khadikar, A., & Jain, A. (n.d.). *Scaling AI in Manufacturing Operations: A Practitioners' Perspective*. Capgemini. https://www.capgemini.com/wp-content/uploads/2019/12/AI-in-manufacturing-operations-2-1.pdf

Chui, M., Hall, B., Singla, A., & Sukharevsky, A. (2021, December 8). *The state of AI in 2021*. McKinsey & Company. https://www.mckinsey.com/capabilities/quantumblack/our-insights/global-survey-the-state-of-ai-in-2021

Chui, M., Hall, B., Mayhew, H., Singla, A., & Sukharevsky, A. (2022, December 6). *The state of AI in 2022 — and a half decade in review*. McKinsey & Company. https://www.mckinsey.com/capabilities/quantumblack/our-insights/the-state-of-ai-in-2022-and-a-half-decade-in-review

Clifford, T. (2020, January 15). *How Moderna is using Amazon cloud to produce personalized cancer vaccines*. CNBC. https://www.cnbc.com/2020/01/15/how-moderna-uses-amazon-cloud-to-produce-a-new-class-of-medicines.html

De Cremer, D., & Kasparov, G. (2021, March 18). *AI Should Augment Human Intelligence, Not Replace It*. Harvard Business Review. https://hbr.org/2021/03/ai-should-augment-human-intelligence-not-replace-it.

Deloitte. (2017, September 20). *Using Blockchain to Drive Supply Chain Transparency and Innovation*. Deloitte, United States. https://www2.deloitte.com/us/en/pages/operations/articles/blockchain-supply-chain-innovation.html.

Hippold, S. (2022, April 20). *How Supply Chain Technology Will Evolve in the Future*. Gartner. https://www.gartner.com/smarterwithgartner/gartner-predicts-the-future-of-supply-chain-technology.

Morley, M. (2022, May 27). *How IoT, AI and Blockchain Will Enable Tomorrow's Autonomous Supply Chain*. OpenText Blogs. https://blogs.opentext.com/how-iot-ai-and-blockchain-will-enable-tomorrows-autonomous-supply-chain/.

Parker, S. (2021, March 14). *How Netflix Is Using Artificial Intelligence And Big Data To Drive Business Performance*. SmartData Collective.

https://www.smartdatacollective.com/how-netflix-is-using-artificial-intelligence-and-big-data-to-drive-business-performance/

Rupareliya, P. (2021, November 26). *How AI and Blockchain Transforming Supply Chain Management?* Intuz. https://www.intuz.com/blog/ai-and-blockchain-in-supply-chain-management.

Vendia, T. (2022, October 2). *Blockchain Could Repair Our Broken Global Supply Chain*. VentureBeat. venturebeat.com/datadecisionmakers/blockchain-could-repair-our-broken-global-supply-chain.

Zabolotnyy, O. (n.d.). *How AI and Blockchain are Changing Businesses*. First Bridge. https://firstbridge.io/blog/blockchain/how-ai-and-blockchain-are-changing-businesses.

Further Reading

Mearian, L. (2018, July 25). *Overstock.com puts a lot of stock in blockchain*. Computer World. https://www.computerworld.com/article/3271078/overstockcom-puts-a-lot-of-stock-in-blockchain.html

3.3

METAVERSE — AN EMERGING CONCEPT AND TECHNOLOGY IN SUPPLY CHAIN MANAGEMENT

Supply Chain 5.0 aims to improve the transparency and efficiency of global supply chain operations, which have long been affected by geographical and spatial limitations. Now, imagine a world where physical distance and geographical borders no longer hinder the smooth functioning of supply chains worldwide. A world where supply chain management is not limited by traditional communication and data sharing channels. This is the world of Metaverse, a concept that is gaining momentum in the business world and a technology that empowers Supply Chain 5.0.

The metaverse is a virtual universe where users can interact with each other and with the digital environment using avatars. It is a 3D environment that mimics the real world, and it has the potential to revolutionize the supply chain industry. The metaverse enables direct coordination with suppliers, reducing production costs and accelerating value chain synchronization. It makes the entire supply chain more responsive and transparent, and it allows for easier negotiations between suppliers and consumers.

But the metaverse is more than just a virtual trading platform. It has the potential to change the way we think about supply chain data. In the metaverse, data are updated in real time, enabling companies to make more precise decisions based on the current situation. The metaverse's ability to bridge the gap between supply chain planning and execution is invaluable for companies looking to optimize their operations and reduce waste.

The metaverse is still in its early stages of development, but it is estimated to generate $5 trillion in value by 2030. Many companies are already exploring the potential of the metaverse for supply chain management. Nike's metaverse, Nikeland, has already shown promising results in reducing the probability of customer returns by enabling customers to visualize shoes of all sizes and match their preferences.

As supply chain management becomes more complex with Supply Chain 5.0 onset, the metaverse offers a solution that can simplify operations and increase efficiency. It provides a new level of transparency and collaboration, and it has the potential to transform the industry as we know it. The metaverse is the next platform of choice for supply chain managers all over the world, and those who embrace this technology early on will have a significant advantage in the market.

Introduction

Metaverse is an emerging concept that has gained prominence over the past year. The concept is derived from science fiction and takes off from current virtual reality and augmented reality technologies. Essentially, a metaverse is a 3D environment that allows users to interact with each other and upload or download data. In 2022, the metaverse investment was $120 billion, as reported by McKinsey, and it is estimated to generate $5 trillion in value by 2030 (Mckinsey & Company, n.d.).

While the concept of a metaverse has attracted a great deal of attention, it is still in the early stages of development. Executives such as Mark Zuckerberg agree with this opinion. They believe that the application scope of the metaverse will be expanded in the next few years, especially in education, training, and customer support helplines. Also, Gartner suggests a cautious attitude about investing heavily in a specific metaverse since it is still nascent (*The Times of India*, 2022).

Essentially, a metaverse is a virtual, 3D environment that mimics our real universe. The term meta-reservoir refers to the creation of a digital copy of the real world. In this way, metaverses can act as alternative sources of energy, food, and water. Such copies can also be used to maintain and create backups of data. These copies can then be accessed from anywhere in the metaverse via an avatar.

All supply chain levels can work more successfully with the metaverse, both internally and externally. Advanced connectivity options enable a direct coordination approach with suppliers, reducing production costs and accelerating value chain synchronization. Thanks to this connectivity, the entire supply chain becomes responsive and transparent, and suppliers and consumers can negotiate costs easily and efficiently. Through extensive cooperation and more precise manufacturing techniques, the margin of production error can be reduced, leading to higher quality products and services. At the same time, it will also reduce customer return rates. Nikeland, the metaverse of Nike, can visualize shoes of all sizes so that customers can find their fit and match their preferences, resulting in a lower probability of return (Spajić *et al.*, 2022).

The role of supply chain data has also evolved. In the metaverse, the data will be updated promptly and adapted to the current situation. As a result, companies can make decisions more precisely, as they have access to the data revealing the "current moment" instead of only the "historical data" (Scaff, 2022). For example, with previously unimaginable computing power and the metaverse's ability to "bend the continuum of time and space," companies can bridge the gap between supply chain planning and execution. You can view your entire supply chain network — from suppliers to end customers — to continuously balance supply and demand in real time. This type of performance specifically requires leveraging the metaverse's ability to bring in increasingly detailed customer and supplier data.

Looking ahead to the future, metaverse, as an emerging concept and technology, is quickly gaining traction in the world of supply chain management. The concept is based on the idea that virtual worlds can be used to facilitate trading, communication, and planning across the entire supply chains. Blockchain, smart contracts, and other cutting-edge technologies have made metaverse the next platform of choice for supply chain managers all over the world.

What is the Metaverse?

The "metaverse," a creation of the internet in science fiction, is made possible by the use of virtual reality (VR) and augmented reality (AR) headsets. It is a virtual world that is accessible to everyone. A "metaverse" is a collection of 3D virtual worlds that emphasize social interaction. The words "meta" and "universe" are combined to form the term "metaverse." Because the term "Metaverse" was first used in 1992 by Neil Stephenson's book *Snow Crash*, that year is significant. Stephenson created a place where the characters could hide in order to escape a dark authoritarian reality in the metaverse world (Algoworks, 2022).

Due to the growing demand for immersion, the development of the metaverse is frequently linked to improvements in virtual reality technology. Web3, a theory for a decentralized internet, has influenced recent interest in metaverse development (Wikipedia, 2023).

According to the metaverse chronology, the intriguing Microsoft HoloLens headsets, which combine augmented reality and virtual reality, made their market debut in 2016. With the aid of this product, a holographic image can be created, brought to life, and used in augmented reality. We also discovered the amusing game Pokemon Go in that same year, which had people scurrying around their residences, campuses, and even workplaces to catch a Pokemon (Algoworks, 2022). The phrase is now used by businesses to describe a variety of improved online environments. These include emerging virtual workplaces like Microsoft's Mesh or Meta's Horizon Workrooms, virtual changing rooms and operating rooms, and online video games like Fortnite. As businesses vie for supremacy, the current iteration of the metaverse is taking the shape of a multiverse rather than a single shared virtual space: a number of unique metaverses with limited interoperability (Tucci, 2022).

This has been a breakthrough in terms of how people interact with each other and with technology. This technology is seen as a platform for user-generated virtual environments that promote collaboration and creativity in addition to allowing users to access content. For example, Meta's Horizon Workrooms allow employees to attend meetings in a virtual office space in the form of avatars instead of wasting time commuting, which makes remote collaboration feasible and effective. Besides, avatars can also enable people to feel comfortable interacting with their colleagues in cartoon versions (*Financial Times*, 2021).

The metaverse is made possible by a variety of technologies, including 3D rendering, AI, and immersive hardware. Many experts see the metaverse as a 3D version of the internet. In essence, it's an online environment that is similar to the real world and a place where everyone uses their avatars to interact with one another and communicate. The metaverse is envisioned as a 3D version of the internet that can be accessed through a single gateway, representing the logical next stage in development (Joshi, 2022).

The metaverse is a place of boundless possibilities, allowing for the creation of entire new worlds and societies, as well as connecting existing online communities together. The metaverse is a world of imagination and fantasy, allowing for the creation of virtual experiences that are as rich and varied as real life.

What is the Difference Between the Internet and the Metaverse?

Mark Zuckerberg indicated that the metaverse is the future of the internet (Wired, 2022). Thanks to the metaverse, some new building blocks are now possible, like the ability to support hundreds of users at once on a single instance of a server (idealistic metaverse predictions assume this number will rise to thousands or even millions, but this may be overly optimistic) or motion-tracking tools that can recognize a user's gaze or the position of their hands. In the metaverse, users can observe the tiny movements and facial expressions of avatars as if they were on the spot instead of staring at the screen. These contemporary innovations have a futuristic vibe and can be extremely thrilling (Wired, 2022).

Virtual reality and augmented reality are two technologies that are believed to be essential to the expansion and development of the metaverse. Precursors, or pre-metaverse solutions, are what we currently have, according to Tuong H. Nguyen, senior principal analyst at Gartner. It's still unclear, he said, "whether VR and AR experiences will end up being the main interfaces of the metaverse" (Tucci, 2022).

A single, shared, immersive, persistent, 3D virtual space where people can experience life in ways they cannot in the real world is what many in the computer industry refer to as the “metaverse”. Some of the technologies that allow access to this virtual world, like virtual reality headsets and augmented reality glasses, are developing quickly (Tucci, 2022).

While it’s still unclear whether virtual reality and augmented reality experiences will become the primary entryways into this metaverse, it is undeniable that these precursor solutions are currently paving the way.

How Does the Metaverse Apply to Supply Chain Management & Emerging Trends?

Consider a customer who is looking to purchase a new vehicle online. To view brands and models online through videos, pictures, or texts without having to visit multiple websites, use the metaverse, which can provide the same experience in a 3D immersive environment. Customers can visit digital stores, interact with staff members, and directly view the (digital) cars they are interested in before making a purchase in this world (Food, n.d.).

Businesses must come up with new ways to make the lives of their customers easier, anticipate and predict market changes and associated risks across the supply chain network, and manage customer expectations if they are to manage business performance and decisions based on a balanced view of growth, profitability, sustainability, diversity and inclusion (Scaff, 2022). Customers can visit virtual stores, explore three-dimensional car models, and get assistance from a chatbot with artificial intelligence that can respond to inquiries thanks to the metaverse.

The metaverse may enable brand-new Supply Chain experiences in the digital world that we have never had before. Most of the top supply chains are modernizing their businesses by going more digital in some areas. Will the transition to digital products and services reduce the significance of the supply chain as we know it now? Or will the metaverse open doors to new opportunities and possibilities?

The creation of a digital space and its translation into reality are the goals of the metaverse. Enhancing the physical supply chain digitally, not just digitally, is the aim of digital operations. The metaverse can improve several areas, including supply chain management. Access to more effective and dependable logistics operations, sophisticated analytics that can better gauge customer needs and expectations, and a platform to link buyers and sellers are all possible benefits.

Efficient collaboration across all tiers of the supply chain

All supply chain tiers can collaborate more effectively thanks to the metaverse, both internally and externally. A direct collaborative approach with suppliers is made possible by increased connectivity potential, which lowers manufacturing costs and speeds up value chain synchronization. The end-to-end chain will become visible and responsive thanks to this connectivity, which will also facilitate seamless and effective cost negotiations between suppliers and customers. The co-managed margins for production errors will produce better-quality goods and services and lower customer return rates with extensive collaboration and more in-depth production-optimized strategies. Companies can expand their capabilities, reducing the costs associated with quality control and the requirement to visit the locations of vendors for inspection and approval. Figure 1 depicts how the Metaverse helps realize the cost-effective collaboration within the healthcare supply chain.

Supply chain transparency

Even for international supply chain management experts, understanding global supply chains is complex and difficult. Now, stakeholders, employees, investors, and clients want to know more about the sources of raw materials, as well as who makes the components and where they are finished. They demand transparency regarding the environmental impact and other side effects of the supply chains they are working with. The metaverse will increase supply chain transparency by providing 3D representations of how businesses create, deliver, and market their goods. As a result, confidence and trust in the supply chain will increase, along with its efficiency, because of this transparency and visibility.

The origin of the raw materials, the manufacturing procedures and technologies, the subcontractors' locations, the impact of emissions on nearby areas, and the marketing strategies of the products can all be very helpful in meeting the demands and ensuring compliance with sustainability laws like the German or EU Supply Chain Act. This visibility and transparency will provide stakeholders with the information needed to make informed decisions regarding the ethicality of their supply chains.

The movement of goods along the entire supply chain can be seen in a virtual environment. To see how the supply chain responds and where it breaks down, problems can be introduced, such as weather events, component shortages, or transportation disruptions. In the event that problems arise, this virtual environment can be used to test potential fixes. These digital twins can assist in identifying and testing improvements at various stages (Scaff, 2022). For example, BMW launched a digital twin factory, which attempted to simulate the entire manufacturing process in real life (as shown in Figure 2) (BMW Group, 2021).

With emerging modern technology, stakeholders can create a digital twin of their supply chain, which allows them to simulate and optimize scenarios before they take place. By using this digital twin, stakeholders can monitor the performance of their supply

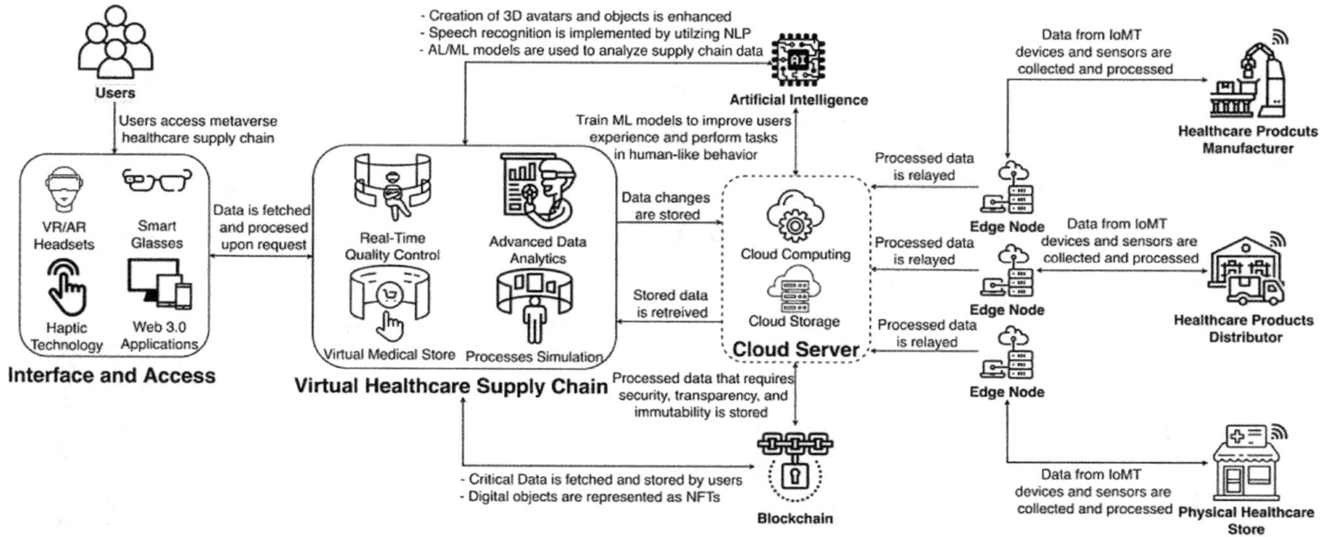

Figure 1. Metaverse in Healthcare Supply Chain (Musamih *et al.*, 2022).

Figure 2. BMW Uses Digital Twins to Reflect Activities in Real Time (BMW group, 2021).

chain in real time and create forecasts for how it will behave in different scenarios to be more consumer-centric and agile.

Customer demand

According to Gartner's prediction, by 2026, 25% of individuals will immerse themselves in the metaverse for at least one hour a day. Correspondingly, 30% of organizations around the globe will provide products and services related to the metaverse (Rimol, 2022). Today, the metaverse is already being utilized by well-known brands like Louis Vuitton, Burberry, Timberland, and Adidas for their exclusive digital products. Hong Kong's "AiR Metaverse" (AiR — Adventure in Reality), a virtual world with a Hong Kong theme, is an interesting use of the metaverse. For instance, in Hong Kong, we have already noticed the entry of shopping centers like Times Square and K11.

As seen from a business-to-business (B2B) perspective, during the past two years of the pandemic, numerous fairs and significant events have moved online, with the China Import and Export Fair (Canton Fair) serving as an example. The COVID-19 pandemic not only altered how businesses functioned in these trying times, but it also undoubtedly hastened the growth of the metaverse (Chow, 2022).

Manufacturing

Customers will have easy access to virtual tools and 3D visualization thanks to the metaverse, increasing accountability, and transparency. This will boost creativity and accelerate the potential for mass customization (i.e. personalized items). For example, the luxury brand Balenciaga and Fortnite co-hosted a Lookbook campaign, where metaverse users could model their own Balenciaga clothes. It was noteworthy that the winning digital assets could be produced in large quantities and purchased in physical stores. Similarly, street fashion pioneer Vans partners with Roblox in Vans World, where you can customize your well-fitting shoes with Vans's authentic shoe collections (Spajić *et al.*, 2022). Additionally, it will make digital product replication simpler, allowing factories and manufacturing processes to advance (Scaff, 2022).

Manufacturing operations will be significantly improved by providing operators with training on new equipment or by enhancing safety measures under current working conditions. Additionally, virtual tools and simulations can be used to test and improve the design of parts and production lines, reducing the number of physical prototypes needed. As conditions can be virtually simulated with the use of AI and operators can be trained in advance of those possible happenings, this will not only help manufacturing become more defect-free, but the digital twin will also help bring up the issues that impede the flow at the shopfloor to the team.

Shorter product lifecycles

In the metaverse, cooperation and sharing of ideas are ideal since companies can build a direct relationship with supply chain members instead of traditional physical products. It will be simple for internal and external stakeholders to collaborate on product designs, present these concepts to manufacturers in the same setting, and receive prompt feedback. As a result, the time it takes for new products to hit the market will be shortened, and the process of creating useful designs will proceed more quickly and shrewdly (Scaff, 2022).

This will create shorter product life cycles, and products will move from idea to market much more quickly. Additionally, there will be fewer iterations in the development of new products thanks to collaboration and idea sharing in the metaverse, which will give stakeholders the chance to have their opinions and input represented in those products.

Moreover, most enterprises have stopped designing products in material form in recent years. Suppose that an automobile manufacturer goes through the following steps to produce a car: carving out a wooden body as an initial mock-up, building a steel prototype, and finally shifting to mass production. By contrast, fashion enterprises design digital clothing and visualize it before releasing it to production, which also means a quicker time to market (McGee, 2022).

Warehouse operations

Every participant, from staff to logistics teams, will be able to take sustainability and Environmental, Social, and Governance (ESG) considerations into account through intelligent planning tools thanks to the metaverse's boundless opportunities for collaboration. Before the physical form is built, warehouse planning can be enhanced, experienced, and tested in the metaverse, saving time and money from concept to reality. This will result in better warehouse designs that are also more effective, as well as better working conditions. Metatechnologies enable local businesses and city administrations to replicate the final iteration of new concepts into their records for accountability and on-going learning (Scaff, 2022).

Strategic operator training will be possible in the metaverse without interfering with regular business operations. Before making a sizable CapEx investment, the flow of any warehouse can be examined, and any necessary modifications can be listed. Additional advantages include improved space utilization through active space modeling and increased location and shelving optimization as the number of stock keeping units (SKUs) rises. The importance of optimization and slotting, which have always been crucial, has grown as fulfillment centers become smaller and even "micro," where storage space is most valuable (Food, n.d.).

Metaverse supply chain: Virtual sourcing

Buyers can comprehend and interact with virtual models of new or updated products with virtual sourcing. This might comprise: By having products delivered to you by the metaverse, you can improve your digital sourcing and procurement procedures (Scaff, 2022). As virtual sourcing offers buyers the ability to view, understand, and interact with products online, it has become an increasingly important tool for optimizing and slotting within small and micro fulfillment centers.

Virtual sourcing also provides buyers with the ability to make real-time decisions regarding product availability and pricing, which can result in more accurate purchasing decisions and improved cost savings.

Metaverse sensing for quality, compliance, and sustainability

For supply chain compliance and customer satisfaction, quality is crucial. In a 3D environment, testing and performing quality control on large quantities of products could be made much simpler: the metaverse enables us to identify and address any supply chain QC, auditing, or compliance gaps (Scaff, 2022).

By using metaverse-enabled sensing technologies, manufacturers, retailers, and customers can ensure that products meet their quality standards while also helping to meet sustainability objectives.

Early Use Cases of Metaverse

Digital connections can be transformed by the metaverse, and this will have a big impact on e-consumer behavior as well as organizational structures, processes, and behaviors. Given that the human mind exhibits the same emotional experiences and reactions in virtual reality (VR)/augmented reality (AR) as it does in reality, it is not surprising to see renowned companies launch online shops for specific product lines. For instance, there is a lot of interest in retail clothing, which already attracts millions of daily users to the various metaverse platforms (Food, n.d.).

Companies are focusing their efforts on creating immersive experiences in which users can shop for and try on clothes without having to physically go to a store. By removing the physical barriers, companies are hoping to attract even more customers and encourage spending. To capitalize on this potential, many companies are leveraging the capabilities of VR and AR. For example, with the help of handheld AR, Ikea's "Place" allows customers to preview how furniture pieces would look in their rooms by merely aiming their cameras at the space they want to fill (Figure 3). Similarly,

Figure 3. Ikea's "Place" App Presents a Preview of Furniture Pieces by AR (Ikea, 2023).

cosmetic brands, such as L'Oréal and Sephora, are using AR to offer customers realistic previews of their appearance when they wear/try different cosmetic products (Chandukala *et al.*, 2022).

Opportunities and Challenges of Integrating Metaverse Into Supply Chains

Improved Visibility

The metaverse will increase supply chain visibility by providing 3D representations of how companies create, manufacture, distribute, and market their products. Interested parties will have a greater comprehension of material sourcing as well as product inputs. In addition, the metaverse can provide more accurate and real-time information on product lead time, logistic costs, delays, and delivery.

Greater Efficiency

The metaverse can also be used to design efficient and effective facilities. The first step is to create a virtual version of a manufacturing facility, a cargo ship, a warehouse, or a distribution center. In this simulated environment, all the processes and flows can be checked, including during peak loading periods or times of disruption. With a warehouse, the flow can be tested (Maersk, 2022). For example, NVIDIA cuOpt used NVIDIA Isaac Sim, powered by the NVIDIA Omniverse platform for simulating and collaborating within virtual worlds and 3D workflows, to create a scalable robotics simulation application showing dynamic re-optimization in a photorealistic environment. In an automated order-picking scenario, the Nvidia robot runs continuously and dynamically re-optimizes in real time; when a robot goes offline, it is re-optimized, and the video report responds in seconds (Fender, 2021) (Figure 4). The report shows, on a scale of 10–1000 locations, the average time savings per route. With the metaverse, we can capture the dynamic behavior of the natural world and optimize logistics.

In manufacturing, Siemens cooperates with NVIDIA, enabling an industrial metaverse with physics-based digital models from Siemens and real-time AI from NVIDIA. Companies of all sizes will be able to employ digital twins with real-time performance data; create innovative industrial IoT solutions; leverage actionable insights from analytics at the edge or in the cloud; and tackle the engineering challenges of tomorrow by making visually rich, immersive simulations more accessible (Siemens, 2022) (Figure 5). This increases the efficiency and accuracy of company decision-making.

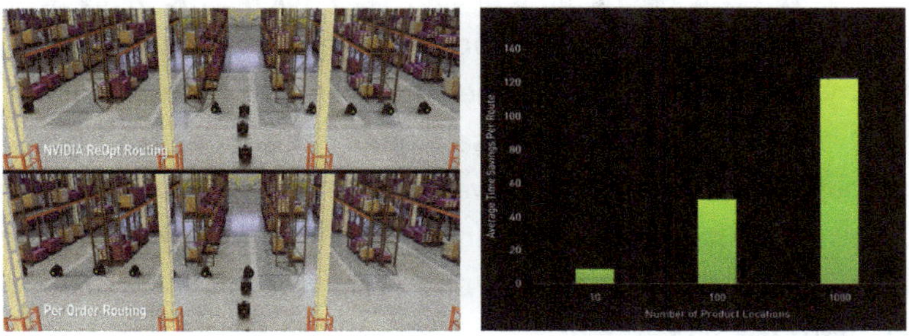

Figure 4. NVIDIA cuOpt Route Optimization (Fender, 2021).

Figure 5. A Full-Design-Fidelity, Photorealistic, Real-Time Digital Twin (Siemens, 2022).

Cost Reduction

A metaverse is designed to seamlessly integrate virtual content with physical reality into an immersive experience and often involves communicating with other people through VR/AR technology (Thompson, 2022). The metaverse significantly reduces expenses by visualizing processes, ensuring data accuracy, strengthening cooperation between all parties, reducing communication barriers, and optimizing or devising products in a virtual environment.

As Mercedes-Benz announced, it is taking the next step in digitizing its production process. By tapping into NVIDIA AI and metaverse technologies, the automaker can create feedback loops to reduce waste, decrease energy consumption, and continuously enhance quality. Developed with digital twins in the Omniverse, Mercedes-Benz planners can access the digital twin of the factory, reviewing and optimizing the plant as needed (Shapiro, 2023) (Figure 6).

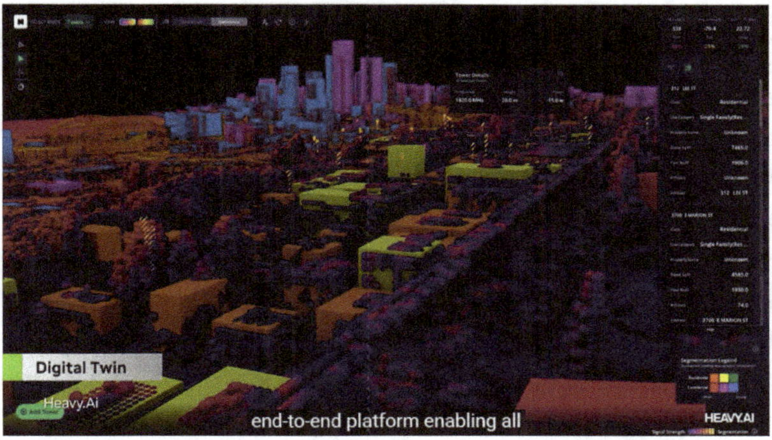

Figure 6. Mercedes-Benz Plant Digital Twin (Shapiro, 2023).

Security and Privacy Concerns

Privacy issues will become a significant concern in the metaverse. Metaverse publishers will control all aspects of their metaspaces, collect vast amounts of user data, and monetize the collected data. Even if there are open-source metaverse worlds that users can host, the publisher who hosts them can still collect and monetize user data (Security, n.d.). As outlined in several metaverse-related works on security and privacy, different types of threats against the metaverse and within it are presented, namely non-fungible token (NFT), Financial Fraud, AR/MR/VR/XR threats, dark verse, privacy issues, cyber-physical threats, social engineering threats, and traditional information and communication (IT) attacks (Rawat & El Alami, 2023), resulting in a substantial financial loss.

The technologies encompassing the metaverse will necessitate the collection of significantly more data than what is currently gathered through social media platforms. This includes, but is not limited to, aspects such as the orientation of an individual's head and the focus of their gaze, which are crucial for accurate display positioning. This is because the metaverse, as envisioned by many in the computer industry, is the next iteration of the internet; a singular, shared, and immersive realm where interactions are deeply rooted in virtual reality and augmented reality experiences.

The metaverse aims to provide a seamless blend of physical and digital realities, demanding not only the current form of data but also more intricate details to create hyper-personalized experiences. The data collected will enable the creation of detailed digital maps of users' movements, interests, and interactions. These maps will not only allow for better positioning of displays but also pave the way for more immersive experiences in the metaverse, built around the unique needs of the industry.

Lack of Industry Standardization

As can be seen in Table 1, the current guidelines for the metaverse are primarily concerned with ensuring that there is

Table 1. Summary of Metaverse Standards.

Standard	Description
ISO/IEC 23005	Standardizes interfaces for seamless information exchange between the physical and virtual worlds, as well as between virtual worlds.
IEEE 2888	Defines standardized interfaces, information formats, and APIs for synchronization and interaction between cyberspace and the physical world.
IEEE P1589	Proposes a standardized interchange format for AR learning experiences, integrating real-world interactions with web applications.
IEEE P2048	Establishes terminology, categories, and levels of the Metaverse to promote its sustainable development and market growth.
IEEE P7016	Provides an ethical assessment methodology and guidelines for developers to prioritize ethically aligned system design in Metaverse systems.

seamless connectivity between the natural world and the virtual world (Rawat & El Alami, 2023). The metaverse is a developing technology that has significant potential for further advancement. Even though there are fundamental conceptual standards, a considerable amount of work needs to be done in the areas of data security and privacy protection, as well as the requirements for implementing the metaverse in a variety of businesses.

Preparing for the Future: Utilizing the Metaverse in Supply Chains

The first step toward metaverse adoption is to build a cloud-native supply chain architecture (Moscardi, 2022) that enables organizations to respond quickly to changes in customer demand, launch new products and services, and offer customers an improved digital experience. This architecture will require adopting new digital technologies like blockchain, artificial intelligence, machine learning, and robotics.

Additionally, companies must invest in advanced analytics capabilities to understand customer behavior and create meaningful insights that can be used to optimize processes and drive better business decisions.

Finally, companies must also prioritize developing a comprehensive data governance policy to ensure the security and integrity of customer data. Therefore, companies must focus on cybersecurity and data privacy to ensure that customer information is securely stored and accessed promptly. Companies should also consider investing in digital-ready infrastructure such as cloud computing and 5G networks to support the implementation of these technologies.

Conclusions

Summary of the Metaverse in Supply Chain Management

We are still in the infant stages of the metaverse's development. In the coming years, several cutting-edge technologies will emerge and grow, encouraging the creation of novel ideas and techniques (but only if they enhance the experiences of users and customers). The obvious capabilities of the metaverse offer a wealth of benefits and applications. Technologies like the metaverse, which enable innovative planning strategies, accelerated virtual experiments, and accelerated time to market for new products, will have a significant impact on executive supply chain leadership decisions (Food, n.d.).

These technologies will also create opportunities to explore new collaborative models across the entire enterprise, connecting suppliers and partners in an ever-growing network of collaboration. Companies can take advantage of the new opportunities to promote products and services as industries shift from physical to digital spaces, like incorporating the metaverse into the marketing strategy and creating unlimited marketing potential (Jain, 2023). In short, the metaverse is a technology that has the potential to revolutionize our businesses and industries in ways we can only imagine. The possibilities of the metaverse are boundless, and its potential to transform our ways of working will no doubt create lasting change across the business landscape.

Future Outlook of the Metaverse in Supply Chain Management

With the support of metaverse technology, which will significantly reduce lead times for all current processes, there is enough evidence to suggest that supply chains of the future will be incredibly efficient and able to respond to customers more quickly.

By removing obstacles such as inefficient communication and physical limitations, the metaverse will open up a world of opportunities for businesses to move faster than ever before. Companies will be able to reduce costs, take advantage of shorter delivery times, and increase collaboration among team members who can virtually communicate without needing to be in the same room. With the development of the metaverse, supply chain management will become a well-oiled machine.

The following is a succinct summary of some metaverse characteristics and much of what we have already covered by Moscardi (2022).

Immersive environments

Most of our supply chains should be living in the cloud, synced with millions of IoT sensors, and largely operating without our intervention by the time the metaverse becomes the platform for conducting global business, so an immersive 3D environment will probably be more of a necessity than a novelty.

Digital twins

Significant advancements in warehouse design and process modeling will be made possible by digital twins (and metaversal immersion), as well as more routine business meetings (which could be held at a conference table on a beach; why just sit in a building in the digital world?). The use of digital twins will also make it possible to model the supply chain in an immersive environment, increasing operational efficiency.

Augmented information

One could argue that the development of the metaverse, its applications, and its eventual adoption depend just as much on the virtual overlaying of real-time rendered 3D information over our real world. It can be argued that this is where the majority of supply chains' meta-value will come from. Depending on where we look, sensors will provide immediate updates as a shipment approaches a waypoint or destination on what it is, where it is coming from, where it is going (if it is not at the final destination), when it is due, whether payment has been processed, and much more. Get an "X-ray" view of the truck (which will be autonomous, of course) to see what is inside, how many units are inside, how they are stacked, whether any units are damaged, etc. Even better, you can instantly see the contents' value and let the system prioritize more expensive or urgent items while always keeping you up to date so you can adjust as necessary.

A broader definition of supply chains

Today, we move goods from one location to another through a series of events until they transition from raw materials to finished products that are ready for consumption. However, that definition is likely to change from a linear model to a collaborative supply network in which supply chains play new and different roles as we move toward a world where many of our activities are virtual.

This new system of supply networks would be more interconnected and interdependent, leveraging a data-driven approach to identify inefficiencies and increase the rate of success. Such a shift would mean that traditional supply chains, which are focused on optimizing cost and throughput, would become less important. Thus, the focus on generating value for the customers takes precedence over dealing with internal inefficiencies and constraints.

The world will possibly have changed when the metaverse comes fully into being. A virtual reality that blurs the lines between reality and imagination, the metaverse has become the ultimate platform for communication, trading, and planning in the world of supply chain management.

It all started with a vision, a vision that was inspired by science fiction but has now become a reality. In the early days, the metaverse was a concept that seemed far-fetched and out of reach. But with the advancement of technology and the tireless efforts of innovators, the metaverse has become a reality.

The metaverse is a digital world that mimics our own, a world that has the power to transform the supply chain industry as we know it. With the ability to create a virtual, 3D environment that acts as an alternative source for energy, food, and water, the metaverse has the potential to revolutionize the way we approach supply chain management.

And it's not just about the products themselves. The metaverse has the power to change the way we communicate and interact with each other. Imagine being able to negotiate costs and coordinate with suppliers directly in a virtual environment, all while reducing production costs and accelerating value chain synchronization. Real-time Asset Twinning emerges as a potent tool, enabling the optimization of physical assets through live digital replicas. This metamorphosis extends further, with agile simulations within the metaverse uncloaking bottlenecks, driving unparalleled efficiency. The metaverse also becomes a realm for risk fortification, orchestrating strategic simulations to safeguard against natural disasters and cyber threats. Immersive customer care takes center stage as businesses revolutionize their interactions, offering prompt and immersive virtual support. The metaverse thrives as a platform for swift design and evaluation, where cost and time-to-market are slashed through VR-driven prototypes and stakeholder engagement within interactive virtual confines. Workforce empowerment embraces immersive learning, allowing tactile skill acquisition and enhanced safety awareness. The metaverse's impact is felt in the proactive realm of virtual commissioning, where preemptive measures eliminate real-world setbacks through virtual facility and equipment replicas. Lastly, this epoch redefines collaboration by creating a virtual nexus where stakeholders engage, communicate, and innovate through virtual conferences, exhibitions, and networking events. The Supply Chain 5.0 era presents boundless opportunities, with the metaverse woven intricately into the fabric of supply chain operations. The possibilities are endless.

But it's not just about the supply chain of today. The metaverse has the power to transform the supply chain of tomorrow. With the emergence of Supply Chain 5.0, the metaverse has become the next platform of choice for supply chain managers all over the world. By leveraging blockchain, smart contracts, and other cutting-edge technologies, companies can bridge the gap between supply chain planning and execution.

The metaverse is not just a concept, it's a game-changer. It's a world where the impossible becomes possible, where virtual reality meets real-world applications, and where the supply chain industry can achieve new heights of success. The metaverse is here, and it's time to embrace the future of supply chain management.

References

Algoworks. (2022, August 2). *Evolution of Metaverse from Beginning to Today.* https://www.algoworks.com/blog/evolution-of-metaverse/.

BMW Group. (2021, April 13). *BMW Group and NVIDIA take virtual factory planning to the next level.* https://www.press.bmwgroup.com/middle-east/article/detail/T0330141EN/bmw-group-and-nvidia-take-virtual-factory-planning-to-the-next-level?language=en

Chandukala, S. R., Reddy, S. K., & Tan, YC. (2022, March 29). *How Augmented Reality Can and Can't Help Your Brand.* Harvard Business Review. https://hbr.org/2022/03/how-augmented-reality-can-and-cant-help-your-brand.

Chow, N. (2022, May 19). *The Metaverse & the Supply Chain: Cracking the 3 Strategic Questions.* LinkedIn. https://www.linkedin.com/pulse/metaverse-supply-chain-cracking-3-strategic-questions-nelson/.

Fender, A. (2021, November 9). *NVIDIA Brings AI to the Supply Chain.* NVIDIA. https://blogs.nvidia.com/blog/2021/11/09/cuopt-ai-software-supply-chain/.

Financial Times. (2021, November 4). The Battle to Control the Metaverse: Microsoft vs Meta. https://www.ft.com/content/46d00829-04bc-4136-992e-856975bbccca.

Food, D. (n.d.). *The Impact of the Metaverse on the Supply Chain.* Board. Retrieved February 2023, from https://blog.board.com/metaverse-supply-chain/.

Ikea. (2023). *Say hej to IKEA Place.* https://www.ikea.com/au/en/customer-service/mobile-apps/say-hej-to-ikea-place-pub1f8af050

Jain, P. (2023, March 2). LinkedIn. https://www.linkedin.com/posts/prateekjain01_contentmarketing-customerrelations-metaverse-activity-7033281699438366720-GJZZ/?utm_source=share&utm_medium=member_desktop.

Joshi, S. (2022, March 15). *What Is the Metaverse? An Explanation for People Who Don't Get It.* Vice. https://www.vice.com/en/article/93bmyv/what-is-the-metaverse-internet-technology-vr.

Maersk. (2022, November 29). *3 Ways the Metaverse Will Transform Your Supply Chain.* https://www.maersk.com/insights/digitalisation/how-the-metaverse-will-transform-supply-chain-management.

McGee, P. (2022, May 26). Tim Sweeney: Epic Will Fight Apple and Google to Keep the Metaverse Open. *Financial Times.* https://www.ft.com/content/e13ce526-0e33-4ca2-9699-184d0138eada.

McKinsey & Company. (n.d.). *Value Creation in the Metaverse.* Retrieved February 2023, from https://www.mckinsey.com/capabilities/growth-marketing-and-sales/our-insights/value-creation-in-the-metaverse.

Metaverse. (2023, February 26). In *Wikipedia.* https://en.wikipedia.org/w/index.php?title=Metaverse&oldid=1141663339.

Moscardi, C. (2022, August 24). *Supply Chain in the Age of the Metaverse.* OpenText Blogs. https://blogs.opentext.com/supply-chain-in-the-age-of-the-metaverse/.

Musamih, A., Yaqoob, I., Salah, K., Jayaraman, R., Al-Hammadi, Y., Omar, M., & Ellahham, S. (2022). Metaverse in healthcare: Applications, challenges, and future directions. *IEEE Consumer Electronics Magazine.*

Rawat, D. B., & El Alami, H. (2023, February 2). *Metaverse: Requirements, Architecture, Standards, Status, Challenges, and Perspectives.* https://arxiv.org/pdf/2302.01125.pdf.

Rimol, M. (2022, February 7). *Gartner Predicts 25% of People Will Spend at Least One Hour Per Day in the Metaverse by 2026.* Gartner. https://www.gartner.com/en/newsroom/press-releases/2022-02-07-gartner-predicts-25-percent-of-people-will-spend-at-least-one-hour-per-day-in-the-metaverse-by-2026.

Scaff, R. (2022, May 31). *4 Ways the Metaverse Will Benefit Supply Chain Networks.* Accenture. https://www.accenture.com/us-en/blogs/business-functions-blog/metaverse-supply-chain-networks.

Security. (n.d.). *9 Security Threats in the Metaverse.* Retrieved February 2023, from https://www.securitymagazine.com/articles/98142-9-security-threats-in-the-metaverse.

Shapiro, D. (2023, January 3*). Manufactured in the Metaverse: Mercedes-Benz Assembles Next-Gen Factories with NVIDIA Omniverse.* NVIDIA. https://blogs.nvidia.com/blog/2023/01/03/mercedes-benz-next-gen-factories-omniverse/.

Siemens. (2022, June 29). *Siemens and NVIDIA to Enable Industrial Metaverse.* https://press.siemens.com/global/en/pressrelease/siemens-and-nvidia-partner-enable-industrial-metaverse.

Spajić, J., Mitrović, K., Lalić, D., Milić, B., & Bošković, D. (2022, September). *Personalized Brand Experience in Metaverse.* MCP-CE 2022 (pp. 21–23).

The Times of India. (2022, April 22). We Are in Early Stages of Metaverse. https://timesofindia.indiatimes.com/business/india-business/we-are-in-early-stages-of-metaverse/articleshow/90989018.cms.

Thompson, Z. (2022, June 30). *How the Metaverse Will Change the Future of the Supply Chain.* ITBrief. https://itbrief.com.au/story/how-the-metaverse-will-change-the-future-of-the-supply-chain.

Tucci, L. (2022, November 18). *What Is the Metaverse? An Explanation and In-depth Guide.* TechTarget. https://www.techtarget.com/whatis/feature/The-metaverse-explained-Everything-you-need-to-know.

Wired. (2022, April 25). *What Is the Metaverse, Exactly?* https://www.wired.com/story/what-is-the-metaverse/.

3.4

INNOVATING THE HEALTH SYSTEM

A LOOK INTO THE FUTURE OF HEALTHCARE SUPPLY CHAINS

The health industry is a multi-billion dollar industry, encompassing hospitals, doctors' clinics, and pharmacies. The range of health services provided by experts in the health industry is extensive. From diagnosing and treating health problems to procuring medical supplies and healthcare equipment, health experts have a lot on their plates. Health supply chains are integral to this industry; they help the health sector innovate and stay ahead of technological advancements.

Health supply chains are the pathways by which products and services move from suppliers to consumers in the health sector. They include all the processes involved, from procuring medical supplies and equipment to transporting and delivering them to patients. In the era of Supply Chain 5.0, healthcare supply chains will undergo transformation, becoming more patient-centric, secure, and efficient in all aspects of their processes.

The primary objective of developing a supply chain is to ensure the timely delivery of essential medical supplies to critical facilities such as hospitals, clinics, and pharmacies. However, it is essential to recognize that healthcare supply chain or supply chain management (SCM) encompasses more than just the procurement and distribution of medications, safety equipment, and other medical necessities. In comparison to traditional supply chains, Supply Chain 5.0 takes it a step further by emphasizing the seamless integration of people and technology.

Within the healthcare sector, the medical supply chain prioritizes technological innovation, collaboration, and knowledge sharing to enhance efficiency, adaptability, and sustainability in the delivery of medical supplies. This approach is aimed at better serving the needs of end patients. Therefore, this supply chain goes beyond the standard requirements and strives to deliver the best possible resources to the ultimate beneficiaries—the patients (Procurement Partners, n.d.).

Digital technology has helped revolutionize the health system in many ways, from patient care to SCM. For instance, it has helped hospitals streamline their supply chains and enhance patient outcomes. In addition, it has enabled healthcare providers to better connect with their patients and implement healthcare programs for specific populations. For example, programs for pregnant women and children under 18 often rely on digital health records, which monitor patient conditions and customize treatment plans for each individual. Automation in the supply chain has also drastically improved the way medical processes are carried out.

Streamlining processes through automation has allowed healthcare providers to track patient outcomes better and improve efficiency. Automated systems enable healthcare providers to monitor vital signs, medications, treatments, and more, all in real time. This allows for quicker and more accurate diagnoses, resulting in better outcomes and improved patient safety. Additionally, using digital technology to automate SCM has allowed healthcare providers to operate more efficiently.

Automated systems can track supplies, orders, inventory levels, and expiration dates, allowing providers to save time and money while improving patient care.

As technology continues to advance, healthcare providers will be able to leverage digital technology to streamline processes further and improve patient care. Artificial intelligence (AI) and machine learning (ML) are also being used to diagnose and treat patients and for research purposes. In addition, the using of robotics and automation for surgical procedures has further improved patient outcomes, enabling them to perform complex tasks with greater accuracy and precision. Automation and AI allow healthcare providers to focus more on patient care and better monitor and manage medications, diagnoses, treatments, and other aspects of patient care.

Overview of the Healthcare Supply Chain

In the healthcare industry, there is a dire need for more efficient SCM. COVID-19 exposed severe flaws in global healthcare supply chains as hospitals were forced to deal with shortages of personal protective equipment (PPE), ventilators, and essential medications. According to Premier's analysis (see Table 1), conducted in March 2021, not only was there a surge in demand for PPE during COVID-19, but raw materials scarcity and port blockages also increased the extent of shortage (Premier, 2021). Automation and AI can play an essential role in improving the healthcare supply chain, allowing providers to better forecast patient needs, identify potential shortages before they occur, track shipments of medications and supplies in real time, and quickly adjust purchasing strategies when needed.

The healthcare supply chain always starts with the manufacturer, who will utilize raw materials to develop and produce products. The manufacturer will deliver the products directly to the institution or use an intermediary. Distributors or group

Table 1. Supply and Percent Change of PPE Among US Health Systems in 2020 and as of March 2021 (Premier, 2021).

Supply	**Inventory days on hand during COVID-19 spikes in 2020**	**Inventory days on hand (March 1, 2021)**	**Percent change in purchase order spending, March 2020 vs. March 2019**	**Percent change in purchase order spending, March 2021 vs. March 2020**
N95s and KN95s	23 days	200 days	+14,302	+715
Surgical masks	30 days	45 days	+1,310	+93
Isolation gowns	20 days	40 days	+428	+96
Exam gloves	15 days	30 days	+51	+225

buying companies can act as mediators in this situation. An organization that works to establish contracts between vendors and stakeholders to lower the overall cost of purchasing goods is known as a group purchasing organization. They only buy products and services used in the healthcare sector. Finally, the stakeholders are given access to the goods and services. The Food and Drug Administration and the insurance companies, like Medicare, keep an eye on the supply chain to ensure that the products being used are safe (Procurement Partners, n.d.). The whole healthcare supply chain is shown in Figure 1.

Hospitals, healthcare providers, pharmaceutical firms, and other healthcare stakeholders can increase the agility and resilience of the healthcare value chain by enhancing the healthcare SCM. This will not only help to eliminate supply chain inefficiencies and unnecessary supply chain expenses, but upstream and downstream partners will be better able to react to unforeseen events like natural disasters or a worldwide pandemic and collaborate more successfully to improve patient outcomes and save lives (Tracelink, n.d.).

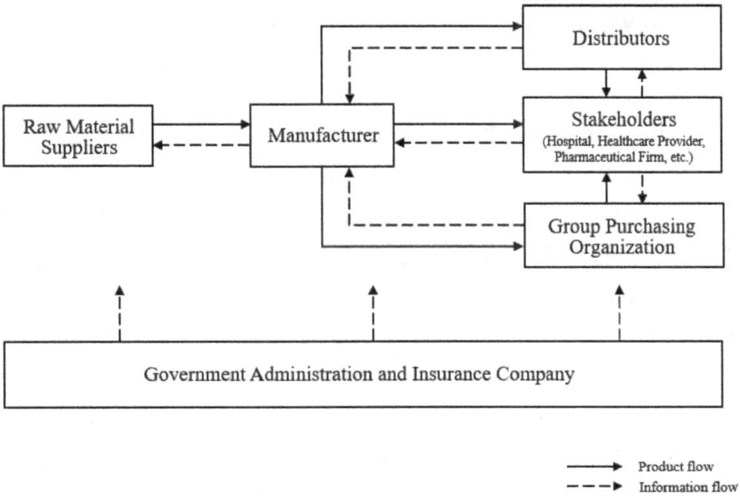

Figure 1. Healthcare Supply Chain.

Transporting medical supplies and approved medications from producers to healthcare facilities is part of the healthcare SCM. The goal of healthcare SCM is to purchase medical supplies and services from wholesalers and provide them to patients while being financially and logistically efficient.

Getting healthcare SCM right means that partners can better detect and resolve bottlenecks, potential disruptions, and other issues arising anywhere in the end-to-end supply chain. It can help improve patient care and safety while at the same time reining in waste and unnecessary spending. The main activities involved in healthcare SCM include monitoring and supporting the flow of medicines, medical supplies, and equipment. They include supply chain quality management and planning, supply chain automation and optimization, supplier relationships, and risk management. Using digital tools and technology to carry out this work can enable firms to continuously adjust and optimize supply chain systems (Tracelink, n.d.).

Latest Developments in Healthcare Supply Chain Technology

Digitizing the supply chain gives healthcare organizations better insight into their supply chains, enables real-time data sharing and seamless communication between supply partners, fosters collaboration, and streamlines the process of integrating supply chain and clinical data, improving the accuracy of demand forecasting and inventory control, and resulting in better patient outcomes (Tracelink, n.d.).

Healthcare supply chains can become more effective and efficient by leveraging digital tools. Additionally, digitizing supply chains enables healthcare organizations to access and analyze data to quickly identify opportunities for process optimization, cost reduction, and waste reduction.

Furthermore, digital technologies such as blockchain and AI have enabled healthcare supply chains to be automated, allowing for faster and more efficient operations. Automating healthcare supply chains also reduces the manual effort required to manage inventory and track shipments, allowing organizations to focus on other critical operations supporting better patient care.

Massive investments are being made in the healthcare supply chain to incorporate AI, wearable AI, robotics, and blockchain to improve patient care. With these investments, healthcare supply chains become more efficient and better able to meet patient needs promptly. This is especially beneficial for patients who need immediate and urgent care and for those with chronic conditions. These investments in the healthcare supply chain reduce manual labor, enhance efficiency, and improve patient outcomes by reducing wait times for vital care services.

Innovations in the Healthcare Supply Chain

Let us begin by examining the challenges in healthcare supply chains (see Figure 2) before we delve into the technologies and solutions for supply chains (Tecsys, n.d.).

ERP and EHR limitations. The enterprise resource planning (ERP) system provides visibility into medical and surgical supplies but misses costly and critical items crucial to managing. The electronic health record (EHR) system documents products used in patient care but only when clinicians enter items into the system. No automated mechanism records the depleted inventory and triggers processes to procure more. In addition, EHR databases can be at high risk of cyber-attacks. One of the most popular methods of accessing health information in 2018 was phishing scams. Hackers often steal confidential information to pay for medical expenses or make illegal purchases (Covetus, 2020).

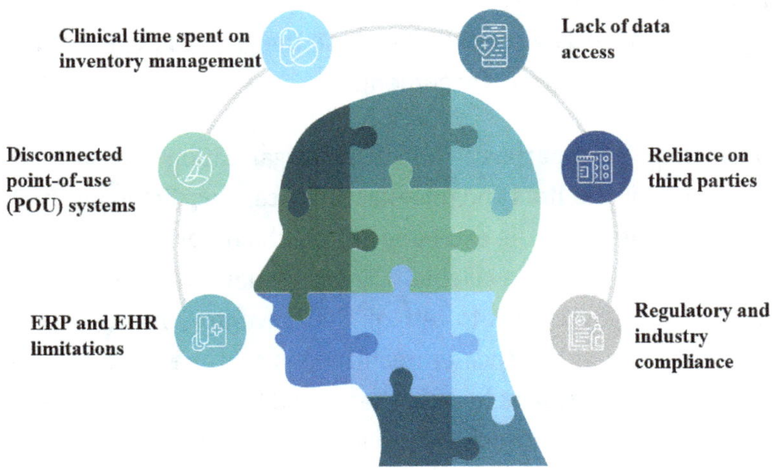

Figure 2. Challenges in the Healthcare Supply Chain.

Disconnected point-of-use (POU) systems: Multiple point-of-use (POU) systems enable supply replenishment for general medical and surgical supplies. The disjointed nature of POUs also presents challenges with recall tracking and adverse event reporting. This can lead to overordering or stockouts, with products expiring on shelves before they can be used.

Clinical time spent on inventory management: Clinicians are left with the burden of managing consignment items not contained within ERP systems. This is usually done manually, with nurses peeling stickers off product packaging during a case. By consolidating your processes and data into a single platform, one-off POU solutions can be eliminated.

Lack of data access: Researchers cannot always access data on hospital outcomes. For example, privacy restrictions imposed by federal law regulate the release of medical information (Norwich University Online, 2020). In an ideal world, the supply chain would have a clear and complete picture of what supplies are used and where they are stored. The supply chain cannot see the big picture regarding supplies, let alone the granular level details required for effective management.

Reliance on third parties: A healthcare organization's reliance on third-party distributors and manufacturers can backfire in times of crisis. Disruptions in the extended supply chain pose the risk that supplies will not be available. COVID-19 has prompted many healthcare organizations to rethink their inventory management practices. 55% of healthcare organizations said they had experienced a third-party data breach, the second highest percentage of all industry sectors. Those third parties have access to sensitive data that is of high value to cyber criminals (HIPAA Journal, 2022).

Regulatory and industry compliance: The ERP system contains only general medical and surgical supplies and, in most cases, lacks item-level details. Because of this, it cannot support the level of traceability required to meet regulations, or perform lot tracking, recalls, or expiration date management.

Use of Blockchain Technology

Research has highlighted the supply chain structure in healthcare based on blockchain, as shown in Figure 3 (Jadhav & Deshmukh, 2022). Blockchain brings noticeable benefits such as serialization, tracing, securing IoT devices, smart contracts, avoiding counterfeiting, and tamper-proof information-sharing systems. Figure 4 showcases various scenarios for blockchain applications in the

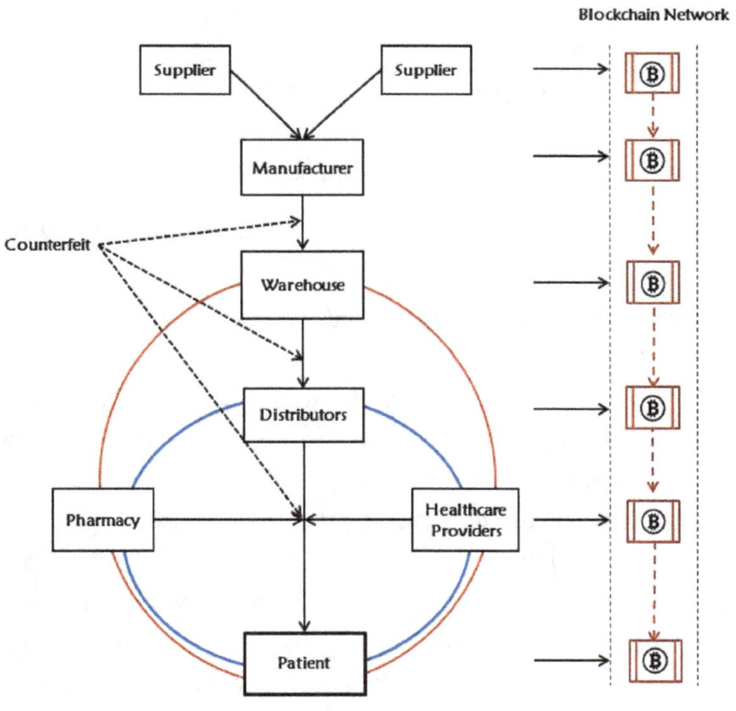

Figure 3. Blockchain-Based Healthcare Supply Chain (Jadhav & Deshmukh, 2022).

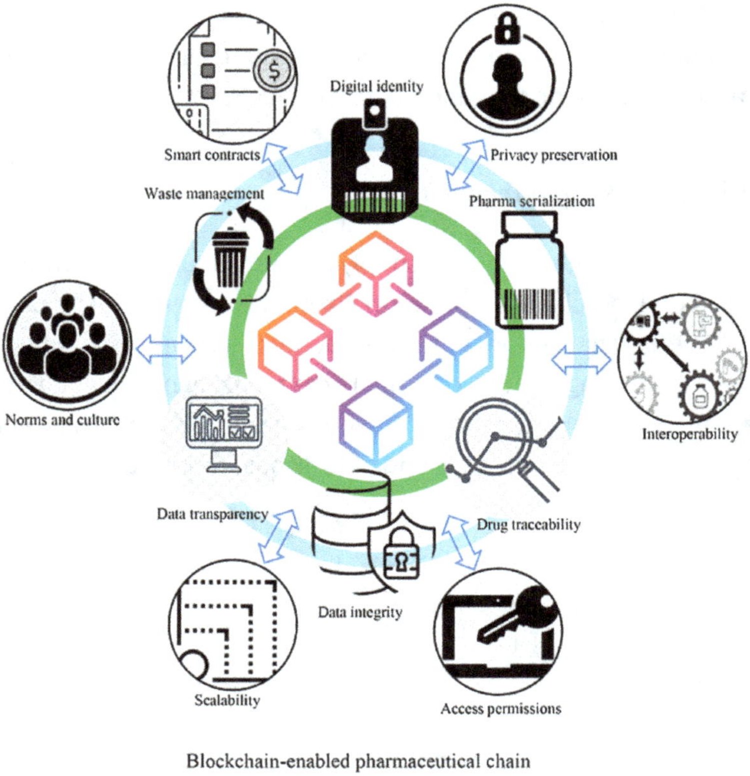

Figure 4. Blockchain-Enabled Pharmaceutical Chain (Bamakan et *al.*, 2021).

healthcare supply chain. These are described in detail in this subsection (Bamakan *et al.*, 2021).

Cryptocurrencies based on blockchain are now well known for their capacity to develop secure and traceable solutions. Healthcare applications are among the new applications and opportunities that are governed by the growing use of cryptocurrencies. In 2021, there were over 23 different healthcare coins (health-based cryptocurrencies) being traded worldwide. Stem Cell Coin, one of the five leading healthcare cryptocurrency ideas, was created to address the need for easier access to qualitative healthcare on a global scale. It aims to develop and promote ways to pay for stem cell treatment in affiliated hospitals and pathological/diagnostic imaging systems (Merchant, 2021). In the health industry, blockchain-based solutions are useful for secure data retrieval and storage, leading to more effective product creation and tracking. Such a system can guarantee the immutability of multi-direction transactions, promote genuine healthcare sector demands, and provide data provenance (Jadhav & Deshmukh, 2022).

Contract adherence is rising as a result of smart contracts. Organizations can hold one another responsible with the help of smart contracts, which ultimately builds trust between them. With these types of transactions, the deal's requirements can be entered into the blockchain and automatically checked against it. This guarantees that each party upholds its end of the bargain. These agreements automatically process orders, lowering the possibility that a crucial component will be overlooked. As a result of the smart contract's inherent level of trust that the other party will uphold their end of the bargain, healthcare organizations may be more willing to purchase supplies from a broader range of vendors. New suppliers might find it simpler to enter the market as a result, which could lead to the introduction of better goods or lower prices (Devine, n.d.).

Blockchain technology can make the process of giving blood safer. Blood can be tracked in a decentralized manner using the blockchain. The amount of discarded donations could be reduced by better tracking and allocating donations to ensure they are used as soon as possible. Additionally, an anonymous link can be made between the donor's personal information and their blood. This indicates that it will be simple to confirm the blood's provenance and safety for use. Donors can also get alerts when their blood is used because the blood will be tracked. The Swedish blood service is working on developing ways to express the importance of blood donors. Donors initially receive a "thank you" text message when they give blood and another when their blood is used (Stone, 2015). As a result, Sweden's blood donation rate has increased, which will ultimately improve patient safety by preventing blood shortages (Devine, n.d.).

One area of the pharmaceutical industry that stands to gain from the distinctive qualities and fundamental tenants of blockchain technology is the drug supply chain. Since these drugs are being distributed to people on the global black market without being detected, counterfeit medications are becoming a bigger problem. The increased risk to human life posed by using fake medications cannot be understated. The World Health Organization estimates that counterfeit drugs cost the pharmaceutical industry over $30 billion annually, making it clear that this is a serious problem (Gerwill, 2019).

The pharmaceutical industry has a complicated supply chain because drugs must travel from manufacturing to distributors, repackers, and wholesalers before they can be sold to consumers. This supply chain has little to no visibility to monitor authenticity. Businesses are already utilizing blockchain technology to improve the global supply chain's integrity, traceability, and transparency. The use of blockchain in this situation can have a number of advantages. When drugs are barcoded or radio-frequency identification (RFID)-tagged, their records can be stored on a blockchain in unchangeable and secure digital blocks after being scanned. These records will be updated in real time as the drugs are transferred from one entity to another in the supply chain. Parties with authorized access, including patients, can check the records at any time (Gerwill, 2019).

Another significant area that can be supported and verified by blockchain technology in conjunction with temperature-tracking devices is cold chain management. This leads to a follow-up comment about device management using blockchain technology, another crucial topic for healthcare, which would be covered in a different chapter about medical management as well as wearables and other injectables that are thriving in the health tech space and that need to be secured as well (Gerwill, 2019).

Application of Artificial Intelligence

AI is able to analyze large amounts of data stored by healthcare organizations in the form of images, clinical research trials, and medical claims, and it can identify patterns and insights often undetectable by manual human skill sets.

The investigation of the relationships between clinical practices and patient outcomes is the main objective of health-related AI applications. AI applications include drug development, personalized medicine, patient monitoring, and the development of treatment protocols. The capacity of AI technology to collect data, process it, and provide the end user with a clearly defined output sets it apart from conventional healthcare technology. AI uses deep learning and machine learning algorithms to accomplish this. These processes are capable of identifying behavioral patterns and developing original logic. ML models require large amounts of input data to be trained in order to produce useful insights and predictions (Wikipedia, 2018).

Top uses of AI in healthcare (see Figure 5) (Kwo, 2021):

1. **AI supports medical imaging analysis**: AI is used as a tool for case triage. It supports a clinician in reviewing images and scans. This enables radiologists or cardiologists to identify essential insights for prioritizing critical cases, avoid potential errors in reading EHRs, and establish more precise diagnoses.

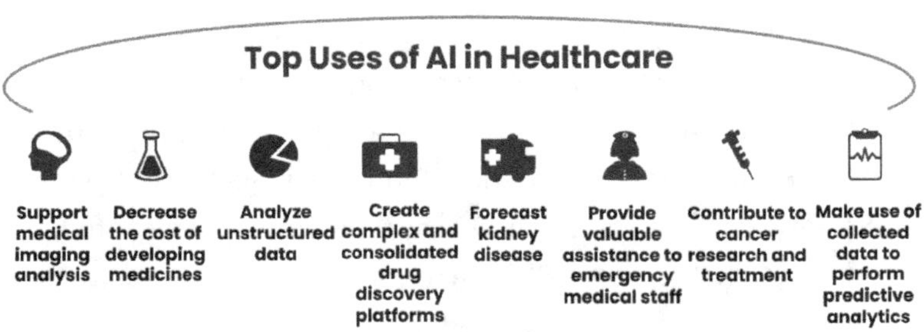

Figure 5. Top Uses of AI in Healthcare.

Hardin Memorial Health partnered with IBM to implement "The Patient Synopsis." This product identifies patient information relevant to the imaging procedure conducted on that patient. The product can be integrated with any medical unit system and accessed from any communication workstation or device in the network.

2. **AI can decrease the cost of developing medicines**: Supercomputers have been used to predict, from databases of molecular structures, which potential medicines would and would not be effective for various diseases. By using convolutional neural networks, a technology similar to the one that makes cars drive themselves, AtomNet was able to identify a safe and effective drug candidate. Atomwise collaborated with IBM and the University of Toronto in 2015, during the West African Ebola virus outbreak, to screen the best substances that could bind to a glycoprotein that blocked Ebola virus entry into cells in an in vivo (in the living body of an animal or plant) test. The compound that was chosen from the ones that were tested was chosen because it had similar effects on other viruses by way of cell penetration. The creation of an Ebola virus treatment was made possible by this AI analysis, which was completed in less than a day instead of the usual months or years.
3. **AI analyzes unstructured data**: Clinicians often struggle to stay updated with the latest medical advances while providing quality patient-centered care. EHRs and biomedical data curated by medical units and medical professionals can be quickly scanned by ML technologies. AI can seek, collect, store, and standardize medical data regardless of the format. The Healthcare Information and Management Systems Society conference HIMSS22 has previously presented its findings that around 80% of data collected by healthcare organizations is unstructured or conversational, including radiological images, doctors' notes, and even social media posts. But one of the most interesting applications of ML and

AI is to take data from unstructured to structured, capturing data generated at an exponential rate with a complete framework (Jercich, 2022).

4. **AI creates complex and consolidated drug discovery platforms**: The company behind the drug discovery platform can generate around 80 terabytes of biological data per week, which is processed by AI tools across 1.5 million experiments. The ML tools are created to draw insights from data sets that are too complex for human interpretation, which decreases the risk of human bias.
5. **AI can forecast kidney disease**: Acute kidney injury (AKI) can be difficult to detect by clinicians but can cause patients to deteriorate very quickly. Early diagnosis and treatment of AKI can have a huge impact on reducing the need for lifelong treatment and the cost of kidney dialysis. VA and DeepMind Health collaborated to develop an ML tool that can predict AKI up to 48 hours ahead of time.
6. **AI provides valuable assistance to emergency medical staff**: Corti is an AI tool that alerts emergency staff if it detects a heart attack. Corti can analyze both verbal and nonverbal clues in order to establish a diagnosis from a distance. In Copenhagen, emergency dispatchers are able to identify a cardiac arrest based on the description provided by the caller around 73% of the time.
7. **AI contributes to cancer research and treatment**, especially in radiation therapy. In some cases, radiation therapy can lack a digital database to collect and organize EHRs, which makes the research and treatment of cancer difficult. Oncora Medical has developed a platform that collects relevant medical data from patients, evaluates the quality of care provided, optimizes treatments, and provides thorough oncology outcomes, data, and imaging. The automatic generation of clinical notes integrated with EHRs led to a reduction in time spent by clinicians managing patient documentation, which improved medical operations and health outcomes.

8. **AI makes use of collected data to perform predictive analytics**. CloudMedX is a company that focuses on decoding unstructured data — data stored as notes. In essence, chronic diseases can be predicted, and their progression rates tracked. Natural language processing (NLP) and ML can read the entire medical history of a patient in real time and connect it with symptoms, chronic affections, or an illness that affects other family members.

An increasing number of organizations are adopting new technologies to support and transform SCM in the healthcare sector. COVID-19 has spurred digital transformation initiatives in the pharmaceutical industry and far beyond. Technology like the digital supply network makes it easier for firms to link up their supply chain systems with EHRs. By connecting supply chain data with EHRs, firms can standardize, streamline, and automate time-consuming business processes. This can reduce costs while also improving patient outcomes. Another technology useful for healthcare supply chain management is multi-enterprise work management software. These applications enable patient-centric orchestration across the end-to-end healthcare value chain. Suppliers and trading partners can share information and actionable insights through standardized, secure, and permissions interfaces. These interfaces help teams work together to further increase visibility into supply chain processes and enhance supply chain resilience. They help supply partners build trusting and mutually beneficial business relationships (Tracelink, n.d.).

Given the intricate web of supply chains that exists today, manufacturers must be able to easily obtain complete visibility of the entire supply chain. A single virtualized data layer provided by a cognitive AI-driven automated platform can be used to identify opportunities for improvement, remove bottleneck operations, and reveal cause-and-effect relationships. Instead of using redundant historical data, all of this is done using real-time data (Jacobs, 2023).

AI and ML principles produce extremely accurate forecasts of future demand when used for demand forecasting. For instance, it is simple to predict with accuracy both the growth of a new product's market entry and the decline and end-of-life of a product on a sales channel (Jacobs, 2023).

In today's connected digital world, maximizing productivity by reducing uncertainties is the top priority across industries. This underscores the need for the industry to leverage the prowess of AI in supply chains. When faced with a pandemic like COVID-19, establishing a good understanding of the impact on supply chains can help manufacturing companies deal with uncertainties in the right way (Jacobs, 2023).

Use of Technology in the Healthcare Supply Chain

Leveraging Data to Improve Healthcare Supply Chains

The volume of big data is projected to increase faster in healthcare over the next few years than in any other field. The expansion of data is accelerating and generating more data of various types (see Figure 6). To reveal meaningful information from high-volume, high-velocity, and high-variety data requires advanced tools — analytics and algorithms. It also requires investing in digital talent and modernizing legacy systems to offer real-time solutions and address security issues (AHA, 2021).

By leveraging the latest healthcare supply chain technology, healthcare organizations are digitally transforming their SCM. They are using this technology to obtain real-time, granular visibility into their supply chains from end to end.

They can use healthcare supply chain analytics to forecast demand more accurately, optimize inventory planning and management, and respond more successfully to shifting market conditions by linking supply chain and clinical data. Digital supply chain management tools can also help increase productivity and

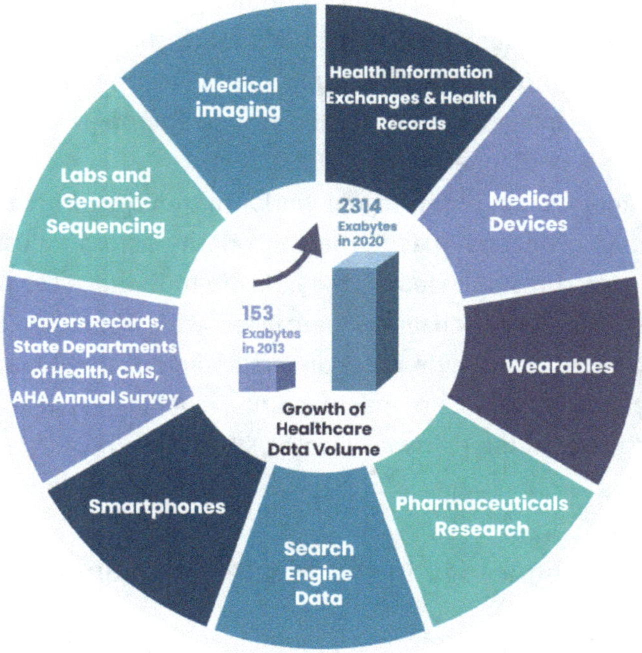

Figure 6. Where are All the Health Data Coming from.

shorten time to market by encouraging improved communication and collaboration throughout the healthcare supply chain. Additionally, by boosting supply chain resilience through increased trust and transparency throughout the supply network, they contribute to the development of a healthcare value chain that is better equipped to face and overcome the difficulties presented by upcoming pandemics and other public health emergencies (Tracelink, n.d.).

Data guarantees that businesses will base their decisions on the truth. Without data, it is impossible to identify the locations, reasons, or activities where processes, transactions, or plans are stuck and how to make them come unstuck (Goosen, 2022). Data-driven SCM tools provide reliable, real-time insights into the health of the supply chain. By unlocking such insights, companies can identify inefficiencies and prioritize investments to improve the overall health of their operations.

Leaders in the healthcare industry are not unfamiliar with the idea of leveraging big data. It can increase organizational efficiencies with the aim of conserving priceless resources in a sector where costs are rising. However, big data's enormous potential to enhance patient experiences and outcomes provides greater value (Edelmann, 2021). With the right analytic tools and algorithms, big data can provide invaluable insights about patient behaviors and preferences, allowing for more tailored treatments. This understanding can empower providers to be proactive in providing personalized care that is truly tailored to the needs of each individual patient.

How Digital Technology can Streamline Operations

AI algorithms, demonstrated in their abilities to filter, organize, and search for patterns in vast datasets and predictive analytics, have transformed aspects of patient care and brought about efficiencies for clinicians, researchers, and students. Additionally, it has enormous potential for using medical imaging analysis and providing patients with individualized care (Edelmann, 2021). Digital technology, such as AI algorithms and predictive analytics, can revolutionize patient care and help providers create efficiencies within the medical field.

The more data handled and collected by professionals, the more effective the solutions we seek when it comes to handling this digital information with care and safety. Axbridge Surgery in Somerset, UK, uses AI to produce a complexity score that is based on underlying health conditions (Edelmann, 2021). This score not only helps clinicians determine the best course of action for individual patients but also gives them an overview of the patient's overall health and identifies which patients are most at risk. Additionally, by using AI algorithms and predictive analytics to assess health data, healthcare providers can identify and treat diseases at an early stage, enabling better outcomes for patients.

A common technological platform, frequently an integrated ERP system, links and shares data from key business functions like finance, purchasing, supply chain, marketing, and others as part of the enterprise-wide initiative known as digitizing the core. By combining the conventional, linear supply chain with a connected, intelligent, quick, and responsive digital supply network, digitizing the core can assist healthcare providers in resolving supply chain issues (Deloitte, n.d.).

Many supply chains are transforming from linear, sequential operations to an interconnected, open system of supply operations. This could lay the foundation for how organizations compete in the future. Digital supply chain networks (DSNs) integrate information from many different sources and locations to drive the physical acts of production and distribution. DSNs enable integrated views of the network and rapid, use-case-appropriate latency responses to changing situations, such as in the oil and gas industry, for example (Deloitte, n.d.).

The traditional structure of supply chains is linear, with discrete steps for design, planning, sourcing, manufacturing, and delivery. Many supply chains today are evolving from a static list to a dynamic, interconnected system that can more easily include ecosystem partners. The end result might be a virtual world that informs and replicates the real one (Deloitte, n.d.).

The primary operating levers within the supply chain life cycle of the sector are plan, source, deliver, and support, and these four component parts or nodes are the primary focus of health provider DSNs operating within an integrated ERP system (Deloitte, n.d.). We can see the differentiation between the traditional supply chain and the digital supply chain in Figure 7.

A supply chain control tower can provide more real-time visibility into these areas and offer powerful AI capabilities. It can build trend analyses that recognize purchasing anomalies in

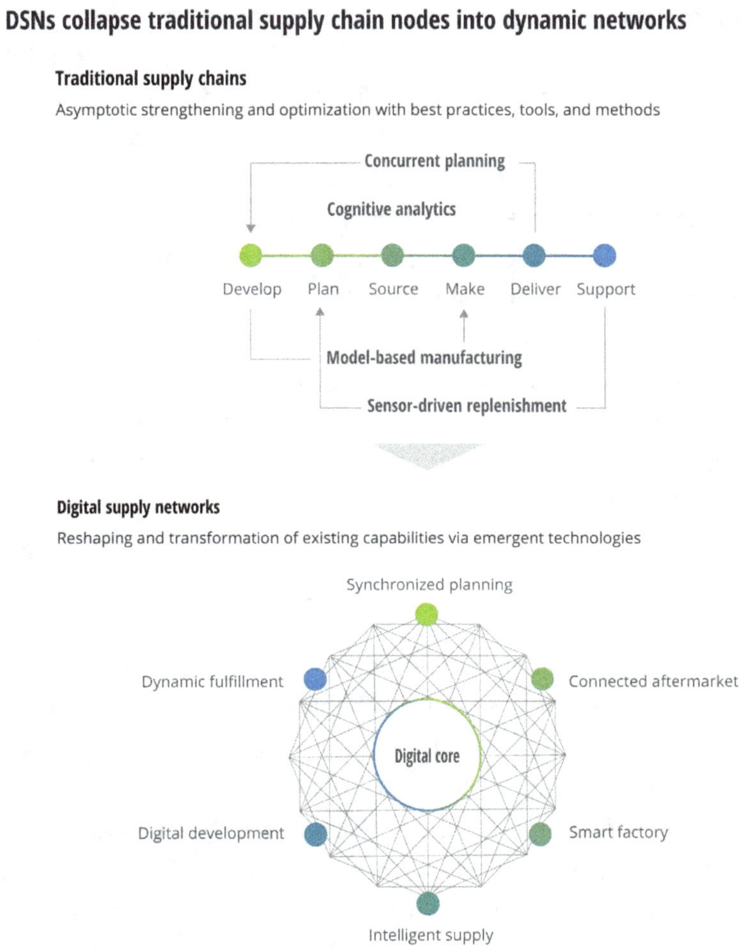

Figure 7. Traditional Supply Chain vs. Digital Supply Chain (Coleman *et al.*, 2022).

real time and promptly alert appropriate decision-makers. A DNS control tower could help solve the healthcare industry's most pressing supply chain issues. A digitally connected control tower enables proactive, strategic data interpretation to better identify low-value activities and facilitate root-cause analysis. The control tower reduces the likelihood of human error by constantly collecting and analyzing data and using its ML capabilities. In addition, the control tower can alert decision-makers when there are deviations from that path. Hospitals and health systems that have solidified their digital core should consider implementing a DSN control tower. This is a scalable, adaptable, and centralized hub using technology, processes, and talent to compile and exploit supply chain data. The control tower can then direct the automation of more menial tasks to free up staff time for more impactful activities (Deloitte, n.d.).

A DSN is one way that hospitals and health systems can move toward a broad, enterprise-level digital transformation. When a DSN is coupled with innovations, such as ML, process automation, data analytics, and 3D printing, organizations can progress in their healthcare provision (Deloitte, n.d.).

Enhancing Patient Outcomes with Automation

In addition to helping people better monitor their own health, wearable health devices are also helping to close gaps in patient data and care. The World Economic Forum (WEF) estimates that over the next 15 years, the five most common chronic diseases — cancer, diabetes, mental illness, heart disease, and respiratory disease — will have a $47 trillion global economic impact. Devices can give clinicians more information than face-to-face consultations do, potentially leading to earlier diagnosis and better treatment guidance. They can also give clinicians more accurate information. These technologies might eventually provide a more accurate picture of a patient's health status than measurements made at a particular time (Edelmann, 2021).

Indeed, tech companies and startups are diligently working on addressing the same problems. For instance, Google is working with health delivery networks to develop big data prediction models that will alert clinicians to high-risk conditions like sepsis and heart failure. Startups like Google, Enlitic, and numerous others are actively developing AI-derived image interpretation algorithms. Jvion provides a "clinical success machine" that identifies patients who are most at risk for adverse events as well as those who are most likely to benefit from prescribed therapies. Each of these could offer guidance to clinicians looking for the best patient diagnosis and care (Davenport & Ravi, 2019).

With the combination of AI and big data, healthcare practitioners now have the opportunity to use data-driven methods to better understand their patient's conditions and make more accurate decisions. These algorithms leverage powerful computational and analytical capabilities to identify patterns in data that would not be apparent to the naked eye.

Effectively designing the "choice architecture" to influence patient behavior in a more anticipatory manner based on empirical data is another area of growing interest in healthcare. The software can customize recommendations by comparing patient data to other successful treatment pathways for similar cohorts using data from provider EHR systems, biosensors, watches, smartphones, conversational interfaces, and other instrumentation. Providers, patients, nurses, call center representatives, or care delivery coordinators may all receive the recommendations (Davenport & Ravi, 2019).

By leveraging powerful algorithms to identify patterns in data, healthcare organizations can design choice architectures to influence patient behavior in an anticipatory manner. Caregivers and health systems can become more proactive in anticipating a patient's needs and developing tailored recommendations and interventions that are most appropriate for the individual.

Conclusions

COVID-19 exposed how the focus on minimizing costs can reduce supply chain resilience and make it difficult to effectively respond to and recover from crises. Therefore, it is essential to ensure that healthcare organizations are leveraging the right technologies and models in order to develop anticipatory care approaches that benefit both the patient and the health system. To facilitate this, caregivers and the health systems must recognize that every patient has different needs and strive to deliver personalized healthcare through tailored recommendations and interventions.

Crises, catastrophic occurrences, and other supply chain disruptions will probably continue to happen in the future, possibly more frequently. For healthcare organizations, it's more crucial than ever to create resilient supply chains that can withstand these disruptions and come out stronger. In order to address the supply chain challenges they are facing, leading organizations should think about figuring out what causes them and then investing in the best mix of people, processes, and technology (Coleman *et al.*, 2022).

The Future of Healthcare Supply Chains

Organizations in the healthcare industry are investing more in technology. A Gartner study found that 61% of healthcare organizations said their new technology investments were a direct response to COVID-19, and 63% said they planned to increase their investment in technology in 2021. According to a 2021 study by Deloitte and the Scottsdale Institute, a non-profit membership organization for the healthcare industry, leaders in digital transformation were most interested in using technology to raise patient satisfaction and engagement, boost care quality, and guarantee better patient outcomes (Coleman *et al.*, 2022).

This industry's ability to improve supply chain visibility and, ultimately, raise the standard of healthcare can greatly benefit from the transparency and information sharing that occurs both horizontally between industry peers and vertically from the point of origin to the point of care (Deluca, 2021). In the face of the pandemic, technology has become a critical part of healthcare.

By leveraging technology to enable access to real-time data and increase visibility into the healthcare supply chain, healthcare organizations can improve their ability to deliver quality patient care while keeping costs low.

The complexity of healthcare supply chain management is being handled by a number of systems, which give businesses in this quickly expanding industry the transparency and end-to-end visibility they require — through real-time information flows, communication tools, and collaborative workflows — to manage a challenging and expanding network of trading partners. Before patients and their bottom line are negatively impacted, it can assist them in identifying and resolving supply and demand problems early on. Additionally, because it resides in the cloud, network participants have the scalability and flexibility they require to implement and take advantage of cutting-edge supply chain technologies like robotic process automation, AI and ML, predictive analytics, and other technologies (Tracelink, n.d.).

Healthcare SCM systems can help provide businesses with the tools they need to effectively and efficiently manage their processes, allowing them to capitalize on the latest advances in technology while ensuring patients receive the best care possible. With these systems in place, healthcare businesses can identify and rectify any underlying issues in their supply chain operations before they have a chance to negatively impact the quality of care that patients receive.

We need to give requestors who are ordering medical supplies better, more accurate information and give them assurance that what they order is available and can be delivered on time. While many healthcare systems have made significant improvements in managing clinical supplies, many others still have a long way to go (Deluca, 2021).

To ensure that medical supply chain operations are efficient and effective, organizations must invest in new technology and systems that enable better visibility, traceability, and data management. By using technology such as supply chain management (SCM) software, healthcare organizations can gain real-time visibility into their supply chains, allowing them to track medical supplies from the moment they are ordered until they reach their final destination.

Optimizing Healthcare Supply Chains for Future Needs

Both patients and the medical community may find the process of supply chain optimization in the healthcare industry an intriguing prospect. The main justification is that, according to research, if these organizations looked to optimize their supply chain processes, they could each save about $11 million annually. The patients would benefit from lower costs for life-saving care thanks to the streamlining of this supply chain (Procurement Partners, n.d.).

Optimizing the healthcare supply chain is crucial to ensuring patients receive high-quality care. While the healthcare supply chain has strict regulatory requirements, there are areas where it can improve. You can enhance efficiency in your supply chain by following these tips:

1. **Improve visibility**: This is by far the most important thing. One should be able to accurately manage inventory and determine where products are located at any given time in the supply chain. Collect all of your data in one place to accomplish this. This process includes gathering data from manufacturing facilities, distributors, suppliers, goods, transportation methods, and the like. Then, using software platforms, AI, or third- or fourth-party services, you will need to completely improve your data analysis skills.
2. **Consolidate the supplier base**. It's simple to optimize your healthcare supply chain by managing your suppliers. If you create win-win partnerships with your suppliers, consolidating

them can be simple. Start retendering to enhance your market awareness, supplier competitiveness, and the potential development of open contracting contracts. You should also start conducting monthly, quarterly, and annual performance reviews.

3. **Center performance**: Establish a hierarchy of valuable supply chain metrics that are outcome-based. An analysis of the trade-offs between key performance indicators should be possible using these performance measurements (KPIs). A KPI model that focuses on the quality, service, expenses, and revenue of your entire supply chain is also an option. Target each link in the organization's supply chain and record performance information in real time.
4. **Put standardization into action**. Healthcare organizations frequently expand by buying other businesses. This circumstance may cause all the various systems and processes to interact with one another. Utilize a framework like the Supply Chain Operations Reference (SCOR) model to standardize the processes for the financial and physical components. One can then apply and enforce standards throughout the entire supply chain by doing this.
5. **Know the expenses**. A better understanding of costs, including their amount and source, would be advantageous to many organizations. Begin by compiling information on your costs for goods and services. One can benchmark, evaluate, and search for patterns in the data using common categories (Nasrallah, 2022).
6. **Partner with a group purchasing organization (GPO)** — A GPO is an organization that uses the collective purchasing power of its members to negotiate low prices for pharmaceuticals and medical supplies. Health systems, hospitals, and other patient care organizations make up its membership (e.g., long-term care facilities, home health agencies, etc.). Partnering with a GPO has advantages in terms of cost and efficiency.

The GPO negotiates on behalf of healthcare organizations, saving them from having to speak with each of their suppliers individually and asking for savings and discounts. Hundreds of facilities are represented by the GPO, giving it much more negotiating power than any one facility could have by itself (Tecsys, n.d.).

What we need to do is find the right balance — a rational balance — that incentivizes the sourcing of critical medical supplies while also capitalizing on an opportunity to improve advanced planning, share information across all industry partners, and find a way to improve supply chain efficiency.

As we move into Supply Chain 5.0, the healthcare industry has an opportunity to take advantage of new technologies to create a more agile and adaptable supply chain. With the use of AI, ML, and the Internet of Things, healthcare organizations can create a more efficient supply chain that can quickly respond to disruptions and provide personalized care to patients. By leveraging these technologies, we can create a more resilient healthcare supply chain that is better equipped to handle crises and provide quality care to patients in need. The future of the healthcare supply chain looks bright, and we have the power to create positive change that will benefit us all.

With every crisis comes an opportunity, and there is optimism that the healthcare supply chain industry will rise to the occasion and make changes that will benefit everyone in the future.

References

American Hospital Association (AHA). (2021). *Leveraging Data for Health Care Innovation.* https://www.aha.org/system/files/media/file/2021/01/MI_Leveraging_Data_Report.pdf.

Artificial Intelligence in Healthcare. (2018, October 8). In *Wikipedia.* https://en.wikipedia.org/w/index.php?title=Artificial_intelligence_in_healthcare&oldid=863084432

Bamakan, S. M. H., Moghaddam, S. G., & Manshadi, S. D. (2021, June 15). Blockchain-enabled pharmaceutical cold chain: Applications, key challenges, and future trends. *Journal of Cleaner Production*, 302, 127021. https://www.sciencedirect.com/science/article/abs/pii/S0959652621012403.

Coleman, T., Petry, J. Kreder, P., Franck, J., & Gerhardt, W. (2022, April 25). *Key Determinants for Resilient Health Care Supply Chains.* Deloitte Insights. https://www2.deloitte.com/us/en/insights/industry/health-care/healthcare-supply-chain.html.

Covetus. (2020, July 17). *Features, Benefits & Limitations of EHR and PHR in Healthcare-Based Services.* https://www.covetus.com/blog/features-benefits-limitations-of-ehr-and-phr-in-healthcare-based-services.

Davenport, T. & Ravi, K. (2019, June). The potential for artificial intelligence in healthcare. *Future Health Journal.* https://doi.org/10.7861/futurehosp.6-2-94.

Deloitte. (n.d.). *How Digital Health Care Can Give Providers an Edge: Building a Digital Supply Chain.* Retrieved March 2023, from https://www2.deloitte.com/us/en/pages/operations/articles/health-care-building-a-digital-supply-chain-examples.html.

Deluca, M. (2021, February 25*). Re-thinking Healthcare Supply Chain in a Post-pandemic World.* Modern Healthcare. www.modernhealthcare.com/supply-chain/re-thinking-healthcare-supply-chain-post-pandemic-world.

Devine, D. (n.d.). *Addressing Healthcare's Supply Chain Challenges with Blockchain*. Huron Consulting Group. Retrieved March 2023, from https://www-cf.huronconsultinggroup.com/insights/healthcare-supply-chain-challenges-blockchain.

Edelmann, S. (2021, February 23). *Leveraging Big Data: Improve Healthcare.* Healthcare Transformers. https://healthcaretransformers.com/digital-health/leveraging-big-data/.

Gerwill, P. (2019). *Blockchain in the Healthcare Supply Chain.* Digital Health Buzz. https://digitalhealthbuzz.com/blockchain-in-the-healthcare-supply-chain/.

Goosen, S. (2022, October 3). *Leveraging Data and Digitization to Overcome Health Supply Chain Disruptions*. PFSC.https://pfscm.org/leveraging-data-and-digitization-to-overcome-health-supply-chain-disruptions/.

HIPAA Journal. (2022, August 3). *55% of Healthcare Organizations Suffered a Third-Party Data Breach in the Past Year*. https://www.

hipaajournal.com/55-of-healthcare-organizations-suffered-a-third-party-data-breach-in-the-past-year/.

Jacobs, T. (2023, February 24). *Unlocking the Value of Artificial Intelligence (AI) in Supply Chain and Logistics*. ThroughPut. https://throughput.world/blog/ai-in-supply-chain-and-logistics/.

Jadhav, J., & Deshmukh, J. (2022, August 23). A review study of the blockchain-based healthcare supply chain. *Social Science & Humanities Open*, 6(1). https://doi.org/10.1016/j.ssaho.2022.100328.

Jercich, K. (2022, March 14). *AI Can Play a Key Role in Turning Unstructured Data into Actionable Insights*. Healthcare IT News. https://www.healthcareitnews.com/news/ai-can-play-key-role-turning-unstructured-data-actionable-insights.

Kwo, L. (2021, July 1). *Contributed: Top 10 Use Cases for AI in Healthcare*. MobiHealthNews. www.mobihealthnews.com/news/contributed-top-10-use-cases-ai-healthcare.

Merchant, S. (2021, January 29). *See How Healthcare Cryptocurrencies Are Transforming Healthcare Management*. Aimblog. https://www.aimblog.io/2021/01/29/see-how-healthcare-cryptocurrencies-are-transforming-healthcare-management/.

Nasrallah, S. (2022, May 18). *The Value of Supply Chain Management in Healthcare*. PathstonePartners. www.pathstonepartners.com/blog/healthcare-supply-chain-management.

Norwich University Online. (2020, May 27). *Current Big Data Challenges in Hospitals and Healthcare*. https://online.norwich.edu/academic-programs/resources/data-challenges-in-healthcare#:~:text=The%20data%20challenges%20in%20healthcare%20are%20myriad.%20Researchers,some%20data%20overlooked%20because%-20it%E2%80%99s%20stuck%20in%20silos.

Premier. (2021, April 1). *Premier Data: The State of PPE Supply One Year into COVID-19*. https://www.premierinc.com/newsroom/blog/premier-data-the-state-of-ppe-supply-one-year-in-to-covid-19.

Procurement Partners. (n.d.). *Healthcare Supply Chain: Everything You Need to Know*. Retrieved March 2023, from https://procurementpartners.com/healthcare-supply-chain/.

Stone, J. (2015, June 10). *Blood Donors in Sweden Get a Text Message Whenever Their Blood Saves Someone's Life*. Independent. https://www.independent.co.uk/news/world/europe/blood-donors-in-sweden-get-a-text-message-whenever-someone-is-helped-with-their-blood-10310101.html.

Tecsys. (n.d.). *Understanding Healthcare Supply Chain Management*. Retrieved March 2023, from www.tecsys.com/understanding-healthcare-supply-chain-management.

Tracelink (n.d.). *Healthcare Supply Chain Management*. Retrieved March 2023, from www.tracelink.com/agile-supply-chain/healthcare-supply-chain-management. Accessed 14 January 2023.

3.5

COLD SUPPLY CHAIN — THE FUTURE OF LOGISTICS AND SUPPLY CHAIN

Picture this: a farmer carefully picking the ripest, juiciest strawberries, a baker perfecting a recipe for the flakiest croissants, and a pharmacist creating life-saving medications. Each of these people has one thing in common: their products require specific temperature conditions during transportation and storage to maintain quality and safety. This is where the cold supply chain comes in; a crucial management process that ensures these temperature-controlled goods make it from production to end-consumer without compromising their integrity.

The term "cold supply chain" refers to the management of temperature-controlled goods from production to end consumer. This type of supply chain is crucial for industries such as pharmaceuticals, food and beverages, and perishable goods that require specific temperature conditions during transportation and storage to maintain product quality and safety.

But with the rise of e-commerce and the growing demand for fresh and perishable goods, the cold supply chain is facing new challenges. Consumers want their groceries delivered within hours, their medications delivered without delay, and their food waste minimized. That's where the future of the cold supply chain comes in, heavily influenced by technological advancements and sustainability initiatives.

Under the framework of Supply Chain 5.0, one emerging trend in the cold supply chain is the integration of cold chain technology. Automation and digitalization will play a major role in optimizing the supply chain process and reducing food waste. The use of sensors and Internet of Things (IoT) devices will allow real-time monitoring and control of temperature, humidity, and other environmental factors, ensuring that products are transported and stored under optimal conditions. Furthermore, with the adoption of advanced logistics management solutions, such as cloud computing and predictive analytics, companies can respond to changing market demands in real time and ensure a reliable and efficient cold supply chain.

Another trend in the cold supply chain is the use of electric vehicles for last-mile delivery, reducing the carbon footprint and promoting sustainability. The development of more efficient refrigeration systems and the use of alternative refrigerants will also help reduce the environmental impact of cold supply chain operations.

The rise of e-commerce and the growing demand for fresh and perishable goods also drive the need for a reliable and efficient cold supply chain. The adoption of advanced logistics management solutions, such as cloud computing and predictive analytics, will enable companies to optimize their operations and respond to changing market demands in real time. It is important to note that the cold chain involves not only the active shipping and handling of temperature-controlled products but the storage as well. Like Royale Cold Storage achieves operational excellence using AEB WMS by transitioning from a paper-based system to digitalized warehouse operations, including automated slot allocation and improved storage space utilization (AEB, n.d.).

As more drugs get approval from the FDA, and especially with so many temperature-controlled products, it is vital that there is freezer space and capacity to keep these products viable (Wayment *et al.*, 2022).

The cold supply chain's future is expected to be shaped by technology and sustainability, resulting in a more efficient, reliable, and eco-friendly system for transporting and storing temperature-sensitive goods. Let's get into some details.

Technology Advances in the Cold Supply Chain

How can Automation and Digitalization Optimize the Processes in the Cold Supply Chain?

Automation and digitalization are revolutionizing the cold supply chain by enabling companies to optimize their processes and increase efficiency. This is being made possible by the emergence of technologies such as autonomous vehicles, cyber-physical systems (CPPSs), digital twins, blockchain platforms, and IoT. These technologies allow for the creation of a digital thread that connects and mirrors a physical supply chain (MacCarthy & Ivanov, 2022). This allows for improved visibility, traceability, accuracy, and speed of transactions between different parties in the cold supply chain. In addition, automation and digitalization are providing real-time monitoring capabilities and the ability to predict supply chain problems before they occur.

Smart factories, warehouses, and logistics, combined with cloud-based` systems and digital platforms, are the main technologies and systems that enable the digital supply chain (MacCarthy & Ivanov, 2022). Analytics, data science, and Artificial

Intelligence (AI) are the primary technologies powering the digital supply chain (MacCarthy & Ivanov, 2022). These technologies help to capture and manage data, detect patterns and insights, drive autonomous decision-making, and optimize operations throughout the supply chain. The digital supply chain provides significant advantages in terms of enhanced visibility, increased efficiency, cost savings, reduced lead times, and improved customer service.

Moreover, blockchain technology integrated with IoT devices advances supply chain automation and creates an ecosystem of immutable transactions that allow for improved audit (Rejeb *et al.*, 2019). This combination enables secure and auditable data exchange within a heterogeneous and context-aware setting, allowing for a fine-grained audit capability where sensor values add additional trust and incorporate real-time and immutable data (Rejeb *et al.*, 2019). In this way, automation and digitalization are optimizing cold supply chain processes (Sorger *et al.*, 2021).

Blockchain technology has emerged as a solution for building a safer, more robust cold supply chain. A multistep distribution process known as "cold chain" requires products to be tracked, examined, quantified, registered, and certified. To deliver goods that are extremely sensitive to high temperatures, like medicine and dairy, manufactured articles are closely monitored and temperature-controlled. When conditions of recall or legal tracking occur, blockchain and health SC consequences, such as ineffective vaccines or contaminated food, not only seriously harm consumers but also cause severe waste, lost revenue, brand mistrust, and high related costs (Food, n.d.).

The combination of digitalization and blockchain technology creates an ecosystem in which immutable transactions are secure and auditable, allowing for a much greater level of efficiency, cost savings, customer service, and lead time reduction. By utilizing blockchain technology and integrating it with

IoT devices, companies can create an automated supply chain system that is not only secure but also provides accurate and up-to-date data.

What Role do AI, Blockchain, and IoT Sensors and IoT Devices Play in Monitoring Conditions?

The modern world is increasingly reliant on technology to manage and monitor conditions, and AI, Blockchain, and IoT Sensors and IoT devices are leading the charge. As a result, the application of such technology in the food sector has become a pressing issue. For instance, Deep Learning (DL) algorithms have been used to improve the accuracy of food products and processes, while Distributed Ledger Technologies (DLT) have been employed to bring transparency to operations (Vilas-Boas *et al.*, 2023). Additionally, IoT sensors and devices can provide real-time monitoring of conditions, while AI can analyze the data generated by these devices to identify any inconsistencies or potential issues.

Similarly, the Industrial Internet of Things (IIoT) collects data from IoT devices and sensors, while Smart Contracts are used to verify tasks according to predefined rules (Khan *et al.*, 2020). Moreover, Digital Twins support the creation of accurate models of physical assets and products in real time (Vilas-Boas *et al.*, 2023). AI, Blockchain, and IoT Sensors and IoT devices also support supply chain visibility, while Smart Contracts with programmable clauses ensure data is trustfully verified (Vilas-Boas *et al.*, 2023). All of these advances in technology have improved the efficiency and accuracy of food production, enabling companies to increase their productivity and optimize their processes.

To address the difficulty of monitoring the cold storage conditions and sending out alarms/reports for the temperature of perishable products in a timely manner, Hua Tech system cooperates with Milesight to integrate intelligence into the cold chain industry in Singapore by using an IoT-based solution: UR72 industrial cellular router, which can realize real-time protection; 24-hours-a-day monitoring through wireless connection underpins the temperature-controlled distribution. The equipment and facilities can best ensure exemplary conservation of cold chain products and increase profitability (Milesight, n.d.).

Advanced deep learning (ADL) techniques also create data that supply chain managers can efficiently optimize and utilize. (Khan *et al.*, 2020). Despite these advantages, there is still room for improvement. For instance, there is a lack of awareness about blockchain technology, and no proper training platforms exist for educating non-specialized people (Khan *et al.*, 2020). Furthermore, many countries have banned cryptocurrency on the state level (Khan *et al.*, 2020), which limits the use of such technology in the food sector. Regulations should be made at the governmental level to allow the use of this technology (Khan *et al.*, 2020).

This lack of awareness and regulation limits the potential of blockchain technology to make a positive difference in the food sector. Despite the potential of blockchain technology to positively influence food production, distribution, and consumption, these factors mean that it is unlikely to become widespread anytime soon. These regulatory challenges limit the extent to which blockchain technology can be used for food production, distribution, and consumption.

Good documentation practices (GDP) policies are primarily designed to standardize and guide the supply of pharmaceuticals from the manufacturer to the end user (the patient).

- Products should always be kept between 2 and 8 degrees Celsius, from manufacturing to the final consumer.
- Considering potential hot climates or an inadequate transportation network, services and deliveries to developing countries should be as effective as those to developed countries.

- Requiring that all companies engaged in the extensive supply and importation of food or medicines have adequate memory infrastructure in place (Food, n.d.).

The IoT integrated Into the Power of Blockchain

To enhance food and health safety procedures effectively, a powerful approach is to integrate blockchain technology with Internet of Things (IoT) tools. With IoT devices capable of monitoring temperature fluctuations over time for each item, consumers gain awareness of products exposed to alarming heat. By utilizing these IoT sensors, coupled with advanced packaging technologies and scanning measures, products at risk can be instantly identified, and safety measures can be implemented along the supply chain.

This is how Korean Air succeeded in managing the vaccine cold chain with Amazon Managed Blockchain. Since 2021, vaccines have become a more important part of Korean Air's transport business. During the transportation, a temperature-controlled container, unit load device (ULD), is used to transport vaccines. A temperature sensor is attached to the inside of the ULD, which periodically measures the temperature even after the container is onboard an aircraft (Yang *et al.*, 2022).

Since the existing system consists of three centralized systems, the transit network, the cargo system, and the web application, and data are stored and managed separately, it is difficult to ensure data consistency and track change history. As a result, Korean Air evaluated blockchains, and ultimately chose Managed Blockchain Hyperledger Fabric (Figure 1), a private network (Yang *et al.*, 2022).

Now, the Korean airline can share temperature history information in real time and verify that there is no forgery or falsification in the entire cold chain distribution process. The airline

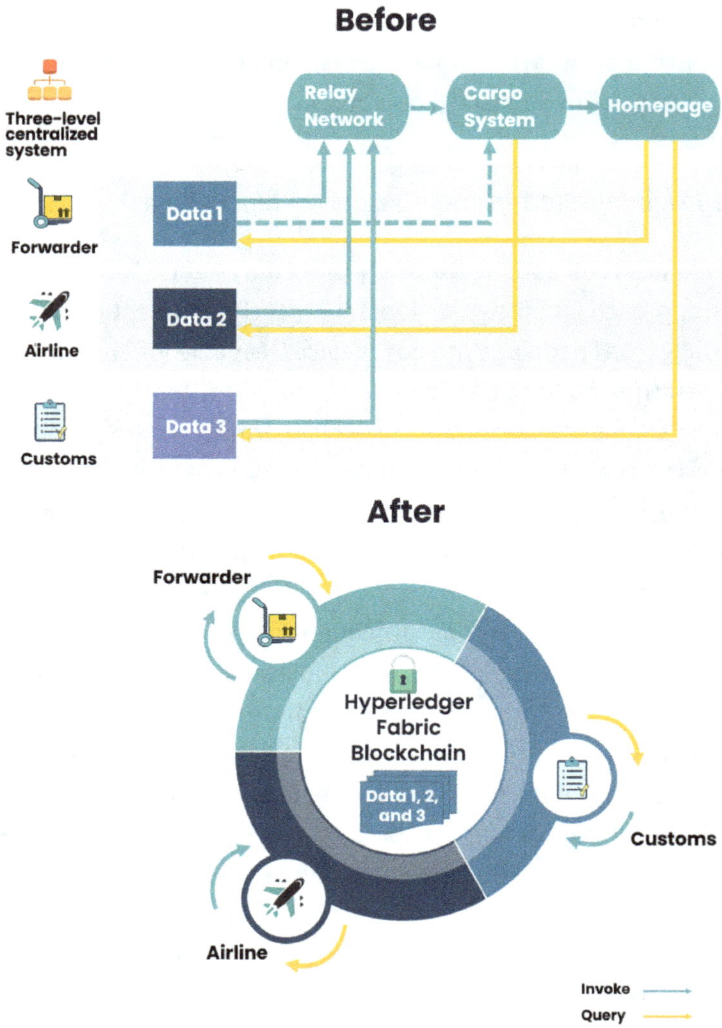

Figure 1. Traditional System and Blockchain Comparison.

integrates blockchain with temperature sensors to ensure the vaccines are properly refrigerated throughout the supply chain process.

Hand-held mobile devices that scan pallets and display information, temperature and humidity sensors that record data in real time, and still more advanced packaging technologies that automatically detect irregularities in the blockchain are a few examples of IoT devices that support cold chains. IoT devices powered by a connected network can also assist in maintaining environments with controlled temperatures throughout. Both tools can incorporate cutting-edge preservation techniques to ensure that all goods are moving through a continuous, uninterrupted cold line (Food, n.d.).

Tracking and Preventing Unsafe Products

Reduced response times and the implementation of effective safety measures rely on achieving end-to-end transparency and traceability in the supply chain. In this context, blockchain technology emerges as a valuable tool to achieve these objectives. By utilizing blockchain, all stakeholders can have access to a secure and immutable record of the supply chain's entire journey, ensuring that the information is accurate and tamper-proof. This enhanced transparency fosters trust, streamlines communication, and enables quick action in case of any safety-related issues or emergencies, ultimately leading to a safer and more efficient supply chain system (Food, n.d.).

Ultimately, AI, Blockchain, and IoT Sensors and IoT devices have proven themselves to be astonishing technologies that take advantage of the applications' needs for a great deal of expertise (Khan *et al.*, 2020). With proper regulation and guidelines in place, these technologies can have a dramatic impact on the food sector, from tracking and traceability to automated payments. However, the regulatory landscape surrounding the use of blockchain technology in food production and distribution is complex, with concerns ranging from data privacy to food safety.

The market for cold chains is anticipated to expand as consumers and businesses become more aware of their advantages. For instance, programs like the Food Safety Vision 2035 of the

Coordinated Global Initiative for Action on Food Safety (CGIAR) aim to increase food safety and reliability by enhancing cold chain management. Companies are also spending money on improved security and efficiency in their cold chain solutions.

Companies like Walmart cooperate with IBM and turn to blockchain for tracking pork in China. It allowed uploading certificates of authenticity to the blockchain, bringing more trust to a system where that used to be a serious issue. Better traceability could help save lives by allowing companies to act faster and protecting the livelihoods of farmers by only discarding produce from the affected farms. Walmart can now trace the origin of over 25 products from five different suppliers using the blockchain system (Hyperledger foundation, n.d.).

Because of rising consumer inflation, the market for the cold chain industry is expanding on its own too. Customers are being encouraged to use more effective cold storage techniques as a result of rising food and other consumable prices. The market is also being helped by the adoption of cutting-edge technologies like radio-frequency identification (RFID) tags and sensors to track food products throughout the cold chain. The cold chain market does, however, face difficulties as a result of consumer inflation. These difficulties include rising manufacturing expenses, rising security risks, and rising environmental impacts (SkyQuest Technology Consulting Pvt. Ltd., 2022).

Challenges and Opportunities for Modernizing a Cold Supply Chain

The challenge of modernizing a cold supply chain is complex and multifaceted, requiring a combination of lean, green, resilient, and agile practices (Al-Refaie *et al.*, 2020). From reducing food waste to improving the efficiency of cold supply chains, new technologies such as blockchain have the potential to revolutionize the food industry and help the healthcare sector, too.

The demand for cold chain logistics is only expected to grow as our world becomes more interconnected through consumerism and e-commerce, combined with the enormous demand for frozen food. To ensure that quality and temperature control are consistently maintained in transit, shipping companies are being forced by the globalization of the cold chain to reevaluate their role in the supply chain (Moreland, 2022).

There is no "one size fits all" approach to cold chain operations because each nation has its own set of laws and specifications for things like food and medical supplies. Knowledge and comprehension of nation-specific transport rules and regulations for temperature-sensitive goods are crucial for a cold chain logistics company to successfully establish itself in this market. Government requirements and standards differ from one country to another, and new regulations seem to be introduced every year (Moreland, 2022).

According to Mukkawar, the overall process of establishing the cold supply chain can be divided into the following major buckets (Mukkawar, 2022).

Dealing with Cold Chain Systems

According to Gartner, creating and managing efficient cold chains necessitates cooperation between a wide range of stakeholders and substantial in-house expertise. That is unquestionably the case, but a lot of it also comes down to making intelligent use of contemporary technologies like the IoT, cloud computing, AI, and machine learning. The challenge of managing intricate integrations is another issue. Because of all this, IT teams, which are already being asked to do more with less, are under a great deal of pressure. No one solution can meet the requirements of cold chain distribution across all industry niches, and siloed solutions are often constrained with regard to customization, integration and data exchange capabilities, leading to frequent change and headaches for logistics leaders in dynamic business environments (Mukkawar, 2022).

Building Solutions with Low-Code

A successful solution must have the capacity to track product location, temperature, and other variables, communicate emergent failures, and interact with industrial equipment. Traditional application development methods are expensive and labor-intensive, but don't be discouraged.

The solution is low-code. Low-code methods reduce a lot of the complexity, allowing IT teams to spend more time delivering business results and less time coding or creating integrations. The application connects suppliers, partners, and customers while streamlining logistics processes (Mukkawar, 2022).

By using low-code to create applications, teams can get more done in less time and with fewer resources. Low-code solutions allow IT teams to quickly build and deploy applications while still achieving the desired outcomes. This increased agility allows businesses to stay competitive by taking advantage of new opportunities quickly without having to go through the time-consuming and expensive process of creating the application from scratch.

Planning and successfully carrying out a cold supply chain's modernization under ambiguous circumstances is crucial to its success. In reality, a number of disruptions can make it difficult to manage the cold chain. Infrastructure, storage, and other physical resources are needed for the movement of material, while information flows are intended to support the coordination of the physical flows and decision-making throughout the supply chain (Comes *et al.*, 2018).

Cold chain failures are attributed to any of the following: information gaps and the inability to manage inaccurate information; failures of decision-making, coordination, or planning; and a lack of or failures of the physical layer (infrastructure, capacity, and goods) causing a disruption in material flows (Comes *et al.*, 2018).

In order to handle the specific temperature requirements, pack outs, and monitoring needed for these extremely sensitive products, the cold supply chain not only requires a consistent workforce but also a workforce with the necessary training. The pharmaceutical industry needs to concentrate on a positive employee experience, which includes excellent onboarding and training, and even partner with other experts when necessary if it wants to compete in the labor market. The hypothetical future cold chain will eventually come to pass. We will arrive at this future more quickly through cooperation and innovation (Wayment *et al.*, 2022).

Drones and solar refrigerators promise to improve capacity and create flexibility for operational decision-makers while monitoring and tracking technologies and information systems can help reduce uncertainty and keep an overview of the situation (Comes *et al.*, 2018). A logistics planning system should continuously update local decision-makers about available refrigeration capacity, refrigerator status, and locations (Comes *et al.*, 2018). This will help to address the challenges of information and decision-making that are currently fragmented, focused on strategic planning, and have long reporting cycles (Comes *et al.*, 2018).

The Future Outlook

The future of temperature-controlled logistics looks bright. According to the Allied Research report, Cold Chain Logistics Market by End Use Industry: Global Opportunity Analysis and

Industry Forecast, the global cold chain logistics market is projected to register a compound annual growth rate of 17.9% from 2019 to 2026 (Coratola, 2021).

Businesses and organizations that ship goods that need cold storage must be aware of the location and management of their shipments. With smart labeling technologies, the cold chain from farm to fork can now be fully traced and transparent, providing suppliers, eateries, and customers with accuracy, assurance, and peace of mind regarding food safety. In the near future, an increasing number of businesses engaged in the cold chain will adopt supply chain network technology to enhance their supply chain visibility. This technology will enable them and their partners to track products in real time, leading to improved efficiency and better collaboration throughout the entire cold chain process (Coratola, 2021).

Entering Emerging Markets

Cold storage providers have a unique opportunity to tap into emerging markets like organic food and COVID-19 vaccine distribution. Concurrently, big pharma companies are actively working on developing vaccines for the coronavirus. Logistics companies, on the other hand, will be devising strategies to venture into these new markets and further expand their presence in established ones. The evolving landscape presents exciting challenges and possibilities for all stakeholders involved (Coratola, 2021).

Custom Packaging Solutions

Businesses will use custom packaging solutions to prevent damage to temperature-sensitive products and manage other risks during transportation. These include battery-operated, portable, programmable heating and cooling devices, and sterile barrier packaging solutions. These solutions can be integrated into freight management platforms to help logistics companies manage and optimize supply chain performance (Coratola, 2021).

For example, the Singa incubator's cold chain delivery is a transportation mode in pharmaceutical international cold chain logistics. An incubator equipped with suitable coolants such as PCM or Dry Ice provides temperature protection for the products.

It can provide temperature recording (every 2–5 minutes in the whole process), monitoring, alarms, and other services for the whole process of the medical cold chain, so as to ensure that the temperature of the whole medical cold chain is guaranteed, while at the same time the temperature data is transparent and traceable. There is no need to open the box to check the temperature of the goods throughout the process. No need to buy a special PDA device; just scan the code with WeChat or an APP to read the temperature record, and the temperature data report is generated immediately and synchronized to the owner's temperature management cloud platform (Singa, n.d.).

Increasing Multi-Segmented Refrigerated Trucks

Logistics companies should invest in multi-temperature refrigerated trucks to provide maximum protection for sensitive materials and meet the highest standards of care (Figure 2) (Coratola,

Figure 2. Customized Refrigerated Trucks (DHL, 2021).

2021). For instance, DHL helps global pharmaceutical leaders move from passive to active cold chain distribution in Turkey. With the growing cost of consumables used in cold chain distribution, expected changes in the new GDP regulations based on European Union standards, and manually intensive processes for product distribution and compliance, DHL designed the first active cold chain pharmaceutical distribution solution in Turkey. By consolidating temperature-sensitive products within the warehouse, customizing refrigerated trucks to enable full visibility into the temperature by the driver and remote personnel, and piloting fully active cold chain distribution in Istanbul prior to the full rollout, the company eliminated consumables costs by 38% and reduced the supply chain's carbon footprint. The elimination of manual processes required to pack the product for transport resulted in additional savings and simplified regulatory compliance (DHL, n.d.).

Information technology in the cold chain sector offers real-time data at various stages of the supply chain, empowering operators to make informed decisions and plan their actions more effectively. The Internet of Things (IoT) will play a crucial role by providing valuable insights into the product's condition and the surrounding environment, including temperature, which helps eliminate potential errors and ensure greater accuracy throughout the process. This seamless integration of technology will enhance efficiency and reliability in the cold chain industry (Tessol, n.d.).

Solar-powered refrigeration units are becoming increasingly popular as industries look for sustainable and eco-friendly alternatives to reefer trucks. Cold storage providers are looking for ways to reduce emissions, cut back on maintenance and costs, and save energy. Diesel engines will eventually be replaced with an all-electric battery-based system, providing better temperature control and reliability (Coratola, 2021).

Conclusions

The cold chain sector is expected to reach a value of USD 340.3 billion by 2025. This growing reliance on the cold chain has aided the sector in bridging the gap between traditional and modern requirements (Tessol, n.d.).

With the rising number of personalized drugs entering the pipeline, many of which necessitate freezer or deep freezer temperatures, the demand for cold storage and handling will escalate. However, this increased need for specialized handling coincides with existing pressure on the supply chain due to the pandemic, evolving online shopping trends, and shifting weather patterns. As a result, addressing these challenges becomes important to ensuring the seamless and efficient distribution of vital medications (Wayment *et al.*, 2022).

As technology improves, cold supply chains will increasingly use Blockchain, IoT, and AI to become more efficient. Blockchain will make it easier to track where each product goes throughout its life cycle. This will make it much harder for anyone to illegally transport or sell contaminated products. IoT will help suppliers keep track of their coolant levels; each container will be equipped with sensors that report on the temperature inside. This makes it much easier for suppliers to check whether or not their items are at the correct temperature before shipping them out. Lastly, AI will make it possible for refrigerators and other equipment to self-diagnose any problems that occur during transport. This will make it much easier to keep items at their proper temperature without any extra work on the supplier's end.

There will be more advancements in this subject as the demand for the cold supply chain increases in the future. Food trends have recently shifted toward more vegan-friendly options, which require more refrigeration space, which means suppliers need something that can keep up with these demands. Additionally, food distribution is becoming more popular around the world; developing nations are picking up on Western diets, and international trade is booming as a result. All of this means there's plenty of room for growth in this field as we move further into the 21st century.

As technology continues to progress, it is becoming increasingly easy for companies to manage their cold supply chains in a more efficient and sustainable way. Automated systems and data tracking can help reduce the amount of waste generated, as well as monitor food temperatures throughout the entire shipping process. Companies like Nestle are already implementing these systems in their factories, with promising results. Furthermore, innovations such as solar-powered refrigerated trucks are reducing emissions during goods transportation and assisting in the long-term viability of these cold supply chains.

In the future, we can expect to see even more advancements in this area. For example, predictive analytics will allow companies to anticipate problems before they occur, helping to reduce waste and energy.

As the world moves toward Supply Chain 5.0, it is becoming increasingly clear that the cold supply chain will play a vital role in the future of logistics and distribution. With advancements in automation, data tracking, and renewable energy, this supply chain is poised to become even more efficient and sustainable.

But beyond the technical aspects, the cold supply chain holds a deeper significance. It represents the delicate balance between the demands of modern life and the preservation of the planet's resources. It ensures that life-saving medicine and fresh produce reach those in need, no matter where they are in the world. It symbolizes the interconnectedness of our global community and the responsibility we all share to protect the planet and each other.

As we move forward, it is imperative to ensure that the cold supply chain continues to evolve and adapt to meet the ever-growing demands of our world while preserving the fragile balance of our environment. It is a challenge we must rise to and one that holds the key to a more sustainable and equitable future for all.

The future looks bright for these chains!

References

Al-Refaie, A., Al-Tahat, M., & Lepkova, N. (2020). Modelling relationships between agility, lean, resilient, green practices in cold supply chains using ISM approach. *Technological and Economic Development of Economy*, 26(4), 675–694. https://web.s.ebscohost.com/abstract?direct=true&profile=ehost&scope=site&authtype=crawler&jrnl=20294913&AN=144576819&h=aCPrYUQN2fV0HMewM%2f8GopP6Guk6lyF3CgnTqecTkP8Bd5akc5o4d0S4nxqQYyKdRnE%2bb3FdIgPlOEpPonptKw%3d%3d&crl=c&resultNs=AdminWebAuth&resultLocal=ErrCrlNotAuth&crlhashurl=login.aspx%3fdirect%3dtrue%26profile%3dehost%26scope%3dsite%26authtype%3dcrawler%26jrnl%3d20294913%26AN%3d144576819.

AEB. (n.d.). *How Royale Cold Storage Achieves Operational Excellence Using AEB WMS.* Retrieved February 2023, from https://www.aeb.com/en/cold-chain-warehouse-management/cold-chain-case-study-technologies.php.

Comes, T., Bergtora Sandvik, K., & Van de Walle, B. (2018). Cold chains, interrupted: The use of technology and information for decisions that keep humanitarian vaccines cool. *Journal of Humanitarian Logistics and Supply Chain Management*, 8(1), 49–69. https://doi.org/10.1108/JHLSCM-03-2017-0006.

Coratola, P. (2021, February 5). *The Future of Refrigerated Logistics in the Cold Chain.* The Network Effect. https://supplychainbeyond.com/future-of-temperature-controlled-logistics/.

DHL. (2021). *Food Logistics: Why It Can Be a Pickle.* https://www.dhl.com/global-en/delivered/globalization/food-logistics.html.

DHL. (n.d.). *Global Pharma Leader Streamlines Supply in Turkey.* Retrieved February 2023, from https://www.dhl.com/global-en/home/our-divisions/supply-chain/thought-leadership/case-studies/life-sciences-and-healthcare/pharma-leader-cold-chain-distribution-turkey.html.

Food, D. (n.d.). *Cold Supply Chain Hand in Hand with Blockchain.* Prophetic Technology. Retrieved February 2023, from https://blog.prophetic-technology.com/cold-supply-chain-hand-in-hand-with-blockchain.

Hyperledger Foundation. (n.d.). *How Walmart Brought Unprecedented Transparency to the Food Supply Chain with Hyperledger Fabric.* Retrieved February 2023, from https://www.hyperledger.org/learn/publications/walmart-case-study.

Khan, P., Byun, Y., & Park, N. (2020). IoT-blockchain enabled optimized provenance system for food industry 4.0 using advanced deep learning. *Sensors*, 20(10), 2990. https://doi.org/10.3390/s20102990.

Milesight. (n.d.). *Milesight Integrates Intelligence into Cold Chain Industry*. Retrieved February 2023, from https://resource.milesight-iot.com/milesight/marketing-collateral/case/cold-chain-singapore.pdf.

MacCarthy, B., & Ivanov, D. (2022). *The Digital Supply Chain.* Elsevier. https://doi.org/10.1016/C2020-0-03788-6.

Moreland, G. (2022, May 27). *4 Trends in Cold Chain Logistics*. SpotSee. https://spotsee.io/blog/4-trends-in-cold-chain-logistics.

Mukkawar, A. (2022, May 6). *How to Better Manage the Cold Supply Chain with Mendix and AWS.* Mendix. https://www.mendix.com/blog/how-to-better-manage-cold-supply-chain/.

Nash, K. (2016, October 19). Wal-Mart turns to blockchain for tracking pork in China. *The Wall Street Journal.* https://www.wsj.com/articles/BL-CIOB-10750.

Rejeb, A., Keogh, J., & Treiblmaier, H. (2019). Leveraging the internet of things and blockchain technology in supply chain management. *Future Internet*, 11(7), 161. https://doi.org/10.3390/fi11070161.

SkyQuest Technology Consulting Pvt. Ltd. (2022, June 27). *Cold Chain Market to Generate Revenue of 436.52 Billion by 2028 Due to Increased Efforts to Reduce Loss of Food Worth $750 Billion.* GlobeNewswire News Room. https://www.globenewswire.com/en/news-release/2022/06/27/2469633/0/en/Cold-Chain-Market-to-Generate-Revenue-of-436-52-billion-by-2028-Due-to-Increased-Efforts-to-Reduce-Loss-of-Food-worth-750-Billion.html.

Sorger, M., Ralph, B. J., Hartl, K., Woschank, M., & Stockinger, M. (2021). Big data in the metal processing value chain: A systematic digitalization approach under special consideration of standardization and SMEs. *Applied Sciences*, 11(19), 9021. https://doi.org/10.3390/app11199021.

Singa. (n.d.). *Incubator Delivery.* Retrieved February 2023, from https://www.singasc.com/productinfo/730660.html?templateId=178835.

Tessol. (n.d.). *Future Trends in Cold Chain Storage and Distribution.* Retrieved February 2023, from https://tessol.in/future-trends-in-cold-chain-storage-and-distribution/.

Vilas-Boas, J., Rodrigues, J., & Alberti, A. (2023). Convergence of distributed ledger technologies with digital twins, IoT, and AI for fresh food logistics: Challenges and opportunities. *Journal of Industrial Information Integration,* 31. https://www.sciencedirect.com/science/article/pii/S2452414X22000607.

Wayment, J., Cook, J., & Health, C. (2022). Building the cold chain of the future. *Pharmaceutical Commerce,* 7(5). https://www.pharmaceuticalcommerce.com/view/building-the-cold-chain-of-the-future.

Yang, S.H., Park, H.Y., Choi, I.Y., & Liu, J. (2022, December 6). *How Korean Air Succeeded in Managing the Vaccine Cold Chain with Amazon Managed Blockchain.* Amazon Management Blockchain. https://aws.amazon.com/blogs/database/how-korean-air-succeeded-in-managing-the-vaccine-cold-chain-with-amazon-managed-blockchain/.

3.6

HARNESSING THE POWER OF RESILIENCE TO CREATE AN AGILE SUPPLY CHAIN

The first lesson supply chain professionals learned at the outset of the pandemic was the importance of resilience. The second lesson was equally important: supply chains must be agile. A global study conducted by Gartner proves the point. The study "discovered that 87% of respondents plan to invest in supply chain resilience in the next two years, while 98% are looking to invest in agility," Geraint John, vice president and analyst with the Gartner Supply Chain practice, observes (DeAngelis, 2021).

The supply chains that are most adaptable and resilient are made to do more than just endure and recover. They are built on procedures and cutting-edge supply chain technologies that let us foresee and act quickly on all potential risks and opportunities in the future.

The entire world's supply chain is under stress from pandemics, wars, and other unprecedented issues impacting businesses. The Fourth Industrial Revolution, the rise of digital commerce, and changing trade dynamics are just a few of the elements upending accepted wisdom about where value is created and how it moves. While many companies are still trying to adapt to these changes, others are starting to think about the next era of supply chain management.

Agility and resilience are two key aspects of supply chain performance. They help manage the speed and complexity of supply chains, respectively. Supply chains are difficult to manage when one or both of these aspects are unchecked. A supply chain needs both agility and resilience to succeed, but which one should be prioritized? This is a challenging question because it depends on the business and the industry. In some cases, a company may need to sacrifice one aspect to gain another.

Agility is defined as the ability to quickly respond to changing circumstances in an enterprise. It also relates to how fast a company can move its products from manufacturing to retail. On the other hand, **Resilience** refers to how quickly a supply chain can recover from disruptions. A resilient supply chain recovers from disruptions faster than a non-resilient one. It's good for overcoming changes in demand, costs, and market trends. However, a weak link in the chain can cause significant delays in shipments for various reasons. Therefore, managing supply chain performance involves balancing agility and resilience.

The success of any business is largely dependent on the efficiency and effectiveness of its supply chain. In today's dynamic and unpredictable business world, it is essential for companies to have an agile and resilient supply chain. An agile supply chain is one that is able to adapt quickly to changes in market demands, while a resilient supply chain is one that can stay operational in the face of disruptions.

Harnessing the Power of Resilience to Create an Agile Supply Chain is the central focus of this section, which delves into effective methodologies for building and strengthening such systems.

The Need for Resilience and Agility in Supply Chains

A resilient and agile supply chain is beneficial for companies in many ways. First, it helps companies mitigate risks associated with disruptions. By having a resilient and agile supply chain, companies can respond quickly to disruptions and minimize losses. Furthermore, companies can also benefit from improved customer satisfaction as they are able to quickly meet customer demands. As McKinsey's case examined, agile transformations resulted in an uplift in customer satisfaction and engagement of between 10 and 30 points (Aghina *et al.*, 2020).

A resilient and agile supply chain also helps companies reduce costs. By having an adaptive and responsive supply chain, companies can reduce the costs associated with unexpected disruptions. Additionally, companies can also reduce costs associated with inventory management and other supply chain activities.

Lastly, a resilient and agile supply chain also helps companies increase their competitive advantage. By being able to quickly and effectively respond to changes in the market, companies can gain a competitive advantage over their competitors. This can lead to increased sales and higher profits. This means that they should be able to scale up or down as required and should be able to source materials, labor, and products from different countries to take advantage of global trade opportunities (SAP, n.d.).

Figure 1 highlights the facets of resilience in a very objective way (Henrich *et al.*, 2022).

Undoubtedly, to maintain a competitive edge and meet customer expectations, supply chains must embody resilience and agility. Resilience enables swift adaptation to environmental changes, while agility empowers rapid responses to shifting customer demands. Embracing these traits is paramount for sustained success in a dynamic and competitive market landscape.

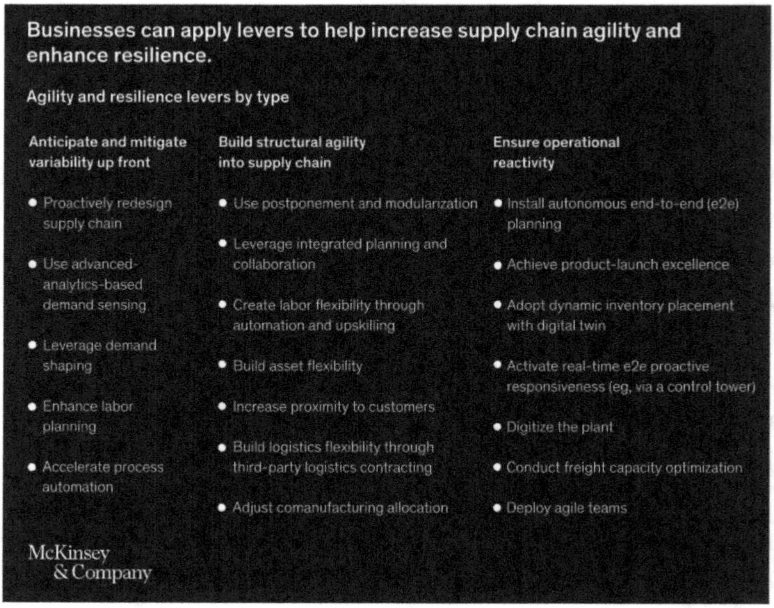

Figure 1. Agility and Resilience Levers (Henrich *et al.*, 2022).

Both of these qualities are essential in order to keep up with the ever-changing landscape of business. The customer is always the king, and it is essential to be close to them in order to understand and serve their needs. However, there is a third element, "efficiency" that also comes into play while balancing agility and resilience (Mussomeli *et al.*, 2022). Efficiency entails utilizing available resources effectively and economically to yield results or reduce costs, while achieving agility and resilience may necessitate certain investments to attain these states. Balancing these factors is essential to optimizing performance and adaptability in a competitive and ever-changing business environment.

If the tripolar supply chain can execute against these three imperatives of agility, efficiency, and resilience successfully, it can go from a corporate expense to a source of competitive advantage and a driver of profitable growth (Figure 2).

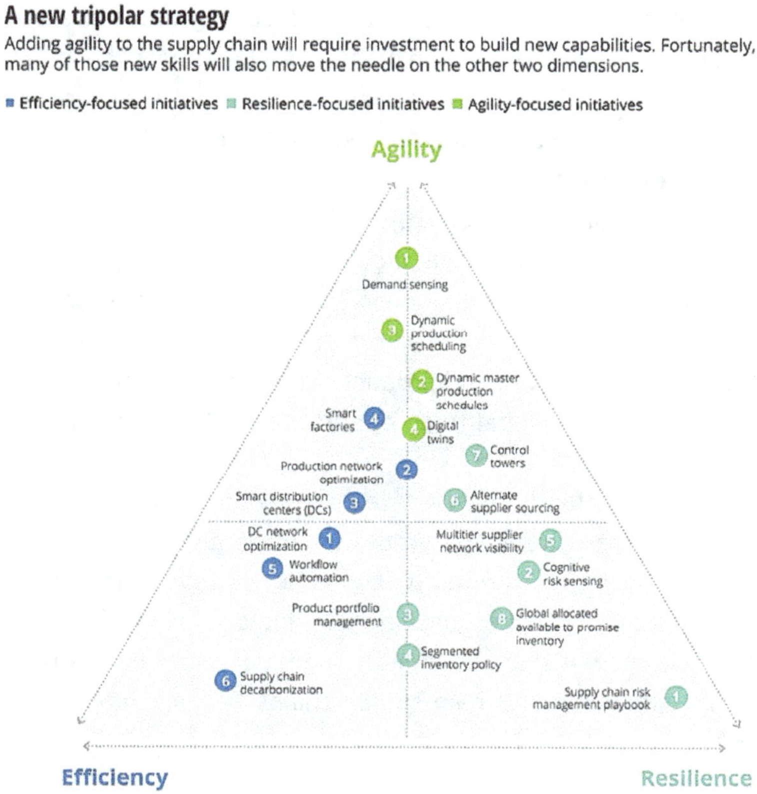

Figure 2. A New Tripolar Strategy (Mussomeli *et al.*, 2022).

To achieve this level of agility and resilience, supply chains need to be restructured so that they are customer-centric rather than product-centric. This means that the focus should be on understanding what the customer wants and needs rather than on producing what is most profitable. We spoke about this element in the first chapter of this book.

It is also important to ensure that suppliers are properly managed. Poor management of suppliers can lead to delays and substandard products, which can have a significant impact on customer satisfaction. Suppliers should be managed on an individual basis and held accountable for their performance. It also entails ensuring that your suppliers are putting into place the most rigorous cyber protection protocols. Increasingly, the attack surface is expanding to include large companies' supplier networks. In February 2022, Toyota idled 14 domestic plants after a supplier of plastic parts and electronics was believed to have been cyber-attacked (PWC, n.d.).

In addition, supply chains should be able to quickly respond to changes in the global economy. This means that they should be able to scale up or down as required and should be able to source materials, labor, and products from different countries to take advantage of global trade opportunities (Mussomeli *et al.*, 2022).

More importantly, the use of technology should be embraced. Automation can streamline processes, while analytics can provide insight into customer needs and improve forecasting. Artificial intelligence and machine learning can also help create predictive models that can identify potential issues before they become problems and help supply chains become more agile and resilient (SAP, n.d.).

Modern Tools for Aligning Business Strategies with Supply Chain Initiatives

Creating a resilient and agile supply chain requires companies to implement strategies that focus on flexibility, responsiveness, and adaptability. Here are some strategies that companies can use to create a resilient and agile supply chain:

1. To start with, companies should analyze their current supply chain processes and identify opportunities for improvement. This can help companies understand where their supply chain is inefficient and what improvements can be made. By doing this, companies can create a more efficient and agile supply chain.

2. Second, companies should establish a resilient and agile supply chain framework. This involves creating a comprehensive framework that outlines the processes and procedures for managing the supply chain. This framework should include strategies for responding to disruptions, as well as strategies for adapting to changes in the market. By having a clear framework in place, companies can ensure that their supply chain remains agile and resilient.
3. Third, companies should strengthen their supply chain relationships and collaborations. This involves building strong relationships with suppliers, distributors, and other stakeholders in the supply chain. By doing this, companies can ensure that their supply chain remains agile and resilient (McKinsey & Company, 2016).
4. Fourth, companies should embrace digital technologies for a resilient and agile supply chain. By utilizing digital technologies such as IoT, AI, and blockchain, companies can improve their supply chain processes and make them more agile and resilient. IBM is a good example. Through investments in geo-mapping, IBM has generated visibility into supply, production, fulfillment, and deliveries across its global network. The technology enables managers to see when a multitier supplier can't ship materials and quickly assess the impact. Ultimately, IBM was able to meet most of its customer demand despite disruptions at various points in its network (Pellathy, n.d.).
5. Fifth, companies should leverage data and analytics for a resilient and agile supply chain. By leveraging data and analytics, companies can gain insights into their supply chain operations and identify potential areas for improvement. This can help companies make their supply chain more agile and resilient.
6. Lastly, companies should mitigate risks and maintain operational resilience. Companies should have strategies in place to mitigate potential risks and ensure that their supply chain remains operational during disruptions (Anderson, 2022).

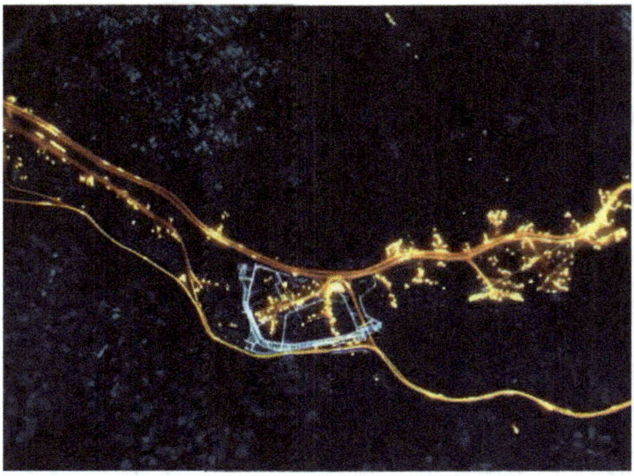

Figure 3. Digital Twin of the Port of Rotterdam (Esri, n.d.).

The activities of the company's own supply chain, as well as those of its upstream suppliers and downstream customers, are all visualized and simulated in real time by a **Digital Twin Model** (Figure 3). This is done by fusing data from various sources, such as ERP and transactional data, weather data, geospatial tracking, and IoT instrumentation. This model offers unmatched visibility and transformative power when combined with a control tower and a personalized dashboard of data, metrics, and events for the entire supply chain. With a digital twin, you can monitor orders, shipments, and deliveries in real time, plan ahead by orchestrating that activity, and even model the effects of suggested changes before putting them into effect (Lam, 2022).

Cisco uses a geographic information system (GIS)-powered digital twin to provide fast, effective technical support. The service delivery insights platform (SDIP) uses business rules and GIS-based location intelligence to send spare parts and technicians from the best warehouse and engineer base in near real-time. Besides, SDIP automatically calculates how far vendors can travel to deliver service in a region and assesses shipping methods for spare-parts delivery. This system lets Cisco's service supply chain adapt rapidly to customer and regional needs (de Gooijer, 2023).

Europe's busiest port utilizes a digital twin to track over 80 ships a day and 460 million tons of cargo per year, generating 3% of the Dutch GDP (Esri, n.d.).

An AI layer can exponentially boost the potential of almost every improvement once that foundation is in place, including demand forecasting, logistics, warehousing, and search. At its core, an AI system tracks and incorporates both conventional and unconventional data sets, including written texts, weather data, and sentiment in the news, as well as historical trends, stock and sales figures, and other financial data. After that, it trains algorithms to link unforeseen and obscure data points, revealing insightful knowledge that is pertinent to one's current needs. Here are a few examples of AI-powered enrichment that improves supply chains significantly; however, the most relevant changes will vary depending on the organization (IBM Consulting, n.d.).

Demand Sensing and Prediction

An AI model can take in a variety of conventional and atypical data sources, including demographics, regional events, weather, and purchasing trends, and predict how demand will change in almost real-time over the course of a few hours to days. With high levels of accuracy, AI-driven insights can also forecast demand based on trends that might not be obvious to particular customers. For instance, the demand for products that people buy on impulse, like carbonated beverages, is highly correlated with ambient temperature forecasts, local events, and promotions. Your company will be better able to meet local consumer demand thanks to improved forecasting, which will increase customer loyalty and revenue.

Intelligent Planning and Risk Mitigation

Businesses can respond to events in almost real-time thanks to predictive insights. Due to a lack of both the necessary data and the knowledge to understand it, supply chain operations have historically not fostered this skill. But today, AI can track the occurrence of disruptive events in real time and use predictive algorithms to better manage their effects thanks to supply chain digital twins. Employees in the supply chain can be much more proactive in risk mitigation, which will enable management to create policies that value and encourage flexibility (IBM Consulting, n.d.).

Deploying Lean Six Sigma to Induce Efficiency and Agility in the Supply Chain at Its Core

Organizations that are looking to become more resilient and agile can deploy Lean Six Sigma strategies to build a more efficient and high-performing supply chain at their core. As a well-known quality management methodology, Lean Six Sigma incorporates different tools and techniques to reduce waste, decrease cycle time, improve productivity, and optimize operations.

In the context of supply chain management, Lean Six Sigma helps organizations identify areas where they can streamline processes, reduce costs, and optimize the performance of their partners. Indeed, an Economist Intelligence Unit survey of 83 manufacturing executives showed that 90% of respondents — the largest group — saw reduced costs as a goal of Lean/Six Sigma programs (Oracle, n.d.). By applying these strategies to their supply chains, organizations can ensure that all interactions are as efficient as possible. This results in faster turnaround times for orders and better customer service overall.

Furthermore, employing Six Sigma means that organizations can monitor their processes for non-compliance or errors in real time. This helps them proactively identify gaps in the supply chain before they lead to issues downstream. As a result, organizations are able to reduce their lead times while also improving customer satisfaction levels.

In order to handle fluctuations in demand and supply, supply chains typically keep safety stocks and extra capacity in the form of warehouse space. However, these first-line defenses (which may have been weakened under lean efficiency drives) are quickly depleted in the event of a sudden, unanticipated shift in input or a significant increase in variability, and the supply chain falters as processes are unable to handle the change in throughput required. The capacity to develop the necessary processes is needed as a second line of defense against such occurrences. For instance, extra picking capacity might take the form of a contract for temporary agency workers hired to handle a surge in throughput (Christopher & Rutherford, 2004).

However, this extra capacity requires funding, so it is suggested that a portion of the cost savings from a Lean Six Sigma efficiency program be put back into risk-reduction strategies that boost process responsiveness. In other words, strive for Lean Six Sigma process performance without going too far in the other direction. A resilient supply chain of strong Six Sigma processes with spare process capacity where it is most needed along the critical path results from the Agile Six Sigma approach (Christopher & Rutherford, 2004).

We have learned from the lean supply paradigm how important it is to lessen variance and facilitate flow, which reduces the need for protective inventory and capacity. But because demand is uncertain and product innovation is increasing, supply chains now need to strategically place capacity and inventory to facilitate flow. This necessitates an all-encompassing viewpoint, especially given how frequently locally driven decisions result in further instability and waste. Investments that preserve material flow rather than only affect the P&L's bottom line (Stratton & Warburton, 2003).

The strategic installation of the "decoupling point" in the supply chain, which helps give the organization the best of both worlds, or a Leagile supply chain, is generally achieved with the combination of Lean, which advocates waste elimination and level scheduling, and Agilie, which needs reserving capacity to cope with volatile demand both in terms of volume and variety. Additionally, this guarantees that the prices are adequately optimized for the required degree of agility and resilience (Carvalho & Cruz-Machado, n.d.).

When used with the utmost seriousness and in accordance with the supply chain objectives of resilience and agility, Lean Six Sigma is a potent approach that has the potential to bring about significant and beneficial changes to the business. With a greater emphasis placed on anticipating demand and understanding customer needs, supply chain strategies must become more sophisticated.

Leveraging Advanced Logistics, Distribution, and Fulfillment Systems

The logistics, distribution, and fulfillment systems of the future must leverage advanced technologies to bring agility and resilience to the supply chain. This would entail the use of automation, artificial intelligence (AI), and data-driven decision-making to ensure that goods are transported efficiently and quickly from

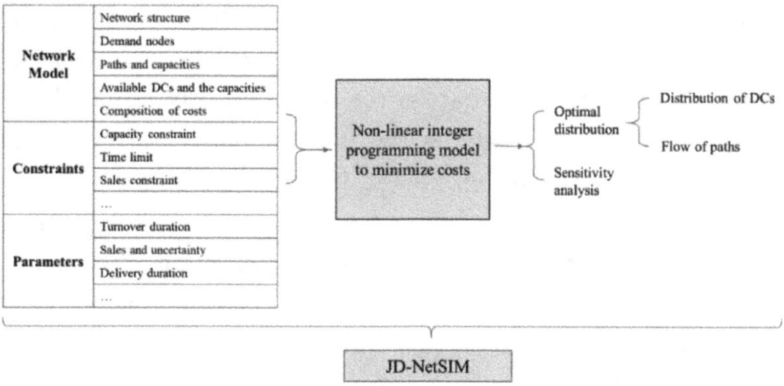

Figure 4. JD-NetSIM (Shen & Sun, 2021).

one point to another without delays or stock-outs. As an example, JD.com's platform, JD-NetSIM (Figure 4), optimized delivery networks during the COVID-19 pandemic. It is a nonlinear integer programming model to minimize storage network optimization costs. Demand, alternative distribution centers (DC), and road nodes make up the model. The DC locations and distribution plan are based on path capacities, transit time, and sales constraints (Shen & Sun, 2021).

Besides, the use of Internet of Things (IoT)-enabled systems would allow for better monitoring of inventories and the tracking of goods in transit.

Robotics, AI, and analytics can transport items through value chains with better speed, reliability, and efficiency, significantly reducing the need for human labor. Rather than completely removing humans from processes, the goal should be to allow them to do what they do best: make critical decisions based on their experience and skill. These technologies, for instance, can free up more time for employees to investigate problems in the system, learn from them, and devise ways to strengthen it (Gandhi, 2022). Restoring the harmony between human and machine intelligence (AI + HI) can hugely benefit supply chains in the future.

Successful firms have already adopted a single, user-friendly interface that enables next-day or same-day delivery, real-time shipment tracking, and hassle-free returns. This streamlined approach enhances customer satisfaction and contributes to their overall success in the market. It's a development that has profoundly altered how businesses view the supply chain. As more consumers choose value-added, premium fulfillment choices, supply chain management is no longer only about cutting costs; it's also about service differentiation, expanding market share, and even boosting profits (KPMG, 2021).

Advanced fulfillment systems could also be used to streamline processes, such as order management, warehouse management, and inventory tracking. By taking advantage of these cutting-edge technologies, companies can increase their agility by enabling them to quickly fulfill orders and deliver products in a timely manner. As Amazon and Walmart fulfillment centers can provide next-day and two-day shipping to meet customer requirements. Additionally, they can also monitor supplier performance in real time, reducing lead times, preventing inventory issues, and increasing customer satisfaction.

Walmart deployed robotics to the new fulfillment center which is a 1.1 million-square-foot facility that features robotics, machine learning, automated storage resulting in increased productivity, better service for our customers, and faster delivery times. It obtains an automated, high-density storage system that streamlines a manual 12-step process into just 5 steps (Moss, 2022).

With these advanced fulfillment technologies, companies have the potential to gain a competitive edge in the market by providing customers with more choices and faster delivery times. Besides, the implementation of these systems can also help businesses reduce operational costs, such as labor and overhead expenses, by eliminating manual processes and automating key operations.

Overall, leveraging advanced logistics, distribution, and fulfillment systems is essential in order for companies to transcend today's supply chains into a resilient and agile future. With the right technologies in place, companies can not only increase efficiency but also ensure customer satisfaction by delivering goods on time — every time! This allows businesses to gain a strategic advantage, remain competitive, and provide customers with an improved level of service that sets them apart from their competitors.

Real-Time Data Integration to Empower Response and Recovery

The future of resilient and agile supply chains will require real-time data integration. Understanding the causes and effects of disruption and acting on them quickly is key to a successful response process, and digital data will enable this to happen.

Consolidating the data the companies generate and currently have access to is the first step to improving decision-making with cognitive technology or machine learning algorithms. Building or purchasing an analytics platform to manage and organize data sources in order to improve current processes and decision-making is an intermediate step. Through data and cutting-edge technology, enhancing supply visibility and transparency may help manage events and risks, improve/remodel network flows, and strengthen business planning procedures. The data will eventually be machine-readable, ushering in more sophisticated cognitive approaches (KPMG, 2021).

For example, Striim is a real-time data integration and streaming platform that supports streaming analytics and the delivery of fresh data to analytics systems. Striim has helped Macy's, a leading retail chain, adopt real-time inventory visibility. Figure 5 shows how Macy's uses Striim to send real-time order

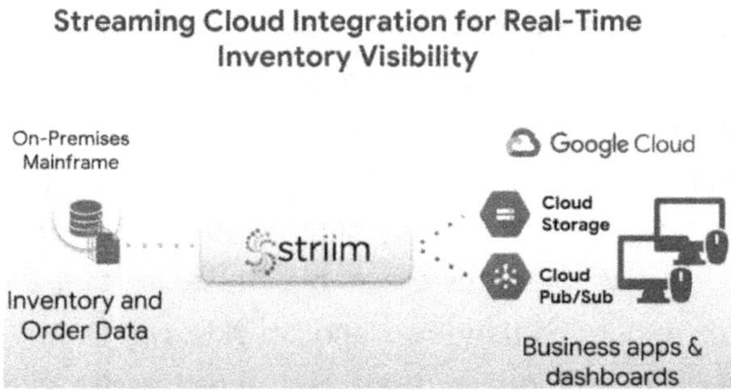

Figure 5. Striim Real-Time Data Integration (Kutay, n.d.).

and inventory data from its on-premise mainframe systems to business applications and dashboards in the Google Cloud. This way, Macy's has streamlined its inventory and been able to adjust stock levels easily (Kutay, n.d.).

Real-time data integration can help organizations anticipate and react faster to changing conditions. It can enable better forecasting, allowing organizations to adjust their supply chain strategy more quickly. This can be done by incorporating advanced analytics and automation into their supply chain management systems (Iakovou & White III, 2020).

The following three data integration strategies increase the resilience of the supply chain and enable it to thrive amid potential disruptions (Radchenko, 2022).

1. **Supply chain digitalization and process automation**: The most important details in this text are that error-prone and inefficient paper-based processes, as well as manual data processing, should be discussed. It is critical to digitize the most critical processes and digitalize data exchange with stakeholders in order to achieve process automation and improve supply chain operations efficiency. Modern cloud-based data integration solutions can help unlock the power

of valuable real-time data to enable data-driven decision-making and process automation. This will enable efficient warehouse management and supply chain execution, allowing for real-time analytics and decision-making to eliminate any inefficiencies in the supply chain before they appear.

2. **Improved supply chain collaboration throughout full integration**: Supply chain integration is essential for achieving close stakeholder collaboration and improved supply chain efficiency. It pulls all stakeholders and business partners out of their data silos to support interconnected and interdependent supply chains. By making supply chain data accessible to all stakeholders, organizations can increase collaboration, leading to a better-organized and reinforced supply chain. Modern data connectivity solutions can make all parties speak the same language without needing to amend IT systems or data formats, making it easy to achieve improved supply chain collaboration and stakeholder integration.
3. **Complete visibility across the supply chain**: Supply chain visibility is essential for organizations to track parts, complete products, and ready-to-sell goods while they are in transit from A to B. By leveraging modern end-to-end visibility solutions, organizations can get a complete overview of their supply chains and enable efficient inventory and production planning. Visibility is essential for improved process efficiencies, reduced risks, increased business profits and customer satisfaction. Full visibility and closer collaboration will help you enhance your supply chain and make it well prepared to combat supply chain issues. For instance, German-based Spotos offers a digital freight forwarding platform that gives shippers access to a vast network of carriers across Europe.

> Corporating with FourKites will give Spotos' clients real-time status updates and predictive ETAs (up to minutes) for their shipments anywhere in Europe, in transit, or at rest, which can reduce dwell and detention costs while optimizing their network as shippers look to manage their costs better (FourKites, 2023).

Such a robust partner network will give you an additional competitive advantage and become a driver for further business growth. This problem is only worsened by a fear of the complexities involved in overhauling paper-based processes and siloed operations and systems.

By incorporating the right technology, organizations can have access to critical data points, such as inventory levels, customer demand, supplier lead times, and transportation times. With this information readily available in real time, businesses will be able to identify both risks and opportunities earlier on, making it easier for them to manage supply chain disruptions accordingly and ensure an effective response.

Conclusions

In the pursuit of a dynamic and adaptable supply chain, the integration of resilience, agility, and efficiency emerges as a critical triad. However, it is paramount to recognize that harnessing the power of resilience lays the foundation for creating an agile supply chain that can withstand disruptions and swiftly respond to evolving market demands. By prioritizing resilience-building initiatives, organizations fortify their supply chains with the ability to recover and bounce back from adversity, creating a solid bedrock upon which agility can be fostered.

When resilience becomes the focal point, it enables businesses to proactively identify vulnerabilities and implement preemptive measures to mitigate risks. This proactive stance enhances the supply chain's ability to adapt and pivot swiftly when confronted with unforeseen challenges, instilling the core principles of agility. With a robust foundation of resilience in place, organizations are better positioned to streamline processes and allocate resources efficiently, striking the right balance between agility and efficiency.

In essence, the sequence of prioritization is crucial. By first reinforcing resilience, businesses bolster their supply chains against uncertainties, enabling them to proactively respond to changing circumstances. Subsequently, as agility takes shape within a resilient framework, the supply chain can react swiftly to capitalize on emerging opportunities and meet evolving customer expectations. Finally, with a resilient and agile supply chain, organizations can then concentrate on optimizing efficiency, ensuring that available resources are judiciously utilized to drive performance and reduce costs without compromising responsiveness.

A supply chain anchored in resilience forms the bedrock for cultivating agility, which, in turn, sets the stage for optimizing efficiency. By adopting this strategic progression, businesses can navigate the complexities of a dynamic market environment with confidence, establishing a competitive edge while sustaining long-term success. The power of resilience should not be underestimated, as it provides the cornerstone for crafting an agile supply chain that is primed to flourish and excel in the new, evolving business landscape.

The Supply Chain 5.0 era will need supply chains to have both complementary capabilities and the resilience to navigate disruptions and uncertainties with ease. It will require a delicate balance of agility and resilience that allows supply chains to respond quickly to changing market demands while also being able to absorb the shocks of unexpected events. With the increasing digitalization of the supply chain, companies will need to leverage data and analytics to create predictive models that enable them to anticipate potential disruptions before they occur. This will require a cultural shift within organizations, as companies will need to embrace a mindset that values agility and flexibility over stability and predictability.

In the Supply Chain 5.0 era, companies will also need to focus on building trust and collaboration across their supply chain ecosystem. This will require a shift away from traditional transactional relationships to more collaborative and strategic partnerships that enable greater transparency and information sharing. By building trust and collaboration, companies can create a more resilient and agile supply chain that is better equipped to handle disruptions and uncertainties. Ultimately, it will be those companies that prioritize resilience first, followed by agility and efficiency, that emerge as winners in the years ahead. By embracing this Supply Chain 5.0 philosophy, businesses can create a transformative and future-proof supply chain that thrives in a dynamic and emerging business landscape.

References

Aghina, W., Handscomb, C., & Ludolph, J. (2020, March 20). *Enterprise Agility: Buzz or Business Impact?* McKinsey & Company. https://www.mckinsey.com/capabilities/people-and-organizational-performance/our-insights/enterprise-agility-buzz-or-business-impact.

Anderson, P. (2022, April 6). Supply chain leaders must optimize their strategy. *Supply Chain Management Review*. https://www.scmr.com/article/supply_chain_leaders_must_optimize_their_strategy.

Carvalho, H. & Cruz-Machado, V. (n.d.). *Integrating Lean, Agile, Resilience and Green Paradigms in Supply Chain Management (LARG_SCM)*. Retrieved March 2023, from https://cdn.intechopen.com/pdfs/15530/InTech-Integrating_lean_agile_resilience_and_green_paradigms_in_supply_chain_management_larg_scm_.pdf.

Christopher, M. & Rutherford, C. (2004, June-August). *Creating Supply Chain Resilience through Agile Six Sigma.* Critical EYE. https://citeseerx.ist.psu.edu/document?repid=rep1&type=pdf&doi=fed07b4acd8ebd3cad0bbc066eeec7b07d6f2b1a.

DeAngelis, S. (2021, March 30). *Creating a Resilient and Agile Supply Chain.* https://www.linkedin.com/pulse/creating-resilient-agile-supply-chain-stephen-deangelis/.

de Gooijer, W. (2023, January 4). *How Cisco Created a GIS-Based Digital Twin of Its Service Supply Chain.* esri. https://www.esri.com/about/newsroom/publications/wherenext/cisco-service-supply-chain-digital-twin/.

esri. (n.d.). *Digital Twin.* Retrieved March 2023, from https://www.esri.com/en-us/digital-twin/overview.

FourKites. (2023, March 6). *FourKites and Spotos Join Forces to Bring Real-time Supply Chain Visibility to European Shippers.* https://www.fourkites.com/press/fourkites-and-spotos-join-forces-to-bring-real-time-supply-chain-visibility-to-european-shippers/.

Gandhi, S. (2022, October 26). Leveraging new tech to boost supply chain resilience. *Harvard Business Review.* https://hbr.org/2022/10/leveraging-new-tech-to-boost-supply-chain-resilience.

Henrich, J., Li, J., Mazuera, C., & Perez, F. (2022, June 14). *Future-Proofing the Supply Chain.* McKinsey & Company. https://www.mckinsey.com/capabilities/operations/our-insights/future-proofing-the-supply-chain.

Iakovou, E., & White III, C. C. (2020, December 3). *How to build more secure, resilient, next-gen U.S. supply chains.* Brookings. https://www.brookings.edu/techstream/how-to-build-more-secure-resilient-next-gen-u-s-supply-chains/.

IBM Consulting. (n.d.). *Building Intelligent, Resilient, and Sustainable Supply Chains.* Retrieved March 2023, from https://www.ibm.com/downloads/cas/VDNJQ20P.

KPMG. (2021, October). *Future of Supply Chain: The Road to Everywhere.* https://assets.kpmg.com/content/dam/kpmg/xx/pdf/2019/11/future-of-supply-chain-the-road-to-everywhere.pdf.

Kutay, J. (n.d.). *Use Cases of Real-Time Analytics in the Supply Chain.* Striim. Retrieved March 2023, from https://www.striim.com/blog/use-cases-real-time-analytics-in-the-supply-chain/.

Lam, B., Calderon, R. F., & Entrup, C. (2022, November 28). *Intelligent Enterprise Fueling the Supply Chain of the Future.* Deloitte. https://

www2.deloitte.com/uk/en/insights/focus/supply-chain/digital-brain-supply-chain-management-with-machine-learning.html.

McKinsey & Company. (2016, October 27). *Supply Chain 4.0 — The Next-Generation Digital Supply Chain*. https://www.mckinsey.com/capabilities/operations/our-insights/supply-chain-40--the-next-generation-digital-supply-chain.

Moss, L. (2022, November 16). *Walmart Deploys Robotics to Compete with Amazon in First of New Fulfillment Centers.* Costar. https://www.costar.com/article/1975310193/walmart-deploys-robotics-to-compete-with-amazon-in-first-of-new-fulfillment-centers.

Mussomeli, A., Delesalle, P., & Kilpatrick, J. (2022, April 1). *The New Supply Chain Equilibrium*. Deloitte Insights. https://www2.deloitte.com/us/en/insights/focus/supply-chain/supply-chain-agility-efficiency.html.

Oracle. (n.d.). *Lean/Six Sigma: The Quest for Efficiency in Manufacturing*. Reliableplant. Retrieved March 2023, from https://www.reliableplant.com/Read/4674/lean-six-sigma-efficiency.

Pellathy, D., Charah, P., & Dittmann, J. P. (n.d.). *How to Avoid the Next Crisis: A New Approach to Supply Chain Agility.* CSCMP Supply chain. Retrieved March 2023, from https://www.supplychainquarterly.com/articles/7478-how-to-avoid-the-next-crisis-a-new-approach-to-supply-chain-agility.

PWC. (n.d.). *Seven Steps to a More Resilient, Agile Manufacturing Supply Chain.* Retrieved March 2023, from https://www.pwc.com/us/en/industries/industrial-products/library/creating-resilient-agile-manufacturing-supply-chain.html.

Radchenko, A. (2022, October 21). *Is Effective Data Integration Critical for Supply Chain Resilience?* Youredi. https://www.youredi.com/blog/is-effective-data-integration-critical-for-supply-chain-resilience.

SAP. (n.d.). *What Is a Resilient Supply Chain? Agility and Risk Management.* SAP Insights. Retrieved March 2023, from https://www.sap.com/insights/what-is-a-resilient-supply-chain.html.

Shen, ZM. & Sun, Y. (2021, October 18). Strengthening supply chain resilience during COVID-19: A case study of JD.com. *Journal of Operations Management.* https://www.ncbi.nlm.nih.gov/pmc/articles/PMC8661997/.

Spotos. (n.d.). *Platform for the Highest Confidence Shipping Experience*. Retrieved March 2023, from https://spotos.eu/.

Stratton, R., & Warburton, R. D. H. (2003, August 11). The strategic integration of agile and lean supply. *International Journal of Production Economics*, 85(2), 183–198. https://doi.org/10.1016/S0925-5273(03)00109-9.

3.7

DIGITAL DEFENSE

PROTECTING SUPPLY CHAINS IN THE CYBER AGE

In 2020, according to the world economic forum, data threats and fraud & cyberattacks were regarded as the sixth and the seventh most likely global risks — after extreme weather, climate action failure, natural disasters, biodiversity loss, and human-made environmental disasters (World Economic Forum, 2020). Cybersecurity and the future of the supply chain are topics that have been at the top of the mind for many organizations for years.

With the emergence of Supply Chain 5.0, the utilization of digital technology and the Internet of Things (IoT) has brought about a considerable increase in the complexity and vulnerability of supply chain systems. Consequently, there is a heightened risk of significant disruptions and financial losses. The most common types of supply chain attacks are ransomware, malware, and data theft. Cybercriminals are increasingly targeting the supply chain, exploiting vulnerabilities in the digital infrastructure, such as unprotected internet connections, weak authentication protocols, and outdated hardware and software.

In comparison to traditional supply chain operations, cybersecurity has acquired critical importance within the framework of Supply Chain 5.0. It plays a crucial role in safeguarding the global supply chain system from malicious activities. Organizations must implement robust security measures to mitigate the risks associated with cyberattacks. This requires a comprehensive approach, including implementing effective security policies, using advanced technologies, and increasing collaboration with suppliers and partners. Organizations must also proactively identify, analyze, and address potential threats.

The global supply chain's future will depend heavily on the success of cybersecurity strategies. Organizations must remain vigilant to protect the supply chain from cyberattacks.

The Current State of Cybersecurity in the Supply Chain

In today's increasingly connected world, many offline work processes have moved online, and it is becoming increasingly common for all parties involved in the supply chain to communicate and collaborate via the internet, which provides cyberattackers with more attack surfaces. Cybersecurity is more important than ever.

What is Cybersecurity?

Cybersecurity is how individuals and organizations reduce the risk of cyberattacks. Cybersecurity's core function is to protect the devices we use (smartphones, laptops, tablets, and computers) and the services we access — both online and at work — from theft or damage (National Cybersecurity Center, n.d.).

Yeboah-Ofori & Shareeful Islam (2019) described that cybersecurity in a supply chain (SC) provides an organization secure network facilities to meet its overall business objectives.

As more and more of our personal and professional lives move online, the risk of cyberattacks grows. This is especially true in the supply chain. The supply chain is increasingly reliant on the use of digital technology to bring benefits to business due to the increased visibility and efficiency it provides, like the development of collaborative online platforms, the growing number of Internet of Things (IoT) devices, and the acceleration of digitalized operations using cloud-based servers. The widespread adoption of digital transformation by all parties in the supply chain has increased the attack surface, resulting in significant company losses. Hence, cybersecurity plays a crucial role in the supply chain.

It takes work to install cybersecurity effectively in the end-to-end value chain. The increased interdependencies among various supply chain parties have brought many challenges, including a lack of third-party audit mechanisms and cascading cyber threats (Yeboah-Ofori & Islam, 2019). Studies showed that in 2021, the average number of cyberattacks and data breaches on 1,200 organizations across 13 industries and the public sector increased by 15.1% from the previous year. Reflectively, a Fortune Business Insights report shows the projected market value increase in cybersecurity reaching 376.32 billion USD by 2029, from 139.77 billion USD in 2021, at a CAGR (compound annual growth rate) of 13.4% (DHL, 2022).

Major Supply Chain Cybersecurity Threats and Cases

Supply chain cyberrisks touch sourcing, vendor management, supply chain continuity and quality, transportation security, and many other functions across the enterprise and require a coordinated effort to address them (National Institute of Standards and

Technology, n.d.). Below are the prominent cybersecurity concerns that organizations face in their supply chain management:

Third-party cybersecurity is inadequate

The growing reliance on third parties in today's supply chains is one of the many factors contributing to the industry's complexity. Third-party risk management is a crucial component of supply chain risk management. Suppliers, contractors, service providers, outsourcers, resellers, brokers, and similar parties fall under the "third parties" category here (Chapman, 2021). Third-party providers or vendors have physical or virtual access to the system and software. Even though many large companies have solid cybersecurity protection, their suppliers and tier suppliers do not have the same awareness or funds to take suitable cybersecurity measures. This allows cyberattackers to identify weak points in the supply chain, launch attacks, obtain relevant customer transaction data, order information, etc., and cause significant losses.

Research shows that organizations share their data with around 730 vendors on average. Of those organizations that share data with third parties, 53% have experienced at least one data breach caused by a third party, with an average cost of about $7.5 million (Reciprocity, 2022).

The SolarWinds attack, for example, was a particularly sophisticated and far-reaching supply chain attack that affected multiple government agencies and businesses in the United States (Biasini, 2020). The attackers could compromise the software of a trusted vendor, SolarWinds, and use it to gain access to its customers' networks. This allowed the attackers to gather sensitive information and disrupt operations for an extended period.

There are many cases where companies were affected due to a breach by a third-party service provider. Organizations such as Target, Home Depot, Fiat Chrysler, T-Mobile USA, the IRS, CVS,

Costco, Sam's Club, Boston Medical Center, and others have suffered cyberattacks because their third-party providers were compromised. It is concerning that third-party breaches have been steadily increasing; a report by American International Group Inc. (AIG) (2013) estimates that more than 60% of breaches occur through a third-party provider (Simon & Omar, 2020).

Digital risk

Digital risks are the unavoidable by-product of digital transformation; the more digital solutions you add to your ecosystem, the more potential network gateways cybercriminals have. Software vulnerabilities could cause these exposures; if left unaddressed, digital risks could develop into the following supply chain threats: ransomware attacks, security breaches, malware infection, process disruptions, and intellectual property theft (Kost, 2023). Malware and ransomware attacks are, unfortunately, becoming more common, and these attacks are designed to steal, change internal data, or destroy sensitive information. (Reciprocity, 2022).

The NotPetya attack, attributed to a government party, was a consequential global supply chain attack (US-CERT, 2017). The attack exploited malware distributed via a software company, granting unauthorized access to the networks of its customers. This malicious software inflicted extensive harm on computer systems, leading to substantial repercussions for the organizations affected.

From 2000 to 2019, a reported 77 cybersecurity-related incidents were uncovered in critical infrastructure, including the process industry, with a vast majority of attacks on the energy and oil production industries (Iaiani *et al.*, 2021). The Colonia pipeline was forced to shut down its 5,500 miles of pipeline after being hit by ransomware in cyberattacks, in which criminal groups hold data hostage until the victim pays a ransom (Figure 1). Ultimately,

Figure 1. Gasoline Shortages After Colonia Pipeline Cyberattack (Wikimedia Commons, 2021).

Colonial paid the hackers $4.4 million for a key to recover their data (Reciprocity, 2022). This cyberattack stalled oil transportation to much of the eastern United States, causing the skyrocketing of gas prices (Tsvetanov & Slaria, 2021) and volatile fuel supplies.

Data breaches

Data breaches are one of the most severe cybersecurity threats organizations face today. In addition to any regulatory or legal repercussions, a data leak or breach typically causes significant financial loss and reputational harm to the victimized organization. Unfortunately, it often takes quite some time for these data breaches to be uncovered.

In 2021, the average cost of a data breach was a whopping $4.2 million. Even with the proper regulatory and compliance standards in place, it often takes organizations a long time to identify a data breach once it has occurred — about 197 days, according to one piece of research (Reciprocity, 2022). The more the parties engaged in collaboration, the higher the potential for data breaches. Unauthorized access via a business email account, lack of encryption, unsecured websites, and improperly stored login information are some of the most common causes of data breaches.

Supplier fraud

Supplier fraud, or vendor fraud, is when a cybercriminal claiming to be a known retailer requests a change to their payment processes. These events are challenging to identify as fraudsters commonly adopt advanced social engineering techniques, including AI-generated voicemails, phishing attacks, and Deepfake video recordings (Kost, 2023).

One example of a cyberattack involved Bazar Loader and Bazar Backdoor, in 2020 (Figure 2). The offenders would use social engineering and target collaborative platforms like Slack and BaseCamp by sending employees at large organizations emails that said they offered important information about contracts, customer service, invoices, or payroll that demanded payment from the business (Lukić, n.d.).

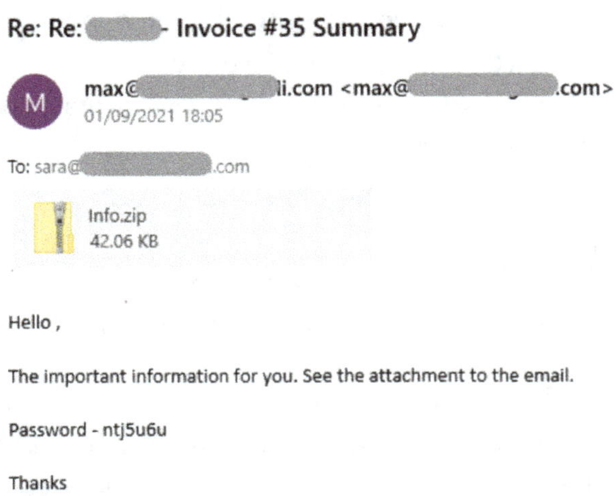

Re: Re: - Invoice #35 Summary

M max@ li.com <max@ .com>
01/09/2021 18:05

To: sara@ .com

Info.zip
42.06 KB

Hello ,

The important information for you. See the attachment to the email.

Password - ntj5u6u

Thanks

Figure 2. Bazar Loader Existing "Email" Correspondences (Shemesh, 2021).

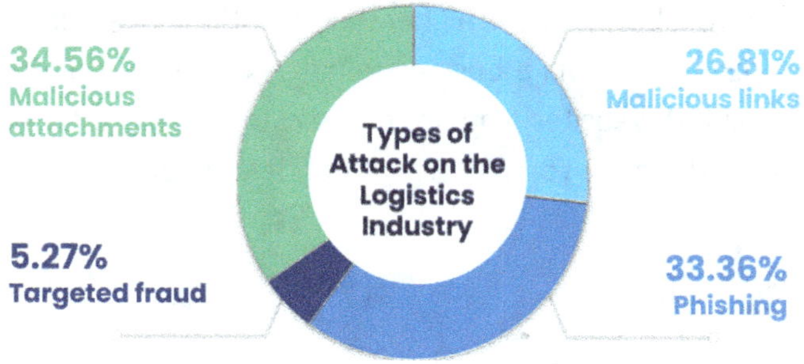

Figure 3. Types of Attack on the Logistic Industry.

These cybersecurity risks are all likely to occur in the supply chain. For instance, in the logistics industry, malicious attachments account for 34.56% of cybersecurity assaults, followed by phishing, which accounts for 33.36%, and targeted fraud, which accounts for 5.27% (DHL, 2022).

In the cases described in Figure 3, the inadequacy of cyberattack prevention endangers the equilibrium of the economy and the environment. The supply chain cybersecurity risk may lead to permanent adverse effects, ranging from reduced service levels leading to customer dissatisfaction, to the theft of intellectual property, and a substantial loss of funds.

According to Cisco Cybersecurity Readiness Index, cybersecurity incidents cost 71% of the affected organizations at least US$100,000, with 41% reporting that the overall cost was US$500,000 or even higher (Figure 4).

Challenges and Opportunities in the Future for Supply Chain Cybersecurity

The future of the supply chain presents both challenges and opportunities for cybersecurity. The increasing complexity of the global supply chain and the proliferation of connected devices will continue to create new vulnerabilities. A growing reliance on supplier-managed cloud services instead of traditional

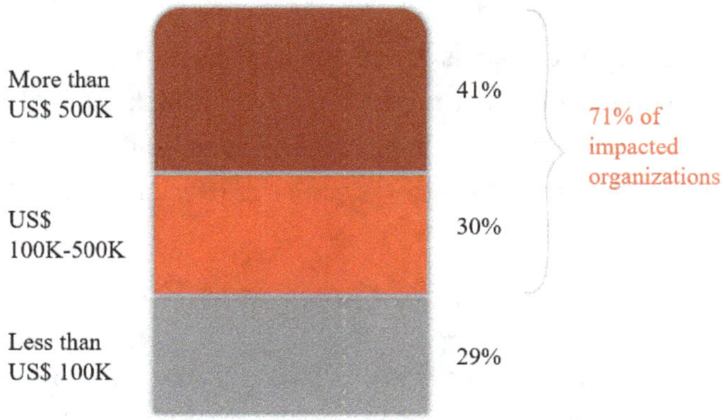

Figure 4. Cybersecurity Incidents Results in Financial Damages (Cisco 2023).

on-premises enterprise software has underscored the need for organizations to gain visibility of the direct and indirect suppliers present in their supply chain.

Vulnerability of the Internet of Things (IoT)

The Internet of Things (IoT) is the interconnection of physical devices, vehicles, buildings, and other items that have built-in electronics, software, sensors, and actuators and are capable of connecting to the network, allowing them to collect data and share it (Lamba *et al.*, 2017). Their ability to connect and be remotely controlled and the lack of extensive security mechanisms make them vulnerable to various attack vectors (Neshenko *et al.*, 2019). Another problem is the complexity of monitoring. Most information security specialists do not know which IoT devices are connected to their networks. In addition, many of these devices are far behind in terms of security from desktop systems and have fixing vulnerabilities, which can take months or even years (Lamba *et al.*, 2017). These characteristics make IoT devices vulnerable to cyberattacks aimed at obtaining required data or installing ransomware.

In 2021, there were more than 10 billion active IoT devices worldwide. Cybercriminals know that IoT security is not at its finest, making it an easier target for a cyberattack. According to IoT-based attack statistics from 2019, the average IoT device gets attacked just five minutes after it goes live (Reciprocity, 2022).

A More Complicated Supply Chain

In addition, sophisticated and geographically interconnected manufacturing processes and services have also created hardware supply chains of rising complexity. For example, producing a single hardware item may involve dozens of component manufacturers and subcontractors, some of which have several degrees of separation from the primary manufacturer (NCSC, n.d.). Complicated procedures and lots of partners make cybersecurity challenging. In 2022, it took an average of 207 days to identify the breach and 70 days to contain it, according to survey data from IBM (IBM Security, 2022). The average time to identify and contain ransomware or a destructive attack was significantly higher than average (Figure 5). A ransomware attack took 237 days to identify and 89 days to contain, for a total life cycle of 326 days (IBM Security, 2022). IBM and the Ponemon Institute report that, on average, a company takes 280 days to detect a third-party data breach (Reciprocity, 2022).

At the same time, new technologies like blockchain and artificial intelligence (AI) can potentially improve supply chain cybersecurity.

For example, blockchain technology has the potential to enhance supply chain traceability and transparency, which can help improve security and reduce the risk of counterfeiting and other illicit activities (Gandomi & Haider, 2015). By establishing a unified digital system, intermediaries are connected from the source of transportation to the destination. Blockchains allow

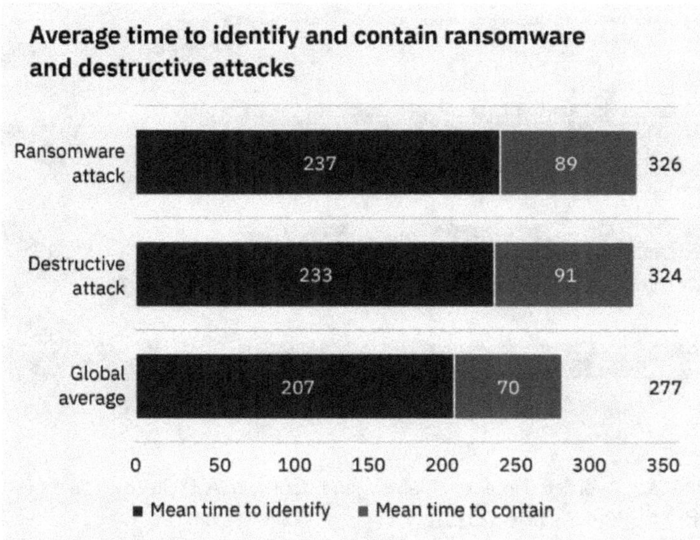

Figure 5. Average Time to Identify and Contain Attacks (IBM Security, 2022).

firms to limit the view and edit privileges afforded to participants, allowing participants only to access those sections of the shared records meant for them. Likewise, it is possible to proof records and audit every supply chain transaction. Blockchains can secure, validate, and guarantee the quality and accuracy of data once it is in the system (Sainathan, n.d.).

AI and machine learning algorithms can also analyze data and identify potential threats in real-time, allowing organizations to take proactive steps to mitigate risks (Kar & Sa, 2018). Companies that use technologies such as AI can reduce the time it takes to identify a data breach by 54 days compared to companies that do not (Figure 6).

As an example, ANDRITZ is an international supplier of plants, equipment, and services for hydropower stations and the pulp, paper, and metalworking industries. The company boasts over 280 production sites and service/sales organizations worldwide. Roughly 50% of its 27,000 employees travel and use the

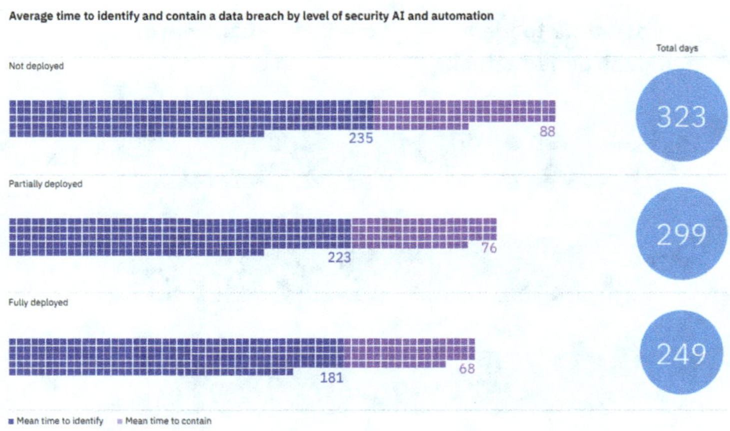

Figure 6. Average Time to Identify and Contain Attacks by the Level of Security AI (IBM Security, 2022).

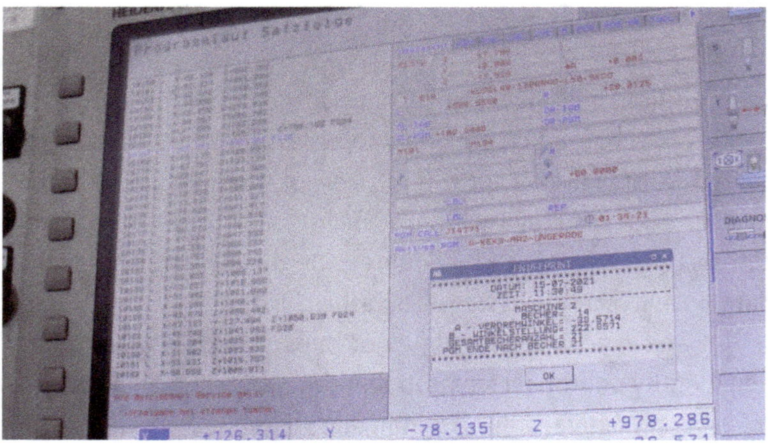

Figure 7. ANDRITZ System (Puleo, n.d.).

company's network and remote connectivity options to access IT resources automatically. Engaging with IBM Security™ and deploying an integrated set of IBM® Managed Security Services (MSS), ANDRITZ has 100% visibility and transparency, solving threats quickly (Figure 7). When the system detects suspicious activity or patterns, such as multiple failed login attempts, it triggers an automated alert. Depending on the severity level, the IBM Security team provides response recommendations (Puleo, n.d.).

Steps Organizations Can Take to Improve Supply Chain Cybersecurity

Complex supply chains can generate expansive assault surfaces, providing opportunities for cybercriminals. If the primary objective of an attacker is a large organization with robust cyber defenses, they may seek an alternative entry point. This could occur through a service provider with access to the target's systems and a vulnerable defense.

Organizations must comprehensively comprehend the cybersecurity risks in their supply chain and develop an effective program to identify, assess, and manage these threats. This includes conducting risk assessments, implementing secure processes and protocols, and providing cybersecurity training to employees. Government and industry organizations also have a role to play in setting standards and regulations for supply chain security.

Identify

Scrutinize the supplier

Evolving supply of digital technologies, such as IoT and cloud services, has made companies more transparent and accessible. Therefore, a process of fully scrutinizing the suppliers needs to be considered.

Every supplier must have a clearly identified owner within the organization (NCSC, n.d.). Typically, identifying risks right from the time of supplier introduction through supplier relationship management, purchasing decisions, and payments is necessary. Maintaining visibility of the suppliers' security measures and communicating your requirements to them are important considerations, particularly for suppliers who are critical to the business.

Identify the critical services and assets

Apply a criticality analysis process according to the importance and priorities of the services and assets (including third-party services), which evaluates the potential harm to the organization caused by disruptions to each of the assets and services, to manage the cyberrisks in your supply chain effectively.

During this process, consider the following factors: Identify the most critical assets and services, the consequences of asset and service disruptions, and access to the most important assets and services (NCSC, n.d.).

Assess

Review the supplier (Third-party) lists and categorize them into levels of risk, prioritizing those who provide critical products or services that pose a high level of risk if compromised or interrupted. Then you can formulate business continuity plans and organize contingencies if a vital supplier disrupts. Developing robust and collaborative security relationships with key suppliers can enhance information flow and coordination during security incidents.

A set of general cybersecurity risk indicators can be used to evaluate any supplier: including information security standards, controls, and procedures; malware protection and threat management systems; identity and access management procedures; audit and compliance procedures; documentation standards; data access controls; data life cycle management; physical security procedures; quality assurance procedures; distribution channel security; and commitment to security assurance throughout a product's life cycle (NCSC, n.d.).

Manage

Organizations must establish a program to manage cybersecurity risk and develop a standard set of policies and procedures that guide all parts of the business undertaking supply chain cyberrisk management activities. Digital technologies like blockchain, AI, and Extended detection and response (XDR) technology can assist businesses in achieving visualization and enhancing cybersecurity.

For example, AI is a valuable tool for improving resilience within the supply chain, especially regarding cybersecurity. AI solutions function like 24/7 virtual security guards, often using pattern recognition and data collection to rapidly identify anything unusual, such as cyber intruders (Tripwire, 2022). IBM report data shows that using XDR technology, a new approach to threat detection and response that offers holistic cyberattack protection to find data breaches is 29 days faster than not using it (IBM Security, 2022).

Testing and validating of supplier performance mechanisms should also be implemented to detect potential problems with suppliers' security issues (such as data breaches). The results should be incorporated into the supplier performance plan to guide future cybersecurity investments. Besides these measures, the company should ensure ongoing monitoring and continuous improvement.

If the organization desires a secure supply chain, all employees must have the same objective. Many cybercriminals will send malicious emails to employees while masquerading as vendors. Implementing a company-wide cybersecurity training program and equipping all personal devices with reliable, up-to-date security software is necessary. Employees should be trained to recognize and respond to cyberattacks and provided with the resources, tools, and direction to respond to and prevent malicious activities.

Government and industry organizations must establish standards and regulations for supply chain security that aids organizations in mitigating the rising risk of supply chain compromise due to cybersecurity and achieving supply chain resilience.

Government policies should use incentives and sanctions to increase awareness and responsibility for cyber security. With cyber threats becoming more sophisticated, silos cannot handle such complex threats. Even the most tech-savvy companies are vulnerable to cyberattacks. This underscores the need for greater collaboration among firms at all levels in the industry to not only present a united front against cyberattacks but also promote knowledge sharing on attack types and best practices. Industry partnerships enable resource pooling, which could lower the cost of fighting the problem (Afenyo & Caesar, 2023).

Conclusions

Addressing the cybersecurity risks in supply chains is complex and daunting. Organizations that embed a culture of supply chain cyberrisk alertness and take a systematic and collaborative approach will mitigate threats, adapt quickly to changes in the business environment, and respond efficiently if an incident occurs.

Organizations must recognize the importance of educating their staff on cybersecurity. Employees must be trained to identify, analyze, and respond to cyberattacks. They must also be given the tools, resources, and guidance to detect, respond to, and prevent malicious activities.

The future of the global supply chain relies heavily on the success of cybersecurity strategies. Organizations must take a comprehensive approach to protecting their supply chain from cyberattacks, including implementing effective policies, using advanced technologies, and increasing collaboration with suppliers and partners. They must also ensure their staff is educated on cybersecurity to protect data. By staying informed and taking the necessary precautions, we can ensure the security and integrity of the supply chain in the future.

This is vital to ensuring the confidence of the business partners, from upstream to downstream, and the customers who place trust in the organization. Data safety enables them to be carefree while doing business with the organization.

In the Supply Chain 5.0 era, cybersecurity will be more critical than ever before. As supply chains become more interconnected and reliant on digital technologies, the risk of cyberattacks increases. Organizations that fail to address this risk will face severe consequences, including financial losses, reputational damage, and regulatory non-compliance.

To address cybersecurity risks in the Supply Chain 5.0 era, organizations must take a holistic approach that includes not only their own cybersecurity but also the cybersecurity of their suppliers and partners. This means implementing comprehensive cybersecurity policies, leveraging advanced technologies like artificial intelligence and blockchain, and building strong relationships with suppliers and partners to ensure that cybersecurity is embedded in every aspect of the supply chain.

Procurement professionals play a crucial role in ensuring the security of the supply chain by integrating cybersecurity as a fundamental criterion when selecting new partners and embracing the digitalization of processes, as discussed in Section 3.1 of this book. As emphasized throughout this section, cyberattacks frequently exploit the weakest link in interconnected value chains, which often involves suppliers or partners associated with the organization.

In addition, organizations must conduct cybersecurity drills involving their suppliers and partners, treating these exercises with the same level of importance as product recalls. While technology plays a pivotal role in preventing such incidents, mock drills serve as valuable tools in creating and validating comprehensive recovery plans should an incident occur. Furthermore, organizations must maintain vigilance by staying abreast of the latest cybersecurity threats and trends.

Proactive identification and mitigation of risks should be a priority. Investing in cybersecurity education and training for employees is essential to ensure that every individual within the organization comprehends the significance of cybersecurity and possesses the knowledge to effectively respond to cyber threats.

In conclusion, cybersecurity will be a critical component of the Supply Chain 5.0 era. Organizations that take a systematic and collaborative approach to cybersecurity will be better equipped to mitigate threats, adapt to changing business environments, and respond quickly to incidents. By ensuring data safety, organizations can gain the trust and confidence of their business partners and customers, enabling them to conduct business in a carefree way. Let's work together to build secure and resilient supply chains that can withstand the challenges of the future as we prepare for the onset of Supply Chain 5.0.

References

Afenyo, M. & Caesar, L. (2023). Maritime cybersecurity threats: Gaps and directions for future research. *Ocean & Coastal Management,* 236. https://doi.org/10.1016/j.ocecoaman.2023.106493.

Biasini, N. (2020, December 14). *Threat Advisory: SolarWinds Supply Chain Attack*. Cisco Talos. https://blog.talosintelligence.com/solarwinds-supplychain-coverage/.

Chapman, L. (2021, December 5). *Third-Party and Supply Chain Risk Management: Then and Now*. Future of Sourcing.

https://futureofsourcing.com/third-party-and-supply-chain-risk-management-then-and-now.

Cisco. (2023). *Cisco Cybersecurity Readiness Index.* https://www.cisco.com/c/dam/m/en_us/products/security/cybersecurity-reports/cybersecurity-readiness-index/2023/cybersecurity-readiness-index-report.pdf

DHL. (2022). *Cybersecurity 2.0.* https://www.dhl.com/global-en/home/insights-and-innovation/thought-leadership/trend-reports/cybersecurity-supply-chain.html.

Gandomi, A., & Haider, M. (2015). Beyond the hype: Big data concepts, methods, and analytics. *International Journal of Information Management*, 35(2), 137–155.

Iaiani, M., Tugnoli, A., Bonvicini, S., & Cozzani, V. (2021). Analysis of cybersecurity-related incidents in the process industry. *Reliability Engineering & System Safety*, 209. https://doi.org/10.1016/j.ress.2021.107485.

IBM Security. (2022). *Cost of a Data Breach Report 2022*. https://www.ibm.com/downloads/cas/3R8N1DZJ.

Kar, P., & Sa, P. (2018). A survey of cyber threats and countermeasures in cloud computing. *IEEE Access*, 6, 70539–70560.

Kost, E. (2023, January 5). *Cybersecurity: The Biggest Security Risks in Your Supply Chain in 2023.* UpGuard. https://www.upguard.com/blog/biggest-supply-chain-security-risks.

Lamba, A., Singh, S., Balvinder, S., Dutta, N., & Rela, S. (2017 January). Analyzing and fixing cyber security threats for supply chain management. *International Journal for Technological Research in Engineering,* 4(5). https://papers.ssrn.com/sol3/papers.cfm?abstract_id=3492687.

Lukić, D. (n.d.). *Cybersecurity in Supply Chain Management, Risks to Consider.* CyberSaint Security. Retrieved February 2023, from https://www.cybersaint.io/blog/cybersecurity-in-supply-chain-management-risks-to-consider.

National Institute of Standards and Technology. (n.d.). *Best Practices in Cyber Supply Chain Risk Management.* Retrieved February 2023, from https://csrc.nist.gov/CSRC/media/Projects/Supply-Chain-Risk-Management/documents/briefings/Workshop-Brief-on-Cyber-Supply-Chain-Best-Practices.pdf.

Neshenko, N., Bou-Harb, E., Crichigno, J., & Kaddoum., G. (2019). Demystifying IoT security: An exhaustive survey on IoT vulnerabilities and a first empirical look on internet-scale IoT exploitations. *IEEE Communications Surveys Tutorials*, 21(3), 2702–2733. 10.1109/COMST.2019.2910750.

Puleo, D. (n.d.). *A United Front Against Cyberattacks*. IBM. Retrieved February 2023, from https://www.ibm.com/case-studies/andritz/.

Reciprocity. (2022, June 22). *Cybersecurity Risks in Supply Chain Management*. https://reciprocity.com/blog/cybersecurity-risks-in-supply-chain-management/.

Sainathan, P. (n.d.). *Blockchain — A Solution for Supply Chain Cyber Security?* Roambee. Retrieved February 2023, from https://blog.roambee.com/supply-chain-technology/blockchain-a-solution-for-supply-chain-cyber-security.

Shemesh, R. (2021, November 18). *What Is Bazar Loader and How to Prepare?* Datto. https://www.datto.com/blog/bazar-loader-attack-what-is-it-and-how-to-prepare.

Simon, J. & Omar, A. (2020, April 1). Cybersecurity investments in the supply chain: Coordination and a strategic attacker. *European Journal of Operational Research*, 282(1), 161–171. https://doi.org/10.1016/j.ejor.2019.09.017.

The New York Times. (2021). Cyberattack Forces a Shutdown of a Top U.S. Pipeline. https://www.nytimes.com/2021/05/08/us/politics/cyberattack-colonial-pipeline.html.

Tripwire. (2022, January 17). *The Supply Chain Needs Better Cybersecurity and Risk Management*. https://www.tripwire.com/state-of-security/the-supply-chain-needs-better-cybersecurity-and-risk-management.

Tsvetanov, T., & Slaria, S. (2021, December). The effect of the Colonial Pipeline shutdown on gasoline prices. *Economics Letters*, 209. https://doi.org/10.1016/j.econlet.2021.110122.

US-CERT. (2017). Alert (TA17-132A). *Russian State-Sponsored Cyber Actors Targeting Energy and Other Critical Infrastructure Sectors*. https://www.us-cert.gov/ncas/alerts/TA17-132A.

Wikimedia Commons. (2021 May 15). *File:2021-05-15 14 33 28 Out-of-Service Gas Pumps Due to Panic Buying after the Colonial Pipeline Cyberattack at the Wawa along Air and Space Museum Parkway in Oak Hill, Fairfax County, Virginia.jpg*. https://commons.wikimedia.org/wiki/File:2021-05-15_14_33_28_Out-of-service_gas_pumps_due_to_panic_buying_after_the_Colonial_Pipeline_cyberattack_ at_the_Wawa_along_Air_and_Space_Museum_Parkway_in_Oak_Hill,_Fairfax_County,_Virginia.jpg.

World Economic Forum. (2020, January 15). *The Global Risks Report 2020.* https://www.weforum.org/reports/the-global-risks-report-2020.

Yeboah-Ofori, A. & Islam, S. (2019). Cyber security threat modeling for supply chain organizational environments. *Future Internet*, 11(3), 63. https://doi.org/10.3390/fi11030063.

Further Reading

National Cyber Security Center. (n.d.). *What is Cyber Security?* Retrieved February 2023, from https://www.ncsc.gov.uk/section/about-ncsc/what-is-cyber-security.

National Cyber Security Center New Zealand Government. (n.d.). *Supply Chain Cyber Security*. Retrieved February 2023, from https://www.ncsc.govt.nz/assets/NCSC-Documents/NCSC-Supply-Chain-Cyber-Security.pdf.

AFTERWORD

Well, there you have it.

The key elements of Supply Chain 5.0 laid bare before your eyes. But before you close this book and put it on your shelf, take a moment to envision a world where supply chains are efficient, cost-effective, and better for people and the planet. It's a world where companies adopt a more holistic approach to their supply chain operations, not just focusing on their bottom line but also the impact of their actions on the environment, society, and economy. This is the future of supply chain as we envision and hope for a positive impact.

Supply Chain 5.0 represents the latest evolution of supply chain management, emphasizing customer-centricity, sustainability, human rights, and advanced digitalization. Recent disruptions, such as the pandemic, climate challenges, and shipping bottlenecks, have highlighted the need to reimagine our supply chain practices. That's where Supply Chain 5.0 comes into play, demanding collaboration among suppliers, manufacturers, retailers, and customers to create a seamless and responsive supply chain that's socially and ecologically responsible. By meeting customer preferences and reducing waste and emissions, we can create a better future.

While the three elements we explored in detail within this book lay the foundation for Supply Chain 5.0, it is crucial to now integrate and understand their nuanced interplay.

In the first element of customer centricity, we discussed the need for personalization, which might seem at odds with sustainability's goal of conservation and reduction. However, the answer lies in the shared economy, where "sharing is the new ownership." Digitalization plays a vital role here, connecting customers to sharable assets through digital platforms. In this new supply chain model, individuals won't need to own every item; instead, they'll have a myriad of choices to use and experience various products, returning them afterward for others to do the same. Circular design, long-lasting materials, and biodegradability will be embedded in this sustainable approach.

One industry that has already embraced Supply Chain 5.0 principles is fashion. Despite the sector's historical environmental impact and ethical concerns, some fashion brands have taken steps towards renewable energy, recycling, and waste reduction, making their supply chains more environmentally friendly. Moreover, fashion industry has fostered satisfaction and loyalty through involving customers in the supply chain process and allowing customization and personalization.

As we step into the future, Supply Chain 5.0 will play a crucial role in shaping the landscape of supply chains. Companies that wholeheartedly embrace these principles will not only achieve their sustainability goals but also positively impact the environment, society, and their own profitability. The right blend of customer-centricity, sustainability and advanced digitalization holds the key to success.

We hope this book has provided you with a glimpse into the future of supply chains, defining the three critical dimensions it encompasses, and inspiring you to take action. Whether you are a supply chain leader, a business executive, or someone passionate about the topic, we all have a part to play in creating a better future.

This is the future we will see, where considerable thinking and remodeling are required to ensure circularity embedded in the design, creation, and supply of any object, along with the principle of long-lastingness or biodegradability. The examples of shared spaces such as Airbnb, shared bikes in many developed cities, clothes libraries, and more are already replete.

The next era of Supply Chain 5.0 demands meaningful education for everyone, including consumers, producers, and government bodies, to embrace wiser choices like the reuse and sharing. Let us all be part of this transformative journey toward a better planet and a more sustainable future.

INDEX

ABOUT THE AUTHORS

Prateek Jain is a highly experienced Supply Chain professional with an impressive career spanning over 25 years in the business world. With a strong track record of success at renowned companies like GSK and Unilever, Prateek has established himself as a trusted brand builder, supply chain expert, and procurement specialist.

During his tenure at GSK, Prateek's expertise as a Master Trainer for Lean Six Sigma propelled him to the forefront of business improvement projects. He not only led numerous successful initiatives but also coached and certified Master Black Belts and Black Belts in Lean Six Sigma.

Beyond his corporate achievements, Prateek has made significant contributions to the wider business community. In 2019, he held a prestigious position as Chairman of the European Chamber of Commerce in Singapore for ASEAN, where he worked to enhance trade and commerce between European businesses and governmental organizations in Singapore. Prateek's inspiring speeches at respected conferences and events, including the Singapore Council for Safety and Health, the Singapore Badminton Association, University of Toronto, and the National University of Singapore, have motivated professionals to embrace modern business practices and drive positive change.

Prateek's influence in the field of supply chain management is undeniable. He co-designed the Supply Chain Holistic Approach, a groundbreaking methodology that serves as the foundation for management reviews at multiple companies through Sales & Operations Planning (S&OP). Additionally, his innovative contributions, such as Flexible Repeat Schedules, supply chain segmentation, layered forecasting, just in case inventory modelling, and digitization, have revolutionized production operations, optimized supply chains, and improved customer service and retention across organizations.

With his expertise in brand creation and supply chain management, Prateek consistently delivers remarkable results. As Commercial Head, he successfully expanded market reach threefold and led the launch of over 10 consumer-centric innovations within three years. Prateek's strategic brand building and expansion strategies not only secured significant market share but also solidified the consumer base across various countries. His ability to align brands with the end-to-end value chain and prioritize customer centricity has been instrumental in driving success.

Currently, Prateek collaborates with consulting firms like EvolveWithUsNow, BCG, Sevendots and others, where he assists clients from diverse sectors in embedding sustainability and strategically aligning their supply chains with customer-centric operations. Moreover, as the Co-chair for the Sustainability Committee in the European Chamber of Commerce, Singapore, he actively works with companies, government organizations, and delegations to promote the United Nations' Sustainable Development

Goals (SDGs) within Singapore and the ASEAN region. He is also the adjunct Senior Lecturer at the National University of Singapore Business School.

In his latest book, "Supply Chain 5.0," Prateek has partnered with senior academics to present an experiential and academic exploration of supply chain management. Drawing on his extensive experience working with various companies and clients across sectors, Prateek offers a transformative vision for the future of supply chain management in the digital era. This book embarks one on a journey of knowledge and innovation as they discover the groundbreaking concepts and strategies that will shape the supply chains of tomorrow.

Mabel C. Chou is an associate professor in the Analytics and Operations department at National University of Singapore (NUS). She received the B.Sc. degree in mathematics from National Taiwan University, the M.Sc. degree in mathematics and Ph.D. degree in industrial engineering and management sciences from Northwestern University. Her research focuses on production scheduling and supply chain analysis. She has published papers for journals such as Operations Research, Management Science, IEEE Transactions on Automatic Control, Math Programming, Production and Operations Management, European Journal of Operational Research, Flexible Services and Manufacturing Journal, etc. Her current research interest is in the application of optimization tools and business analytics for engineering, service, and supply chain management problems. She is an associate editor for Operations Research, a senior editor for Production and Operations Management and an associate editor for Pacific Journal of Optimization. She has also consulted for companies such as GSK, Caterpillar, P&G, SIA Engineering Company, National University Hospital, Tan Tock Seng Hospital, Lenovo, Supreme Components International, etc. and conducted courses for 3M, the Logistics Institute – Asia Pacific, and the Singapore Institute of Manufacturing Technology.

www.ingramcontent.com/pod-product-compliance
Lightning Source LLC
LaVergne TN
LVHW010334220926
848484LV00004BB/893